THE YOUNG LITIGATOR

Tips on
Rainmaking,
Writing
and
Trial
Practice

AMERICAN BAR ASSOCIATION
Section of Litigation

FIRST
CHAIR
·PRESS·

Cover design by Monica Alejo / ABA Publishing.

Printed in the United States of America.

15 14 13 12   5 4 3 2

Library of Congress Cataloging-in-Publication Data

The Young Litigator: Tips on Rainmaking, Writing and Trial Practice /
by the Young Lawyers Leadership Program.
    p. cm.
  ISBN 978-1-61632-985-3
  1. Practice of law—United States. 2. Law—Vocational guidance—
United States. 3. Lawyers—United States—Marketing. I. American Bar
Association. Young Lawyers Leadership Program.
  KF297.Y678   2011
  340.023'73—dc22

                                     2011016522

Discounts are available for books ordered in bulk. Special consideration is given to state bars, CLE programs, and other bar-related organizations. Inquire at Book Publishing, ABA Publishing, American Bar Association, 321 North Clark Street, Chicago, Illinois 60654-7598.

www.ShopABA.org

TABLE OF CONTENTS

Introduction   vii
The Young Lawyer Leadership Program   ix

Rainmaking   **1**
Introduction   1
Douglas E. Motzenbecker

Bringing in Business   **5**
Gearing up for Rain: A Junior Associate's Guide to Rainmaking   5
Sania Anwar
Can I Make Rain?   10
Paula W. Hinton and Sara Holtz
Ethical Considerations in Rainmaking   13
Tamara L. Traynor
Young Lawyer's Perspective on Rainmaking: A Timeline for Success   20
Amy Messigian and Bronwyn Roberts
Young Lawyers   **25**
What They Didn't Teach You in Law School:
How to Establish a Clientele   25
Gerald Giaimo
Making Rain: A Newly Minted Associate's Perspective on
Developing Business   28
Effie Silva
Using Online Social Networking Sites to Make It Rain   30
Griselda Zamora
A Dozen Marketing Tips for the Time-Starved Lawyer   34
Ellen Ostrow, Ph.D.
Business Plans—Business Development   **38**
Don't Wait, Create! Networking & Business Development for
Younger Lawyers   38
Michelle N. Lipkowitz
A Business Plan: Why Every Associate Should Have One   44
Laura Cullison
Mentoring   **49**
The Dark Side of the Mentoring Relationship   49
Kathleen B. Havener
A Mentoring Checklist to Help Make the Mentoring
Relationship Productive   52
Amy Messigian, Anne Marie Seibel, and Lu Ann White
Accelerating Career Development Through Multiple
Mentoring Opportunities   59
Nan E. Joesten
Where Have All the Role Models Gone?   63
Coke Stewart

iii

Writing   **65**
Introduction   65
   C. Pierce Campbell

Clarity and Persuasion   **67**
48 Litigation Writing Rules   67
   Peter R. Silverman
If You've Got It, Flaunt It: Persuasive Brief Writing   72
   Evelyn Storch
An In-Depth Look at the Legal Argument   **76**
Writing a Winning Legal Argument: What TO Do and
   What Not TO Do   76
   Lawrence D. Rosenberg
Quick Tips for Successful Writing   **103**
Young Lawyer's Spotlight Ramblings on Writing:
   "Like A Lawyer" Not   103
   Rick Alimonti

Trial Practice   **109**
Introduction   109
   David Sterling

Trial Preparation   **111**
The Trial Lawyer's Motto: Be Over-Prepared
   A "How To" Guide To Trial Preparation For
   The New (And Experienced) Trial Lawyer And
   Her/His Invaluable Support Staff   111
   Reena M. Sandoval and Jane K. Manning
Final Trial Preparation   126
   Hon. Christopher T. Whitten
In Support of the "To Do" List   135
   Hon. Samuel A. Thumma
General Advice   **139**
The Young Lawyer's Corner Lessons Learned at
   My First Criminal Trial   139
   David M. Burkoff
Young Lawyers Advice to New Lawyers
   (And Important Reminders for the Rest of Us)   142
   James E. Scarboro
Tips for Working with "Difficult" Opposing Counsel   145
   David S. Coale
Judge's Column
   Basic Litigation Pointers And Courtroom Etiquette For
   Bankruptcy Lawyers   147
   Douglas O. Tice, Jr.

What Judges Want   153
Mark A. Drummond
A Judge's Guide to Protecting Your Reputation   160
James G. Carr
The Road to Lead Plaintiff: The Basics   171
Aimee Williams

Oral Argument—Comportment in the Courtroom   **175**
A Few Do's and Don'ts of Oral Argument   175
Thomas J. Donlan
Young Lawyer Focus: "A list of the things, in no particular order,
    that I wished I was told and was not . . . and the things I was
    told but only really understood during or after the argument"   183
By J.D. Barnea, Gabrielle Bina, Elisabeth Brown, Ethan Glass,
Adam Gromfin, Doug Keller
Method Acting for Lawyers   187
Kathleen B. Havener
Using The Lessons Of Aristotle To Present Outstanding
    Oral Arguments, Part I   191
Lawrence D. Rosenberg
Using the Lessons of Aristotle to Present Outstanding
    Oral Arguments: Part II   211
Lawrence D. Rosenberg
Lasting Impressions: The Role of Closing Argument   227
Linda L. Listrom

Motion Practice   **236**
Effective Motion Practice In Trial Courts   236
Luther T. Munford and James W. Shelson
Reflections on Motion Practice   245
Louis B. York
New Standards of Legal Sufficiency To Survive A Motion
    To Dismiss?   248
Judge Samuel A. Thumma

INTRODUCTION

A young lawyer entering into the practice of law can be overwhelmed by the amount of information he must necessarily obtain to create and maintain a productive and successful law practice. Most practicing attorneys know that the education received in law school is only a small portion of the knowledge that is needed, and needed as quickly as possible. Continuing education, new lawyer programs, and firm-sponsored training and mentoring all seek to provide new attorneys with the tools they need to succeed. This work is a compilation of articles, chosen by younger practicing lawyers, that seeks to guide young lawyers in their first days, months, and years in the practice of law.

This book is the final product of a project that began as an attempt to compile the numerous resources published for young lawyers by members of the American Bar Association Section of Litigation. Section of Litigation entities, First Chair Press, whose mission includes publishing books of interest to young lawyers, and the Young Lawyer Leadership Program, which develops future leaders for the Section, resolved to produce a book of great interest and worth to young attorneys. First Chair Press and the YLLP worked together to compile this set of articles originally published in various newsletters, journals, websites, and other sources by the committees and task forces of the Section of Litigation. First Chair Press saw the need to bring these works, written by many well-respected attorneys from around the country, into a single volume; the YLLP provided the manpower over several years to review, analyze, and select works from past Section publications. Hundreds, if not thousands, of articles were reviewed, and the best were chosen.

In deciding how to create the book most likely to be utilized by young lawyers, First Chair Press was forced to choose only a few great articles. The selections for this book, arranged under the topics of Writing, Trial Practice, and Client Development, are timeless and universal in their appeal. A litigator cannot fully succeed without the ability to gain and manage clients, write persuasively, and conduct a trial. Even in the world of decreasing jury trials, increasing ADR, and written communication by email or texting, these skills are essential. Whether at a large or small firm, in-house or outside counsel, rural or urban, and regardless of practice area, these three topics affect all litigators. For that reason, they were selected.

While this book was published with the young lawyer in mind, certainly there are very few attorneys who could not use a bit of a refresher on the topics covered herein. The goal of this book was not to become a definitive guide on the practice of law, but instead to be a forum for sharing viewpoints of successful practitioners on some of the most basic concerns of the practice of law for any litigator. Any litigator is likely to find new or forgotten lessons in the articles contained herein.

Committees and task forces within the Section of Litigation are the groups who made this work possible. The Section's committees do a marvelous job of encouraging their members to produce works of interest to litigators in a professional manner. The education received in reviewing the hundreds of articles considered was invaluable to those involved. The ongoing transition of the Section's newsletters and journals to electronic format will create access to these great articles where it has not existed previously. The reader is encouraged to take full advantage of this new opportunity and take note of this tremendous resource available to members of the Section of Litigation. To the committee chairs, journal editors, and authors who made this possible, a great thank you! Your efforts are invaluable to the mission of this organization.

It is hoped that this will be the first in a series of similar publications. There are other topics of timeless appeal which can be included in future volumes including ethics, law practice management, and discovery. Additionally, articles of note to practitioners in specific areas such as products liability, constitutional law, commercial litigation, amongst many others, are in the Section's vast library. The perspectives expressed by the many authors of these articles are invaluable, and a compilation thereof can help provide the additional base of knowledge and information all new lawyers (and many not-so-new lawyers) need to reach their full potential as successful litigators.

C. Pierce Campbell, Douglas E. Motzenbecker, and David Sterling
First Chair Press

THE YOUNG LAWYER LEADERSHIP PROGRAM

The Young Lawyer Leadership Program is committed to increasing participation of young lawyers in the Section of Litigation by: (1) involving young lawyers in the work of the Section with the hope that they will develop into future leaders of the Section; and (2) enhancing the image of the Section among young lawyers, including those who are members of the Section and the Young Lawyers Division of the ABA. Now in its eleventh year, the ABA Section of Litigation's Young Lawyer Leadership Program (YLLP) has been a resounding success in helping young lawyers become actively involved in the Section's meetings and committees. YLLP representatives become members of a Section committee or task force, engage in substantive work, and are paired with a mentor from the Section's experienced leaders. Also, each year YLLP representatives attend three leadership meetings during which important work of the Section is conducted, as well as the Section's Annual Meeting and the ABA Annual Meeting.

RAINMAKING

Introduction

By Douglas E. Motzenbecker

The problem with rainmaking is that attorneys in private practice are expected to bring in business, but nobody tells you how to do it. This handbook is intended to give you some valuable insights on the rainmaking process.

There is a first day of practice for every lawyer, but it is never too early to begin working on your rainmaking abilities. I often compare client development to trying to use a plastic spoon to dig a tunnel under a highway: each step seems in vain and there is so much more to do. Stated differently, Rome wasn't built in a day. To many attorneys, the project of building client relationships is so daunting they never get started.

Don't let that happen to you. The hardest part about rainmaking is mental—taking the first steps—but where do you begin? To get business, you have to see rainmaking as your second job, the work you do for yourself. Most law firms are really just small businesses. As an owner of the firm, or as someone who wants to eventually be a partner, you are not only practicing law but you are also in sales—selling yourself and your intellectual inventory. Business generation requires you to not only have the skills to do the work but the persistence, personality, and finesse to close the deal.

And, like any small business owner, in private practice you are not simply going to be working nine-to-five. If you owned a restaurant, car

Douglas E. Motzenbecker is a shareholder with Podvey Meanor, P.C., in Newark, New Jersey, where he has an active litigation practice emphasizing labor, employment, insurance coverage, securities, and other complex litigation. Mr. Motzenbecker has been Editor-in-Chief of Litigation News, a publication of the American Bar Association's Section of Litigation, and serves on the book publishing board of First Chair Press, an imprint of the Section of Litigation.

dealership, or other small business, you would be spending nights and weekends promoting your products, developing marketing strategies, hiring and firing employees, managing and improving your inventory, outdoing your competitors, processing paperwork, and putting out fires every day.

Why would law be any different?

The reality is that developing a book of business requires time and persistence. Okay, but how much exactly? The unofficial rule of thumb is that attorneys seeking to build a client base must invest at least ten percent of their professional time in marketing; however, devoting twenty percent is more likely to yield results. You must plan to spend at least 200 hours a year on rainmaking, although it is probably going to take more like 400 hours. The other unstated reality is that business development means getting off the clock and going to a prospective client's office for a free consultation, or to the library, a seminar, or a bar association meeting.

Faint heart never won fair maiden. Although you will land some clients easily, others will usually take much more time. Come to think of it, there actually *are* a lot of lawyers out there. The competition is fierce and clients can be ponderously slow in choosing counsel. It can take four to six years before a client will send you your first case—and don't expect it to be much. Since you are an unknown quantity, no sane client is going to send you a big case at first. Trust and relationships are built gradually. Clients want to know whether this new lawyer they have never worked with is going to gouge them on the bill, meet deadlines, take surgical and effective action, and end this case on favorable terms. In short, six months into the case, are they going to think you were the right lawyer for the job?

Getting business also requires you to declare a major—that is, to decide which specific areas of the law you are going to master. That decision is yours alone to make (what, you are waiting for a partner to come to your office one morning and anoint you a bankruptcy specialist?). To make rain, you are going to need specialized knowledge and skill in a chosen area of the law. Since litigation can be cyclical, it is important to focus on more than one area.

But as a new litigator assigned to a partner's cases, you will typically be assigned a broad range of assignments ranging from answering interrogatories, performing legal research, reviewing thousands of documents, eventually taking depositions, and—if you are lucky—going to court, if only in a second-chair capacity. You may get assigned to an antitrust case one day, to a bankruptcy preference action another, and to an employment discrimination suit the next. After five years of this, you will usually know a little about a lot—that is, if you let your firm's and its clients' meandering needs drive your career for you. You will ordinarily have conducted only that research which the case required, but never have quite gotten the full picture, particularly since the client was not going to pay you to research academic matters.

To fill in the gaps in your knowledge, the key is to determine which areas of the law interest you most, not to mention those that are in demand and—why not say it?—pay well. Once you identify those areas, make it your business to become expert in them by reading as much as you can about each subject and then writing down what you have learned. If you are going to be successful in marketing your practice, it helps enormously if you can show—through your scholarly articles, papers, and even books—that you know what you are talking about. Don't think for a minute that your clients want to pay you to teach yourself how to litigate their cases. Like a patient looking for a doctor, they expect you to be an expert—and right now.

But, as an associate in your present law firm who is getting a substantial salary, the attorneys you work for might expect you to bill 2,500 hours annually or something approaching that to justify your salary. If you are in a law firm that assigns you interesting work that is helping you develop as a professional, great. But if your firm requires you to bill 2,500 hours and gives you only rote and mundane assignments, where do you find the time for practice development? By leaving for a firm that requires only 2,000 hours and gives you interesting work that allows you to become a lawyer with first-chair skills and experience. If you are doing work that you would not be a little bit proud to describe for a client, you are not in the right firm, or at least not getting the right experience. Believe it or not, you will eventually have been practicing for ten years and the partners you work for are going to start to expect you to bring in business. Yeah, but I was selling my soul for *your* cases, you say, and I never got started.

Revisit my earlier advice: don't let that happen to you. Many new attorneys run into another problem: they are working on pieces of an enormous case, but are ten years out and have yet to try a case. And, having no trial experience, how can they ask a client to entrust them with a lawsuit that may have to be tried? The fact is, they can't, and, thus, they are afraid to ask for the work.

So, since you say you want to be a litigator, you are going to need to get trial experience. But you are as green as grass and no one wants to give you a $5 million case. How do you beat this Catch-22? By taking on pro bono matters, getting your name on the public defender's pool of outside counsel at low wages, saying yes when a court asks you to represent an indigent client in a litigated matter, and seeking out every small case in your firm that allows you to get on your feet in court. The non-paying cases are, well, non-paying. But, unless you burn the nights, weekends, and holidays to get the invaluable experience this work can give you, it is going to be a lot harder to make rain down the road. And, if you don't become expert in at least one given area, you are going to run into trouble at or about the ten-year mark. Ironically, whether you invested nights, weekends, and holidays to build your future, those ten years will be gone either way. You should at least have something to show for them.

As Hyman Roth says to Michael Corleone in *Godfather II*, this is the business we have chosen. And, having chosen this profession, I urge you to make the full commitment. You will have more fun and find litigation a whole lot more rewarding. Happy hunting.

RAINMAKING

Bringing in Business

Gearing up for Rain: A Junior Associate's Guide to Rainmaking

By Sania Anwar

In today's competitive environment, law firms are reinforcing their rainmaking expectations, not just from senior-level attorneys but also from junior associates. In an economic downturn, it may be more challenging for attorneys to generate business, but it is also more valuable to a law firm. The simplest way to conceptualize rainmaking is to break it down into the two elements necessary to bring in business: Relationships and Marketing, the R and M in rainmaking. Whether a marketing budget is available or not, successful rainmaking requires (1) making contacts and maintaining relationships and (2) creating and implementing an individual marketing plan.

Junior associates, especially those in their first two or three years of practice, tend to consider rainmaking a professional virtue that is expected to make its appearance much later in their careers. However, successful rainmaking can never start early enough. The foundation should be laid during law school, where relationships are formed that an associate can cultivate and develop through the early years of his or her law firm career. A junior associate shouldn't believe that successful rainmaking requires an aggressive law firm marketing plan with participation from all levels within the firm. Although a built-in rainmaking support system allows junior associates to draw upon marketing resources to expand and develop their contacts, the key to successful rainmaking

From the **Woman Advocate**/Winter 2010/ABA/Section of Litigation

at any firm is a comprehensive individual marketing plan that adapts to the marketing support provided by the firm.

BUILDING RELATIONSHIPS

The key to future rainmaking is to forge relationships at every step of your legal career, beginning in law school. Often, law students are either overwhelmed by educational endeavors or they have a myopic understanding of law firms. To be better prepared for the future, however, law students should understand that law firms have two components: the practice of law and the business of law. In today's competitive market, the ideal candidate has an appreciation for and the ability to contribute to both. What is expected of law students and junior associates from early on in their careers has expanded over the years to include not only scrutiny of what goes out of the firm (*i.e.*, their work product) but also of what comes in (*i.e.*, their business and marketing contacts).

START BUILDING CONTACTS EARLY

Making contacts and forging relationships in law school begins by actively seeking out people you are interested in getting to know. Searching through the law school's alumni network is one place to start. Law school alumni are often eager to share their experiences and perspectives with law students during "informational interviews." You should also call upon the career offices and networking support available at your law school. These resources can help you make the right contacts, which can potentially turn into long-term relationships.

PARTICIPATE IN THE COMMUNITY

This recommendation holds true for both law students and junior associates. Participating in events that bring together members of the community from different generations and backgrounds is one of the best ways to develop contacts and relationships.

Law students and junior associates should consider actively participating in Inns of Court, local bar association committees, or law student or young lawyers' divisions of specialty bars or programs. This will allow you to make a seamless transition once you begin practicing or when you advance further in your career.

VOLUNTEER, INTERN, OR CLERK

Law school presents numerous volunteering opportunities that can lead to networking with other attorneys and members of local organizations that are supporting the same cause. During and after law school, you should also consider internship or clerkship opportunities at corporations, law firms, and courts. These are excellent opportunities to develop relationships with people who are willing to offer exceptional learning experiences and networking resources.

SEEK OUT MENTORS

The most gratifying and supportive relationships for a legal career are those between mentors and mentees. These relationships are the best examples of initial contacts that later yield business opportunities. Law schools expend ample resources developing mentorship programs. The importance of such programs is recognized by members of the community, who contribute their time and efforts to form long lasting bonds with the students. Junior associates should look for inspiring individuals who can serve as mentors both within their firms and within organizations they belong to. Most specialty bar associations also routinely create mentor-mentee opportunities. Your mentor can naturally pass on his or her contacts and relationships to you for your own business development.

INDIVIDUAL MARKETING PLAN

Every junior associate should design and implement an individual marketing plan that takes into account already existing relationships, the process of identifying potential contacts, and the marketing resources available from within the firm.

From as early as your first year at a firm, compose an individual marketing plan and include accountability checks at various points to make modifications to your plan. Make it a habit to routinely check the status of your progress and set concrete goals to comply with your plan.

IDENTIFY POTENTIAL CONTACTS

As a junior associate, the key to successful rainmaking lies in creatively identifying and seeking out potential clients. Not only should junior associates make use of any network opportunity that presents itself to them, but they also must actively create such opportunities to ensure a constant stream of contacts. This requires creativity and resourcefulness.

Do not delete newsletters or correspondences from bar associations and specialty programs that make their way into your inbox; scan them for networking events and interesting articles you can share with contacts. Think beyond the bar. Join business and trade associations or your local chamber of commerce. Professional associations are ripe for the picking. Do not overlook the six degrees of separation: Ask people you know to spread the word and introduce you to the organizations to which they belong. You can be a guest at local alumni events of schools other than your own if the event includes professionals you are targeting. Dip into the legal community for referrals and generate cross-referrals. Request that other lawyers send you conflict work or work they do not handle.

KNOW WHAT YOU OFFER AND TO WHOM YOU OFFER IT

The most crucial element of marketing is knowledge—knowledge of what the law firm has to offer and of potential clients who may benefit from the firm's services.

As a junior associate, you have to embrace the fact that not only are you marketing yourself, especially to long-term relationships, but you are also representing the law firm at all times. The key is to understand that as a salesperson, your role is to market the brand you are part of—the law firm. Interview and chat with people at the top of the law firm to really understand what it has to offer clients and what niche it targets. Know about the key players at the law firm and how you can market their success. Investigate significant wins and high-profile former or current clients to offer as evidence of the quality your firm offers.

You must also have knowledge of your target clients' industry. Be an expert in what your target clients do and what they need. Ask to attend organizational meetings or serve on committees so that you have a better understanding of their day-to-day issues. Only then can you efficiently and convincingly cater to the specific needs of current or prospective clients with the tools and services provided by the firm.

ESTABLISH YOUR PRESENCE

Visibility and presence of junior associates within the legal community strengthens brand recognition for the law firm, making it easier to market the firm's recognized and quality legal services.

Practice making initial conversations with prospective clients. Always carry your business card and keep those you receive in an organized manner. Recognize that not everyone files away your card for future reference, so follow up with an email, which is easier to track and reinforces the initial contact.

Be a prolific writer: Contribute to journals, local newspapers, and blogs. Find out if a relevant trade or professional organization has a newsletter and contribute to it regularly. Organize workshops and seminars and send invitations to potential clients. If your firm creates opportunities for client interactions, make the most of it each time by asking the right questions and exhibiting your knowledge of the client's business and concerns.

DILIGENTLY MAINTAIN CONTACTS

One common mistake junior associates make is to get too focused on the volume of contacts and networking. A contact is only good as long as it is maintained.

Learn to add value to every communication you have with a client or prospective client. Keep track of your important contacts and maintain a contact database. If someone has an interesting background, make a note of it and review your notes before your next meeting. For example, if someone shares his or her plan for a much-awaited vacation, ask during your next communication how it went. Think of ways to cater to clients' or prospective clients' needs, even without an invitation. Offer to do seminars for an organization you are hoping to bring in as a potential client. If something relevant crosses your desk—a news article or a proposed bill—send it to your contacts as a "thought-you-should-know."

Although rainmaking was traditionally left for later years of practice, law firms are now starting to place an emphasis on skills for creating business opportunities at earlier stages of a law firm career. In a business where time is the unit that measures performance, most junior associates choose to set aside rainmaking activities for a later date. However, the keys to successful rainmaking at any stage of a legal career are to understand that you can begin marketing as early as law school, to make contacts that develop into relationships, and to draw on those relationships with creative and efficient marketing.

Can I Make Rain?

By Paula W. Hinton and Sara Holtz

As a young associate, brand new to your career and to a law firm, you are mistaken if you believe that making rain isn't part of your job description. The process involved in making rain starts from the first introduction, whether it be personal or professional. Your fellow associate one day might be the general counsel of a Fortune 500 company, or another young attorney may wind up as a major decision maker in a potential client. Chances are someone you interact with today will be in a position in the future to hire or recommend you. You want to have created the right impression from day one and have formed a relationship with that individual.

You are responsible for your personal career development. Each of you has the potential to be a rainmaker. The key is to build strong relationships—both inside and outside of the organization in which you work.

As a young attorney, you will have the opportunity to attend a variety of community and professional events. These may seem daunting at the outset. No one is particularly comfortable when faced with a room full of strangers. But if you look at these events as a chance to practice your relationship-building skills, you may be surprised to find out how easy it is to transform these events into a rainmaking tool. Here are a few tips to make the most of your attendance at such events.

These are opportunities to meet clients, prospective clients, and referral sources. Chances are most events you will be invited to or asked to participate in will include one or all of those potential resources. That can even apply to an event at your child's school—find out in advance who is invited and who your potential audience will be.

Set a specific objective for each event. You might decide to meet two new people, reconnect with a former client, and conduct a little market research. Be sure you attend the event with an objective in mind.

Invite a client or prospect to attend the event with you. The basics of building a relationship are spending time with someone. Even if they don't accept the invitation, it has given you an opportunity to contact her and stay on her screen.

Formulate a response to the inevitable "what's new?" before the event. Before you go to the event, think about what is new in your prac-

From the **Woman Advocate**/Winter 2007/ABA/Section of Litigation

tice and something interesting that someone may want to hear about. Don't just give the typical "oh nothing," response. There's bound to be something interesting in your practice that you can generally describe that might interest the people attending the event.

Have a client-focused response to "what do you do?" Rather than responding with the "oh, I'm a lawyer" in an apologetic tone, which is unlikely to encourage conversation, try something like "I help nursing homes and hospitals raise cheap, long-term money," or whatever else might be a nice summary of something interesting you are working on or which describes what you do from a potential client's perspective.

Arrive early. If you arrive as dinner or lunch is being served, you are going to miss the best opportunity for mingling. Those 15–30 minutes before an event begins are really the prime time to meet new people and have an opportunity to touch base with those you have met in the past. If you are really pressed for time, show up for the reception and mingling time, talk to a few people you don't know, and leave before the meal. Just don't leave your client or prospect sitting alone at the table.

Don't hang with people you know. Despite the fact that we all want to spend our time with the people we already know, if you are talking to your fellow associates, you are both wasting your time. Unless the people you know are clients, potential clients, or referral sources, reach out, get out of your comfort zone, and introduce yourself to new people and be prepared to talk about them.

Prepare in advance three topics to talk about if there is a lull in the conversation. With all that is happening in your world today, there are clearly three things to talk about. Better still, think of three good questions you can ask the people you meet that might engage them into discussing things that are near and dear to their hearts. Those might be issues related to their work, their family, their children, or their interests. The more you find out about the people you meet, the more opportunities there are to form relationships and opportunities for your advancement in the future. Be an active listener and act on what you hear.

Follow up with those you meet. What good does it do you if you connect with all those people but don't stay in touch? Send a short handwritten note to tell someone you enjoyed meeting him or her. Follow up with an invitation to lunch or to get together in the future. Just make sure you follow up. You have invested the time to meet new people; now get to know them.

Opportunities will arise in the future, and you should put yourself out there.

Despite the conventional wisdom to the contrary, women are very well suited for rainmaking. They are nurturers and naturally assist people with their personal and professional needs. Their strong relationship-building skills can form the basis of their business-building approaches.

It's not too early to start developing your rainmaking skills. Rainmaking can expand your opportunities personally and professionally. View making the most of the events you attend as another opportunity to excel, as you have done to this point. As Eleanor Roosevelt said: "The future belongs to those who believe in the beauty of their dreams."

Ethical Considerations in Rainmaking
By Tamara L. Traynor

Ethics guide our practice as attorneys and also should be a fundamental part of developing business. In a desire to distinguish yourself to attract new clients in a legal environment that is increasingly competitive, do not lose sight of the fundamental rule that a lawyer must be competent in representing a client.[1] Such competence is established if the lawyer has the legal knowledge, skill, thoroughness, and preparation reasonably necessary for the representation. Thus, devoting time and care in perfecting your craft as a lawyer will further your abilities and overall wealth of experience in serving clients. You should keep abreast of new developments in the law that affect your practice, which may also affect the advice you give to clients. You should ensure that you comply with all the requirements for maintaining your license to practice law in the state(s) in which you are admitted, including continuing legal education courses.

Investing the time to hone your legal skills, achieving great results for your clients, acquiring additional skills and experience in developing a specialized practice, and striving to achieve perfection in producing quality legal work will be the foundation of the reputation that you will present to the marketplace in developing your own book of business. Be mindful of the ethical rules that pertain to marketing yourself to potential clients, existing clients, and referring attorneys or other professional colleagues.

WHAT'S IN A "BIO"?

When it comes to communicating your services and capabilities or achievements to others, Model Rule 7.1 provides that all such communications about a lawyer's services shall not be false or misleading. For example, when you describe your background on a website "bio" or in a brochure to prospective new clients, saying that you have "experience in handling bankruptcy matters," after handling only one such case, may be misleading to the unsuspecting consumer. The term "experience" implies a degree of knowledge and skill in a particular legal field in handling many cases over some time and becoming familiar with the law and statutes governing that practice area. Merely "dabbling" in a

---

From the **Woman Advocate**/Fall 2007/ABA/Section of Litigation
[1] MODEL RULES OF PROF'L CONDUCT R. 1.1. The Model Rules form the basis for many states' ethics rules.

particular area of law should not be presented as an established specialty if you want to avoid the risks of violating the ethical rules on communicating your services to prospective clients. Certainly, if you become specialized in a particular area, that experience will enable you to represent truthfully your qualifications in marketing and generating new business.

Model Rule 7.4 provides that you may communicate the fact that you are specialized in a particular field, or fields, but, again, such statements must conform to the general "false and misleading" rule in Model Rule 7.1. Some jurisdictions, or accredited organizations such as the American Bar Association, provide opportunities to become a certified specialist in a particular field (*e.g.*, "Certified Trial Attorney"). Model Rule 7.4(d) provides that you can communicate the fact that you are a certified specialist if you clearly identify the name of the certifying organization.

Be particularly careful before using other designations to communicate your background and achievements, such as "Super Lawyer," because they have come under attack in certain jurisdictions. In New Jersey, the Committee on Attorney Advertising, appointed by the New Jersey Supreme Court, issued Opinion 39 on July 24, 2006, in which it concluded that advertising oneself as a "Super Lawyer" or a "Best Lawyer in America" violates New Jersey's Rules of Professional Conduct 7.1(a)(3) and 7.1(a)(2), which proscribe misleading communications that compare a lawyer's services with another lawyer's services and are likely to create unjustified expectations in the lawyer's abilities or the results she can achieve. The committee believed that superlatives such as "super" and "best," by their nature, create an unreasonable expectation that a lawyer can deliver legal services superior to those of a lawyer who has not been designated a "Super Lawyer" or "Best Lawyer in America." Certain other designations, such as "AV rated" through Martindale-Hubbell, are not considered false or misleading and do not require additional explanation because they can be independently verified.[2] The unsettled question and current debate over the proper use of superlative descriptions or designations should give you pause before you use them in your marketing efforts.

BRANDING

As firms search for new ways to differentiate themselves in the legal market, "branding" has become the method of the moment to reinvigo-

---

[2] Mason v. Florida Bar, 208 F.3d 952 (11th Cir. 2000).

rate a firm's image and to attract new clients. To that end, firms are shortening their names, coming up with catchy slogans and sleek logos, and updating their websites in a multimedia effort to establish a brand image. On an individual level, the notion of branding, in terms of marketing a lawyer's practice area or expertise, likely will follow suit and become more commonplace. If you pursue branding in generating business, you should be sensitive to the guidelines for truthfully communicating your services set forth in Model Rule 7.1.

"BLAWGS," WEBSITES, AND EMAIL

A web log (blog) is an up-to-the-minute Internet site that is updated often to reveal new content, information, or "breaking news" on a particular subject. Blogging is the latest digital communication method to mass-publicize a person's knowledge or expertise. Further, blogs allow the public to participate in the discussion and to add content through commentary about postings on the site. Successful blogs have many repeat visitors and are cross-referenced in major search engines such as Google.

Legal blogs, called "blawgs," are seen as a way to develop new business, get visibility for current issues in particular practice areas, and establish a niche brand image for attorneys who can grasp the new technology and devote the time needed to maintain a relevant blawg that is visited often by the public. Websites and targeted emails, newsletters, or brochures remain tools that most lawyers rely upon to get their message (and credentials) out to a mass audience in generating business.

Some people question whether blawgs are risky from an ethical and professional liability perspective. Indeed, legal press articles have discussed concerns raised by professional liability insurance carriers as to the "insurability" of blawgs operated by lawyers and/or law firms.[3] The concern is that the lawyer or firm, in answering questions through the blawg, will be seen as giving legal advice. Thus, the lawyer or firm may unintentionally establish an attorney-client relationship with the recipient of the information. To avoid any confusion, blawgs should have strong disclaimer language advising those who view the site that the information given in the site is not legal advice and that an attorney-client relationship is not established with anyone who views the site. You might give thought to including the statement that the blawg reflects the personal views of the lawyer who publishes it and that the site is pub-

[3] *See, e.g.,* Lisa Brennan, *Law Firms' "Dear Abby" Blogs Kiboshed by Insurer*, N.Y. LAWYER, April 17, 2007.

lished in the lawyer's individual capacity. The firm associated with the blawging lawyer can disclaim any responsibility for the content of the site and, therefore, minimize the impact of any liability that might flow from its operation. Websites, like blawgs, also must be carefully reviewed and monitored to be certain that viewers of the site are warned that information appearing on or given in the site is not legal advice and that an attorney-client relationship is not formed by visiting the site and providing information or posing questions to lawyers through the site.

Other ethical concerns in using the newer forms of media through the Internet to generate business are the risks that confidential client information may be revealed and that blawgs, websites, or email communications may provide the attorney with confidential information from a prospective client. Model Rule 1.6, concerning protection of client confidences, provides that a lawyer should not reveal information relating to the representation of her client without the client's consent. Accordingly, when describing your past accomplishments or experience, you must take care to use only general descriptions without revealing specific information that is reasonably likely to disclose the identity of the client or client's situation. Protecting a client's confidences is at the heart of the attorney-client relationship, and the duty to protect those confidences continues even after the attorney-client relationship ends. With the advent of real-time electronic communication over the Internet, care must be taken not to reveal information or details concerning clients, client matters, or, indeed, anything relating to the client representation.

A blawg or website provides opportunities for unsolicited information from people seeking legal advice or services. Through the Internet, the lawyer or firm may obtain confidential information that should be protected by the rules of ethics. Model Rule 1.18 addresses a lawyer's duties to prospective clients. A "prospective client," as defined in Model Rule 1.18(a), is a person who discusses the possibility of forming a client-lawyer relationship in a particular matter with the lawyer. In analyzing the ethical obligations of a lawyer or firm under these circumstances, the focus is on determining whether the prospective client had a reasonable expectation of forming an attorney-client relationship with the lawyer or firm. Under Model Rule 1.18(b), if you actively solicit and obtain any personal or confidential information from a prospective client, you may not reveal such information even if no attorney-client relationship is formed, except as may be allowed under Model Rule 1.9 (relating to duties to former clients). To prevent the reasonable expectation that unilateral, unsolicited information from a person will be held in confidence by the lawyer or firm, the blawg or website should have a "pop-up" dialogue box that states clearly that the person revealing the information understands and agrees that the lawyer or firm will have no duty to keep the information confidential and that an attorney-client relationship is not formed until the lawyer or firm takes steps to formally meet with the person.[4] Ideally, that dialogue box should appear before the person submits the information, and the person should have to affirmatively "accept" or "agree" to the terms before submitting any information on the blawg or website. Although cumbersome, this and similar protective measures can reduce the likelihood that a person would be deemed to be a "prospective client" under Model Rule 1.18. Giving appropriate warnings to viewers of the blawg or website supports the argument that the person should not have had a reasonable expectation of forming an attorney-client relationship with the lawyer or firm.

CONCERNS IN SOLICITING NEW CLIENTS

In addition to detailed disclaimers, blawgs, websites, or marketing email communications must conform to the specific ethical rules governing solicitation and advertising in your jurisdiction. Under Model Rule 7.3(a), concerning solicitation of prospective clients, a lawyer cannot directly solicit business from prospective clients through in-person, telephone, or real-time electronic contact when the "significant motive" for such solicitation is the lawyer's pecuniary gain. The exception to Model Rule 7.3(a) is that a lawyer may, through direct contact, solicit business from another lawyer or persons with whom the soliciting lawyer has a family, close personal, or prior professional relationship. Model Rule 7.3 also proscribes any form of solicitation of a prospective client who has made it known he or she does not wish to be contacted by the lawyer and solicitation that involves coercion, duress, or harassment. The rule also advises that proper solicitations, whether a recorded oral message or in writing, must include the words "Advertising Material." Under Model Rule 7.1, any solicitations must not be false or misleading. New York recently enacted strict attorney advertising rules.[5]

---

[4] *See* Kathryn A. Thompson, *The Too Much Information Age*, A.B.A. J., July 2007 (discussing Model Rule 1.18 and the ethical debate over handling unsolicited information received by persons seeking legal services).
[5] You can access the rules by visiting the New York State Bar Association's website at http://www.nysba.com and clicking on "Professional Standards for Attorneys." You will find a link to "Lawyer Advertising Regulations."

Although some of the new advertising rules have recently been struck down as unconstitutional,[6] the other provisions concerning methods of advertising and soliciting new clients have been preserved. For example, under the New York advertising rules, a law firm's website shall be labeled "Attorney Advertising" on the home page, and emails, under certain circumstances described in the rules, must state "ATTORNEY ADVERTISING" in the subject line.[7] It is incumbent upon you to be informed of the advertising and solicitation regulations that govern in your jurisdiction.

REFERRAL FEES AND "GIFTS"

The Model Rules of Professional Conduct allow an attorney to give referral fees to another attorney provided that the total fee is reasonable; the fee arrangement is proportionate to the services performed by each attorney; the client agrees to the referral (or fee splitting) arrangement, including the share amount to be paid; and the client's agreement is confirmed in writing.[8] Model Rule 7.2(b) states that a lawyer "shall not give anything of value to a person" who recommends the lawyer's services to potential clients subject to certain exceptions, including that the lawyer can pay the reasonable costs of advertising allowed by the Model Rules and can enter into a nonexclusive referral arrangement with another attorney about which the client is informed. Under the ethics rules, giving and accepting *de minimis* gifts among referring attorneys may also be permissible. You should research the ethics opinions in your state or local bar association to determine whether such gifts are proper. In the "post-Enron" era we live in, much attention has been paid in the for-profit corporate world to conflicts of interest and the appearance of impropriety created when professionals and/or company executives give or accept gifts, junkets, and other things of value in the course of doing business. If you have any hesitation in giving or accepting gifts from clients or other attorneys in connection with generating business, simply do not do it. You are wise to give very serious consideration to potential risks that may be involved in making any financial arrangements or exchanging gifts with potential referral sources.

---

[6] Alexander v. Cahill, 2007 WL 2120024 (N.D.N.Y. July 23, 2007) (slip copy).
[7] N.Y. COMP. CODES R. & REGS. tit. 22, § 1200.6(f).
[8] MODEL RULES OF PROF'L CONDUCT R. 1.5(e).

YOUR REPUTATION IS YOUR STOCK IN TRADE

Being ever mindful of and vigilant in conforming to the particular rules of professional conduct that govern in your legal community is the very foundation of forming a professional reputation that will bring in new business. Attorneys whom others see as trustworthy, above reproach, and ethical will be the ones to whom clients are referred. When marketing your practice and in generating new clients, be certain that you are scrupulous in following the ethical rules. The extra time and care you take to be sure that your business development activities are appropriate will not be in vain.

Young Lawyer's Perspective on Rainmaking: A Timeline for Success

By Amy Messigian and Bronwyn Roberts

Having clients of your own has certain benefits that are not always available to lawyers who are serving firm clients. Unlike their "service lawyer" peers, "rainmakers" can be selective about the firms at which they want to work, the people with whom they want to work, the type of work they want to do, and the clients they want to serve. They are also generally compensated for their rainmaking efforts. Accordingly, becoming a "rainmaker" is an important goal for the lawyer seeking to be in charge of her destiny. To this end, we propose a timeline for new lawyers looking to become rainmakers down the road.

LAW STUDENTS

You do not need to wait until you have finished law school to begin networking or getting involved in legal associations. Join local and national bar associations, and seek out leadership positions for law students. In many cases, you will be able to maintain a leadership role in the committee you join after you have graduated, and you will have already established a budding network with other attorneys. Attend any local bar association meetings you can.

Get a social life. Don't let all your classes keep you from reaching out to community and personal interest groups. The people you meet in social settings could very well become clients or referral sources at some point in the future.

FIRST YEAR

As soon as you begin your new position, reach out to law school classmates to meet for lunch and compare notes about your respective experiences. Keep updated contact information for your classmates, understand the legal work they are performing, and make sure they know where you are and the type of work you are doing. In a few years, these classmates will likely become excellent referral sources.

Get your name known in the legal community by offering to coauthor an article with a senior lawyer in your firm. Even in cases where you do not receive authorship credit, showing an interest in article de-

From the **Woman Advocate**/Fall 2007/ABA/Section of Litigation
The authors would like to thank Nan Joesten for her contributions to this article.

velopment now and contributing to the research or editing of an article will pay off later when that same partner is looking for a coauthor on a different article. Also, use downtime between work to write on your own. You never know when you will have the opportunity to publish down the road, and researching a topic of interest to you will provide additional clarification and understanding of part of your practice.

Avoid collecting continuing education credits alone. Rather than rack up your continuing education credits online or via telephone, attend as many continuing legal education seminars in person as possible. Focus on topics that interest you and expand your knowledge of a particular area of law. Remember to have a supply of business cards handy to exchange.

Law firms frequently buy tables at community and bar association events. Seek to secure a seat at your firm table when possible. And again, bring those business cards!

SECOND YEAR

Many of you will be approaching a high school reunion in the first three years of practice. As much as you may not want to remember your high school hairdo or significant other, you should attend your reunion. You will meet and reconnect with numerous people in varying businesses and careers, many of whom may look to you now, or in the future, for legal advice.

Although you will have far less time to do so later in your career, during the early years, you may be capable of taking on pro bono work, often with the blessing of your firm. Even though this may not seem to be the best way to make rain, taking on pro bono work allows you to perfect your craft and often gives you the ability to start and finish a matter with little outside assistance. Being able to survive legal minefields on your own builds the confidence necessary to appear before judges and jurors and will serve you well when you are called upon to take on the challenge in the future.

Ask the senior associates and partners with whom you work to send you to court hearings that they would otherwise cover with a telephonic appearance, such as status conferences and minor discovery hearings. Appearing will lessen your fears of speaking before court in the future when you have something more to say than "Ms. Messigian for the Defendant, Your Honor." Again, although this does not directly create rain, it will improve your public speaking—something quite necessary to the litigator who hopes to bring in clientele of her own.

Seek guidance from your mentors. Many law firms have established programs pairing junior lawyers with more experienced attorneys who are tasked with mentoring new lawyers. If you are paired with a great rainmaker as your mentor, good for you! Take advantage of the opportunity by asking for advice on what you can be doing to become a rainmaker and for his or her support by including you in your mentor's rainmaking activities. Seek out firm rainmakers and ask about how they built their practices, and what they would suggest you do at this stage in your career.

THIRD YEAR

Join and become active in local civic associations or trade associations. Attend their meetings and offer your assistance in projects. When you join such associations, make sure that the people you meet know the type of legal work performed by you and your firm.

FOURTH YEAR

Watch and learn from "rainmakers" in your firm by participating in firm marketing events. Assist in the planning and presentation of a seminar updating clients on important trends in your field.

Continue to keep track of your law school classmates and determine whether they could be referral sources in the future. Also, send holiday cards and news articles of interest to prospective clients with whom you have connected along the road and clients of the firm with whom you have enjoyed a working relationship. Let these prospective clients know that you are interested in and concerned about their business needs.

FIFTH YEAR

Add value to your personal stock by beginning to develop a unique expertise in a particular field. In addition, look at your firm's clientele and determine whether any major clients or prospective clients do business in another state, and seek admission to that state's bar. Many states allow you to apply for admission without examination after five years of practice in another jurisdiction.

Create your business plan. Set aside time to draft your marketing goals for each quarter or year, such as getting published, attending local bar events, or going out to lunch with a client, and hold yourself accountable for reaching those goals. Even better, get together with colleagues who have similar rainmaking aspirations and agree to hold one another accountable for achieving your interim goals each week or month. Similar to a marketing mentoring circle, having a group to check in with is great for inspiring you to put the time into achieving your goals, helping you overcome obstacles along the way, and sharing creative rainmaking ideas.

SIXTH YEAR

Become very knowledgeable about the depth of services offered by your firm. Be on top of recent firm work and success stories. Get to know your firm colleagues outside your practice area and be ready to make appropriate introductions of your colleagues to your prospective clients.

Take prospective clients out for lunch and listen to the issues they may have. Offer to introduce them to people who could assist them in their businesses.

SEVENTH YEAR

Having coauthored articles with more senior lawyers in your earlier years, now is the time to branch out and seek to publish something that you have written on your own. Get an idea for an interesting piece and contact bar journals and trade journals to determine whether there might be a place for your proposed article. Even if you are unable to get your article published, you may be able to use it as a client alert that you could send to clients and prospective clients of the firm.

Speaking engagements are another great way to build your name recognition while meeting people interested in your area of expertise. Make sure that the attorneys you look to for mentoring know that you are interested in an opportunity to speak, and get their suggestions on how you can improve your chances of being asked to participate on panels at various events.

EIGHTH YEAR

Having cemented your relationship for several years with local or national organizations, seek a leadership role within a section of the bar association, your alumni association, or other organizations in which you have been active.

NINTH YEAR

By now, you likely have had the good fortune of having someone ask for your legal assistance. Even if the matter is a small one that might not meet the profile of your firm's typical clientele, take it. You will find that good work on a small matter will lead to opportunities for larger matters; it will also likely lead to lucrative referrals.

TENTH YEAR

In your tenth year, you should be well versed in how to market yourself and how to start building your own client base. You will have presented at bar association events, written articles of interest to your target client base, dined with prospective clients, made important introductions for clients and prospective clients, and likely will already have some business of your own. Now is the time to set aside four to five hours per week and devote them to marketing and increasing your client base. You will likely continue to do almost all that you have done in the preceding years, but you will now know what works best for you. If you have found that article writing is not bringing in the business you had hoped it would, but that your weekly luncheons have, scale down the writing and make your lunch dates more frequent. Similarly, if you find that speaking engagements are particularly uncomfortable, but you still have a message to get out, cut down on your public speaking and focus on your writing. Figure out what works best for you, set aside the time, and get out there and build a practice. The rain may not be flowing yet, but the forecast looks good.

Young Lawyers

What They Didn't Teach You in Law School: How to Establish a Clientele
By Gerald Giaimo

One learns very quickly after passing the bar exam that there is a core element to the practice of law that is not taught in law school or covered on the exam: generating a clientele. Distinguishing oneself among attorneys with long careers is, ab initio, difficult enough for the young lawyer. It is particularly true, however, in construction law, where the practice has become increasingly a niche business, with more and more attorneys holding themselves out as "specialists" in the field. In surveying my colleagues, though, I have discovered success stories that prove it can be done. Indeed, rainmaking in this field is not the exclusive province of the senior lawyers. The business development key for the young attorney, in the final analysis, is both to embrace the fundamental habits of good lawyering and to adopt a modern business strategy, marketing directly to industry-relevant prospects.

Qualities that constitute successful lawyering apply indiscriminately in the profession. Invariably, we are reminded that business generation, client retention, and client satisfaction all begin with the following few good habits.

BE RESPONSIVE

Although it might seem obvious, client communication must be the highest priority. Always answer your telephone if you are available. Return missed calls the same day if possible or, at the latest, within 24 hours. Nothing detracts from client satisfaction with greater force than a client's feeling of neglect. Adopting such call-back rules is a simple and easy way to keep the client happy.

BE PROFESSIONAL

In these days of "business casual" attire, it is easy to lose sight of the fact that clients are very sensitive to the manner in which you present your-

From the **Construct!**/Summer 2007/ABA/Section of Litigation

self to others. Although some expect aggressive advocacy, you should act in a civil and reasonable manner at all times. Whether you are in the courtroom, in a meeting, or on the telephone, your client is watching and digesting—consciously or unconsciously. You will always reap greater respect and confidence from clients (and potential future clients) for treating others with respect and dignity.

BE YOURSELF

Embrace your natural personality and style. Both your legal work and marketing methods suffer when you adopt a style that does not comport with who you are. Every attorney has a different style, and one size does not "fit all." Not being afraid to do what feels natural and comfortable shows confidence, which, in turn, translates into success. Without question, these habits will help you level the playing field with your colleagues to a certain degree. It is not realistic, however, to expect the local media to contact you for comments and quotes or to expect to receive a leadership appointment in construction law associations or bar committees. Indeed, to distinguish yourself as a rainmaker in the construction law field, you need to pioneer industry territory.

Any litigation in which you represent a party will, by necessity, involve two or more construction-related entities. Whether adverse or not, relationships are created in the course of a case—good or bad—from which reputations follow. There is no greater opportunity to demonstrate your construction law skills than before an audience of these entities. In general, counsel have long memories, and a successful result for your client might lead to a phone call for future work from another party—even an adverse party—impressed by your competence and professionalism.

Although the competition to publish articles or to teach seminars on construction law topics can be fierce within the bar community, there are often wonderful opportunities available to provide training or educational seminars directly to potential clients. Small contracting companies, which rarely have the resources to attend large industry seminars, would welcome free materials or seminars marketed directly to them, offered at a time or in a form that synchronizes with the busy schedules of small business owners.

One colleague and friend, Christopher Huck, a young partner at the Connecticut construction law firm of Michelson Kane Royster & Barger, P.C., offered another example of overlooked industry marketing: "You have to keep in mind the process by which outside counsel are brought into a dispute. Surety bond agents, project accountants/auditors, and industry expert witnesses are often involved with claims and disputes before they escalate to litigation. Nurturing relationships with individuals who have these roles can generate a bounty of referrals. "Of course," he added tongue-in-cheek, "it doesn't hurt to have a good golf game, too."

Young attorneys would be mistaken to assume that rainmaking in the construction law field is reserved for those who are well-known and seasoned. The beauty of the ideas and strategies presented here is that they are equally available to young and seasoned attorneys alike. Although it is unlikely that the bar exam will ever include a section on business development acumen, the young lawyer would be well-served to study up and hit the ground running; it is never too early to start making rain.

Making Rain: A Newly Minted Associate's Perspective on Developing Business

By Effie Silva

After a record 143 days without precipitation, a steady rain began falling the day I arrived in Scottsdale, Arizona. I ran for cover in what would be my first regional meeting as a recent lateral into the litigation practice group. That was the day I learned the basics needed to land my first client—something I did while preparing this article.

RAISE YOUR PROFILE

Attend industry and legal functions, join key professional/community organizations, and volunteer for some pro bono projects. The firm's existing clients may know who you are because they pay your bills, but certainly no one else will learn about you or your talents if you don't leave your desk. It's challenging, true, but networking is critical to raising your profile and ensuring future referrals. I met my first client by pushing myself into a women's business conference that my firm was sponsoring.

JOIN IN FIRM PROPOSALS/PITCHES

You must demonstrate that you have a solid understanding of your practice group's business plan and the services the firm can provide. Only then will they let you venture into the world of planning a business campaign. Volunteer to conduct industry-specific research and prepare information for pitches. Identify cross-selling opportunities with existing clients. For example, if you are a litigator, evaluate whether one of your litigation clients requires assistance with a corporate transaction or real estate matter. After consulting with more senior lawyers, suggest to those clients what additional work could be performed for them.

PUBLISH

Write articles, internally or externally, related to your group's practice. I started by writing a summary of two recent Eleventh Circuit opinions for my firm's *International Litigation and Arbitration Newsletter*, which has been submitted to the ABA Section of Litigation's *International Litigation Newsletter*. Your publication might just lead you to securing a speaking engagement to corporate executives exhilarated to learn about your topic.

From the **Woman Advocate**/Fall 2006/ABA/Section of Litigation

SECURE A MENTOR

Good mentors are hard to find. If your firm has a mentoring program, you will be paired with someone in your office whom you may or may not like. Regardless, you must seek out someone who would be willing to guide you through your formative years. Comfort level is key. Find someone you trust to give good advice on ethical questions and who will, without judging you, answer the stupid questions that we all have from time to time.

FIND A NICHE THAT MATTERS TO YOU

Personally, I have always been interested in international relations and world politics. I majored in international relations at Wellesley College and took several international classes in law school. Today, I practice commercial litigation at a premier international law firm. Several of the cases I currently work on have some international aspect. Whether it is preparing a Taiwanese client for a deposition or suing a company for a breach of contract that originated from the development of a Brazilian power plant, I wake up every morning excited about the cases that I am working on. Start building a niche as early as you can; this will allow you to develop expertise in a specific field, and you will be the obvious choice when clients need help.

Using Online Social Networking Sites to Make It Rain

By Griselda Zamora

Using online social networking sites as part of your professional rain-making toolkit makes sense. After all, reaching out to contacts, making connections, and then turning connections into long-lasting relationships is part of making it rain. We build long-lasting relationships through various mediums. In today's marketplace, online social networking must be one of them. Facebook alone has over 300 million active users.[1] Ignoring this wealth of potential contacts would be remiss. You would never ignore a highly attended conference targeting your client base. Why would you ignore a highly attended social networking site that also reaches those same contacts? The use of online social networking sites will only grow and continue to be refined, and it should correspondingly grow in prominence as part of your rainmaking toolkit.

Many of you have received emails from business associates, clients, or colleagues inviting you to friend them on Facebook, join them at LinkedIn, or follow them on Twitter. Online social networking sites promise connections organized by interest, workplace, school, or community. Social networking sites are great places to learn about people or topics that interest you, to ask others for assistance, and to develop initial contacts within your client base.

Sites such as Facebook, LinkedIn, and Twitter are well-known online social networking sites. Although each site differs in focus, they all provide users with a platform that allows them to network in a social and professional capacity. Facebook users add friends or contacts electronically and are then able to send personal and professional updates to their network of friends. LinkedIn focuses on helping its users build an online professional network that can further their careers. Twitter, on the other hand, allows users to post updates (*i.e.*, tweets) via a blog format. Followers subscribe to individual Twitter feeds based on topic or person of interest and then receive the latest information via tweets.

PITFALLS TO AVOID: THE ILLUSION OF PRIVACY

However, as with any rainmaking tool, pitfalls exist and must be avoided. Two of the biggest pitfalls with online social networking sites

From the **Woman Advocate**/Winter 2010/ABA/Section of Litigation
[1] Facebook Press Room Statistics, www. facebook.com/press/info.php?statistics (last visited Sept. 30, 2009).

are the great illusion of privacy and forgetting the need for constant consciousness of who we are and what we do.[2] Failing to focus on the positive uses of social networking sites—and not recognizing the major pitfalls—can seriously hinder your online professional image, not to mention your career.

For some unknown reason, when we get behind a computer screen, we seem to forget there is no real privacy in what we do. You can expect privacy in your communications when you close your office door. That cannot be said of online social networking sites. It is inherent in the nature of social networking sites to make users as public and accessible as possible. After all, you are using social networking sites to make as many connections and contacts as possible. People take great pride in letting others know about the number of online friends, connections, or followers they have. Keep that in mind the next time you hit the send button and you let slip that comment about a senior associate at your firm whom you dislike. Know that all of your friends, the ones you so proudly gathered, will immediately read your comment and then share it with all of their friends. You can rest assured that in less than 10 minutes, your comment may likely end up in the senior associate's email inbox.

As an online social networking site user, you should be prepared to have your friends' online behavior reflect on your professionalism. Simply put, as your mother once warned, be very careful who your friends are, as you must take caution and care when accepting online friends. Your friends' behavior directly impacts how you are perceived, both personally and professionally, whether in real life or online. For example, take an attorney with a large DUI defense practice. All the effort and care she took to establish an online presence as a top-notch professional DUI defense firm would be seriously undermined if a "friend" in her network posted a profile picture in which she is holding a beer in each hand. The friend may find it amusing to share her drinking habit with the world, but the attorney's other clients would not (not to mention the reaction of opposing counsel).

Unfortunately, what your friends say and do on online is inextricably linked with your own online image. Take great care to ensure that you accept only friends whom you know and trust and who fit the image you want to portray on your social networking site. Make sure you regularly monitor your social networking site and remove friends who do

---

[2] Interview with Gregory J. Dhuyvetter, Assistant Principal, Academics, Mater Dei High School, in Santa Ana, Cal. (Sept. 18, 2009).

not reflect your site's professional image. You should also be a good friend to others by monitoring your own online behavior.

Also remember to take the time to understand and use the advanced privacy features and settings found on social networking sites. Doing so will allow you to better filter, manage, and limit access to your site's content. For example, Facebook allows you to set different privacy levels based on contact group type. Setting a higher privacy level for professional contacts will limit their access to personal information, yet still allow you to share family photos with your family contact group.

FOCUS ON THE POSITIVE WHEN YOU REPRESENT YOURSELF ONLINE

Because privacy is not guaranteed on social networking sites, you should also make an effort to blend your personal and professional online images. This will present others with a complete picture of who you are. Acknowledging that you are a professional with personal interests and hobbies makes you accessible. Sharing the fact that you enjoy playing tennis does not detract from your professional online image. On the contrary, it can enhance it. Shared interests and hobbies provide another good avenue to make an initial connection with a potential client.

Realizing that online privacy is just an illusion will also help you avoid another major pitfall—forgetting the need for constant consciousness in all you do. You must always remember who you are and what you are doing while on social networking sites. We have all heard horror stories of dubious pictures posted online that come back to haunt the subject or about a job or scholarship lost because of something someone posted on a blog or in a public profile. Remember that everything you do online is a direct representation of who you are and, in turn, also represents your firm. If you would not say something to a senior associate or partner while standing in front of him or her, you do not want to say it in your profile, post, or tweet. If you find you have the time, you may want to consider the use of two different profiles on social networking sites: a personal profile and another for professional use. Your goal on social networking sites should be to make as many positive professional connections as possible. If you focus on the positive aspects of social networking sites, you can avoid the pitfalls.

One such positive aspect is keeping others up to date on your professional endeavors. A great way to stay connected would be to send a tweet to your client base inviting them to an interesting seminar related to their area of business, or to inform your Facebook friends about an interesting article you recently read or wrote yourself. Whether it be learning about a new area of law you are considering practicing or solving a professional dilemma, social networking sites provide you with connections to those who have faced similar situations.

When using social networking sites, remember to make posts only when truly necessary. Keeping your posts professional in content, succinct, accurate, clean, and easy to read will quickly build professional online credibility. Always remember to follow your jurisdiction's professional ethical guidelines and requirements as applied to online social networking sites, and do not breach any confidentiality duties through online networking. If you keep your focus on the positive aspects of online social networking sites, you will avoid common pitfalls and make it rain.

A Dozen Marketing Tips for the Time-Starved Lawyer
By Ellen Ostrow, Ph.D.

It is the greatest of all mistakes to do nothing because you can do only a little. Do what you can.

—Sidney Smith

Every man [sic] takes the limits of his own field of vision for the limits of the world.

—Arthur Schopenhauer

Many of the lawyers I coach feel stymied in their efforts to market their services successfully. Some are blocked by their perceptions of what marketing entails. They see it as a succession of uncomfortable cold calls—as anything but professional. Most feel that it's simply not possible to fulfill billable-hour requirements, attend to their families, and also find time for marketing activities.

One of the interesting things about this situation is that most of these attorneys actually have many opportunities to market their services. These opportunities don't require the burden of substantial amounts of extra work. Marketing is much easier if you are aware of the things you already do that have the potential to promote your work and realize the marketing opportunities that occur in your day-to-day interactions with others.

Here are 12 tips for the lawyer who needs to market but doesn't have the time.

REDEFINE MARKETING

Marketing is developing a sense of yourself and your strengths and communicating this to others with the goal of helping them solve a problem. Many lawyers avoid marketing because they think it is repugnant. Few attorneys go into law to make cold calls or push to close a sale. Cold calling is one marketing strategy you could choose, but there are many other ways to communicate your unique expertise and talent.

Stop telling yourself you have to be a superstar to market. There is no "one right way." Marketing is only effective if you do it, and you're far more likely to do it if your marketing activities fit comfortably in your life.

From the **Woman Advocate**/Fall 2005/ABA/Section of Litigation
The author's email newsletter, Beyond the Billable Hour,™ *is available at* www .lawyerslifecoach.com.

TAKE CONTROL

These days it's not realistic to say that you don't have time to market. Instead, consider how you can best use the time you have to do what must be done. Ask yourself, "If my life depended on getting around this 'reality,' what would I do?"

Even more importantly, marketing is the best way to implement your career plan and control your life. Clarifying your vision of the "perfect" client and developing a solid sense of your strengths and the work you want to do empower you to further your success. Designing your career, developing a network consistent with your goals, and acquiring a client book are the pathways to real career autonomy.

CHOOSE THE RIGHT STRATEGY FOR YOUR GOALS

Before they can hire you, prospective clients must be aware of you and perceive you to have the expertise they need. You can become more visible and credible by writing articles for publications that your market reads, giving speeches at their trade association meetings, sending newsletters to targeted companies, and hosting seminars for industry leaders. Direct contact is essential for building the relationships you'll need to get hired.

Credibility alone isn't enough. Cold calling, making warm calls, arranging an appointment, sending a personal letter of introduction, and meeting for lunch or coffee all are ways of making contact. The single most important part of your strategy, however, is networking.

NETWORKING DEVELOPS AND MAINTAINS MEANINGFUL RELATIONSHIPS

Networking is a sincere and consistent effort to help others with the hope that they will, in turn, help you. You can help people in your network by providing them with information, introductions, ideas, referrals, advice, emotional support, and free public relations. Your hope is that they will reciprocate.

The most important skills in relationship building are active listening and showing that you understand the other person's situation and experience. Women, in particular, usually have finely honed these skills. It's useful to remember that many marketing activities come quite naturally to you.

FOLLOW THE "RULES OF ROMANCE"

Management consultant and author David Maister encourages lawyers to approach prospects and clients as people with whom they'd like

35

to have a long-term romantic relationship. The following are Maister's rules:

- Communicate honestly.
- Listen and work to understand.
- Communicate frequently.
- Be supportive and understanding, not critical.
- Genuinely care about the relationship.
- Express appreciation.

PLANNING IS ESSENTIAL

Without a plan, most lawyers won't market because they view it as difficult or unpleasant. But developing an individual marketing plan enables you to make optimal use of the time you have and to avoid time wasters that don't fit with your priorities.

A marketing plan also allows you to stop thinking about marketing as an overwhelming project and instead to break it down into small action steps that you can easily accomplish. Many lawyers find that coaching enables them to develop a realistic plan, break marketing activities into manageable action steps, and successfully follow through.

PLAN MARKETING WITH YOUR WHOLE LIFE IN MIND

To achieve career success without sacrificing a fulfilling life, it's critical to design your career by taking your whole life into account. At least once a year, take the time to write out your important life roles (as parent, partner, child of aging parent, lawyer, friend, community member, person who needs to nurture your health, and someone with outside interests). Ask yourself what you want to accomplish in each of these roles during the coming year. What do you have to do to accomplish these goals? Refer to your life plan as you complete your monthly, weekly, and daily planner.

EMPHASIZE ACTIVITIES THAT FULFILL MULTIPLE GOALS

Changing your concept of marketing can change your feelings, attitudes, and behavior. Once you've redefined marketing, you can become aware of the opportunities for marketing that were there all along.

You can find a multitude of activities that allow you to be with your family and contribute to your community while marketing your skills. What if you took your children to a fundraiser for a homeless shelter that was sponsored by a company in your target niche?

Marketing is more of a mindset than the ability to devote time to particular tasks. Once it becomes a natural part of your daily activities, time becomes less of an issue. You begin to realize that you have opportunities to market in almost every context in which you interact with people.

BALANCE AND FLEXIBILITY ARE CRUCIAL

When people allow work to consume their lives, they tend to become myopic and ungenerous. A normally thoughtful, considerate person can find herself being brusque, not returning phone calls, or focusing only on business matters when talking to a client who's just told you that her mother is critically ill. It's essential to maintain sufficient balance and flexibility to behave like the caring person you really are. Simply treat others the way you'd like to be treated.

LEVERAGE

A single work project can be recycled into a plethora of marketing activities. Consider inviting a group of clients to a presentation about the ways in which your project is relevant to them. Submit an article about the project to your niche's industry publication and make sure it's published in your firm's newsletter as well. Contact organizations like Fulcrum and offer to speak on the topic. You can make this the core of a speech you deliver at other meetings your niche attends. Leveraging is a way to get maximum usage out of the work you're already doing. It's a great time-saver.

RECOGNIZE THE RESOURCES YOU ALREADY HAVE

To begin, make a list of the people you used to know, those you currently know, those who know you, and those you would like to know. It's often the case that if you list all the people connected with your network members, you'll find a route to the people you want to meet, such as the new corporate counsel of a major player in the industry you represent.

To build and maintain relationships with selected people in your network, you can sit on boards, participate in volunteer activities, serve on industry committees, and maintain regular contact through phone calls, email, and lunches. If a particular relationship deepens, consider inviting that person and his or her family to your home.

BE PATIENT

Don't expect instant results from your marketing activities. If you do, you'll get discouraged and give up too quickly. Keep in mind that it takes a long time for marketing activities to bear fruit. Right now you're just planting seeds. Persistence and patience are key.

Business Plans— Business Development

Don't Wait, Create! Networking & Business Development for Younger Lawyers

By Michelle N. Lipkowitz

Ages ago, the sole responsibility of a younger lawyer was to focus on billable hours and honing research and writing skills. Those days are long gone. Success as a younger lawyer today is no longer bestowed solely by the billable hour fairy or based exclusively on quality work product. Rather, it is equally tied to the ability to market oneself effectively—internally and externally.

Younger lawyers today need to recognize the importance of prioritizing business development and networking during their early years rather than waiting and finding themselves behind when it comes time to be considered for partnership. We should not wait for opportunities to arise—we need to create them.

In order to succeed in networking and business development as a younger lawyer, begin with two main principles: Visibility, because people have to know you to consider choosing you, and credibility, because people have to be confident that you will do a great job in order to choose you. By keeping these principles is mind, you can create your own recipe for success using the following plan and ingredients.

PERSONALIZED MARKETING PLAN

Create, act on, evaluate and consistently revise a personalized marketing plan (PMP). Your PMP should identify both short-term (1 year) and long-term (5 to 10 year) goals. Importantly, you need to determine a way to quantify your progress. For example, track the number of hours spent on professional activities, specific leadership positions attained and re-

From the **Environmental Litigation Committee Newsletter**/Fall 2005/ABA/ Section of Litigation

lated initiatives and accomplishments; the number of articles written and presentations given; communications with current clients, with particular attention to new matters generated through your relationship with the client; and the number of contacts made with potential clients. Conduct biannual reviews and update your PMP accordingly.

STEP 1: CREATE YOUR MISSION STATEMENT

Why a mission statement? As highlighted in Stephen R. Covey's time management handbook, *First Things First: To Live, to Love, to Learn, to Leave a Legacy*, writing a personal mission statement offers the opportunity to establish what's important to you and determine how to stick to it throughout your career. Or, it enables you to chart a new course when you are at a career crossroads. This reasoning is adaptable to a personal mission statement for a younger lawyer. For example, Covey talks about imagining what all of your friends and family would say about you at your 80th birthday or 50th wedding anniversary. For the young lawyer, in the law firm environment, imagine the partnership meeting at which the firm's partners will vote on your election to partnership. What do you want them to say about you?

Similarly, Covey refers to crafting a mission statement as "connecting with your own unique purpose and the profound satisfaction that comes in fulfilling it." Younger lawyers need to do the same thing in crafting their legal career path. We need to look internally and consider: Why am I practicing law? Where do I want my practice to go? What unique strengths do I bring to the table? Be true to yourself and create opportunities you will enjoy.

Younger lawyers need to be introspective while balancing this with focused efforts on the task at hand—reaching clients and potential clients. It is important to always consider your target population: the clients themselves. One should consider: what do my clients and potential clients read and watch? Where do they congregate for business and social purposes? What issues are important to them? For me, the overarching goal is to build long-term, mutually beneficial relationships with clients and referral sources based on honesty, integrity, and credibility.

STEP 2: OUTLINE YOUR ACTION POINTS

Now that you have completed your mission statement, you need a mechanism to set targets and quantify your progress. This is also the place to identify your short- and long-term goals. Sample action points include taking a few potential clients or referral sources to lunch or dinner each month, writing two articles per year within your substantive area, giving four speeches or presentations within the year and/or present two CLEs or seminars before the end of the year, and joining a community organization or board.

STEP 3: IDENTIFY THE "WHO"

"The Who" is all of the people and organizations which will help you to meet your action points and achieve the goals of your mission statement. Just like a healthy investment portfolio, "the Who" of your PMP needs to be diverse.

Bar Associations

On the national level, a young lawyer can become active in the American Bar Association. As an introduction into the ABA, a younger lawyer can become active in the Young Lawyers Division, which is open to all ABA members under the age of 36 or admitted to practice less than five years. You can also become active on a committee within an ABA section related to your practice area (*e.g.*, the Section of Litigation, which has also established a Young Lawyer Leadership Program).

Many State Bar Associations and City Bar Associations also have young lawyers' sections or divisions.

The key to any bar association becoming a viable source of networking and business development is simple: participate! Active participation offers ample networking and business development opportunities for a younger lawyer. Merely showing up for the annual meeting is not enough. All of the aforementioned bar associations produce publications, put on CLEs, and host various other networking events, all of which are opportunities for a proactive younger lawyer to approach bar association leadership and say, "put me to work."

Alumni Memberships

Contacts from school can be one of the best sources of referrals and potential clients for younger lawyers. But don't limit yourself to law school and college. Widen your scope and consider friends you have maintained since childhood. A younger lawyer can reap a significant return on a relatively small investment by becoming, and remaining active with, their law school, college, and possibly even high school alumni association(s). Many times, these alumni associations include affinity associations for members with shared cultural, religious, or geographic backgrounds that tend to offer a cohesive network that is ripe for client development and referrals.

"Internal" Clients

One area of development that many younger lawyers tend to overlook, to their detriment, is internal client development. This refers to building relationships within your office, region, and, if applicable, greater firm. Internal clients include all of a younger lawyer's colleagues—partners, senior counsel and associates, and peers—and also office staff.

Internal client development can be viewed as a type of cross-selling. There is a reason so many businesses focus on cross-selling: it's effective. On a rudimentary level, cross-selling is the strategy of pushing new products to current customers based on their past purchases. Cross-selling is designed to widen the customer's reliance on the company and decrease the likelihood of the customer switching to a competitor. Younger lawyers can adapt this cross-selling strategy for use in their own career development.

Here are some goals for a younger lawyer's internal cross-selling strategy: increase visibility and credibility with internal clients; expand internal client relationships by assuring that the internal client is completely satisfied with your service, and inquire about additional business and legal issues the internal client has; and familiarize yourself with the internal clients so that you can better anticipate their business objectives and legal strategies.

NON-LAWYERS

It is imperative that younger lawyers integrate non-lawyers into their PMP. After all, and particularly in the law firm context, your client in-house counsel in turn services their corporation's business people, who are mostly non-lawyers. Many cities around the country have some sort of young professionals networking group. Join one. These young professional networking groups (often targeted to young professionals under the age of 40) host networking events and coordinate volunteer activities. Such events offer younger lawyers opportunities to make contacts outside the legal community, including other young up-and-coming leaders who will ultimately be in decision-making positions, and capable of influencing the selection of counsel, either within their own corporations or through referral. Because of the ever-looming billable hours, there tends to be a dearth of lawyers participating in young professionals networking groups. But, proactive younger lawyers can use this under representation to their advantage, becoming a bigger fish in a smaller pond.

STEP 4: IDENTIFY THE "HOW"

Now that you have completed your mission statement, identified your action points, and outlined the "who," we need to give your PMP legs by identifying the "How." In essence, the "How" identifies how you are going to meet your action points and personify your mission statement. Suggestions include: (1) renew contacts and cultivate relationships with potential referral and client sources; (2) become active in a bar association and/or community organization, and volunteer to take on leadership roles; (3) become active internally within your firm—at the office, regional, or firm-wide level; and (4) increase visibility through print and presentations.

Simple ways to renew contacts and cultivate relationships with individuals who are potential referral or client sources include inviting them to lunch, dinner, or a sporting event and following up punctually with a telephone call, letter, or email. Becoming active in bar associations and community organizations, and volunteering to take on leadership roles, begins with researching the applicable organizations, expressing an interest and attending meetings. The next step is to build visibility and credibility by actively participating in the organization by organizing meetings and events and by chairing and cochairing committees and subcommittees.

Younger women and minority lawyers can become active in diversity focused organizations such as the Minority Corporate Counsel Association (MCCA). The MCCA advocates for the expanded hiring, retention, and promotion of women and minority attorneys in corporate law departments and the law firms that serve them. The MCCA provides great networking and business development opportunities to younger lawyers through their diversity dinner series, regional networking panels and receptions, CLE expos, and diversity conferences. In order to get more involved in your firm, seek opportunities to become active in recruiting and hiring, the summer program, or associates committee.

There are several ways to increase visibility through print, including not only writing articles for business publications, legal publications, and firm publications, but also for your law school magazine or newsletter or college magazine or newsletter. The reach of these writings can be increased by sending them to your contacts. Similarly, many potential clients and referral sources are pleased to receive information of interest, articles and recent caselaw—even if it is not your own work—from a younger lawyer who is anticipating their needs. This applies to both internal and external clients.

In order to increase visibility through speaking, a younger lawyer must speak whenever and wherever he or she can. One way to get a leg in the door is to volunteer or ask to present with someone senior to you. Another option is to be part of a panel rather than trying to debut as the main attraction. The reach of a younger lawyer's speaking engagements can be increased by inviting his or her contacts. Sample speaking engagements include CLE seminars and substantive area seminars, both internal and external.

CLOSING THOUGHTS

In addition to a PMP, younger lawyers need to keep their profiles updated and keep a working file for all articles, presentations, major achievements, and kudos. You should focus on building credibility by consistently producing top-notch, quality service and work through preparation, and returning calls and emails promptly—even if the response is that you need to research the issue and get back to the client. Younger lawyers should hone their skills in anticipating client needs and being respectful of client schedules. This is particularly important when sending documents to clients for review. Along the same lines, younger lawyers need to focus on understanding expectations, always meeting deadlines, being budget conscious, and providing consistent status updates, without needing to be asked for one. It's not rocket science, but it does take effort, time, and commitment to accomplish your goals. Start by taking two hours of quiet time this weekend and write a mission statement. You will be amazed at how much progress will flow from that simple effort.

SUGGESTED READING

Effective Marketing for Lawyers by Christine S. Filip, Esq., New York State Bar Association, 1996.

First Things First: To Live, to Love, to Learn, to Leave a Legacy by Steven R. Covey, A. Roger Merrill, Rebecca R. Merrill, Firseside, 1994.

Lions Don't Need to Roar by D.A. Benton, Warner Books, 1992.

Marketing the Law Firm by Sally Schmidt, Law Journal Seminars' Press.

Rainmaking: An Adventure in the Law by Jerry Sears, Associates Publishers, 2001.

The Art of Winning Conversation by Morey Stettner, Prentice Hall, 1995.

The 7 Habits of Highly Effective People by Stephen R. Covey, Simon and Schuster, 1989.

Who Moved My Cheese by Spencer Johnson, Kenneth H. Blanchard, Penguin Putnam, Inc., 1998.

A Business Plan: Why Every Associate Should Have One

By Laura Cullison

I developed my first business plan about two years ago. Why? Because that was when I started getting feedback about career advancement from a mentor outside my firm. The first thing I realized was that none of the partners I was working with knew that my unswerving goal was to make partner. How could they? I was so busy working on their cases that I never talked about my future goals. Heck, I was so busy working on their cases that I never even thought about my future goals. I assumed that my hard work made clear what my goals were.

My mentor pointed out to me that although the associates I work with generally do outstanding work for the partners, not all of them want to, or do, make partner. "In order to advance," he said, "you need something more than skill and hard work."

"What is the something more?" I asked.

"That is what you need to figure out," he said. "The answer depends on you and where you fit within your firm." I came away from the conversation realizing that I needed to devote some serious thought to my career development. In my case, my large law firm maintains a number of formal and informal programs designed to assist associates in their career development goals. This article is intended to be of assistance to anyone who may or may not have that level of support.

I concluded that the best place to start would be with a document that would reflect where I am as a lawyer, what I have to offer, and where I want to go. Luckily, this was not a unique idea; it is called a business plan, and every lawyer should have one.

Initially, the thought of drafting a business plan was like visiting the dentist—do it when you have to, when you are a partner, but it will not be pleasant. A business plan seemed too much of a "salesman" concept. I reached the conclusion that I would never be in sales when I was a teenager trying to raise funds for new band uniforms by selling cleaning products. I knew I was never going to be the one to close the deal, bring in the business, or sell the brand when it came to soap.

Instead, I became a lawyer at a large law firm. I happen to love what I do. As a young associate, I could not imagine being any luckier or happier in my work.

From the **Woman Advocate**/Winter 2010/ABA/Section of Litigation

As I started interacting with clients, and as I began attending seminars and presentations on career development, though, it became impossible not to hear about networking, business plans, client development, and taking part in business pitches. Of course, I thought, these development activities were not my responsibility. Networking and pitching—which seemed a lot like sales to me—were carried on only at the most rarified senior levels of our large law firm, I told myself. After all, my clients are the partners I work for, and that other stuff is irrelevant, right?

As my mentor made clear, I was wrong. Setting aside the few chosen ones who have success fall into their laps, I concluded that most associates need to learn all those suspiciously salesman-like activities (e.g., networking, pitching, and business planning) to advance in their careers. Stated another way, creating a business plan to help develop such skills was a way to claim control of my career. My mentor helped me realize that my career does not belong to my firm or to the partners I work with—it is mine. Even with the specter of large-scale layoffs, associates are intelligent, skilled individuals with the ability to adapt and find ways to achieve their career goals. Having a business plan that includes the contingency of a layoff at your current firm is not pleasant, but it will put you in a much better position if the worst happens. Every unemployed associate has a resume, but very few have a business plan.

HOW DO I WRITE A BUSINESS PLAN?

A business plan is like a snapshot that you update on a regular basis—a snapshot of what you have accomplished, who you know, who you would like to know, what you are doing, and what you would like to do with your legal career. Each topic area typically addressed in a business plan is listed below along with some suggestions on how to write it up. There is no one-size-fits-all business plan, so you can take this generic template and customize it to fit your goals and needs.

STATUS AND GOALS

Since an associate's status is typically measured by year, status is pretty straightforward. However, if your firm takes a nuanced approach, feel free to reflect that in your business plan. But what about your goals? Be honest here. As a first or second year, do you want to work with a specific partner? Handle a pro bono case? Is your goal simply not to get caught in the next round of layoffs? As a mid-level associate, do you want to have taken a certain number of depositions, joined a community organization, or taken a leadership role in a bar-related activity? As

45

you get more senior, your goals may change to something like developing a book of business in a specific area or exploring in-house opportunities with a particular client—it's your plan, so you decide what fits.

CONTACTS

As a first year, even the thought of developing a relationship with someone with an eye toward future legal business is probably a bit beyond your horizon, and that is OK. Creating and maintaining a contact list is an area I struggle with. I have always been put off by the thought of viewing people through the lens of "what this person can do for me and my career." But if your goal is to develop as a lawyer, being aware of who you know, and who you would like to get to know, matters. So long as you treat all people with respect and kindness, maintaining a contact list will not turn you into a megalomaniac.

Early in your career, focus on keeping in touch with the people in the legal community that you know and are getting to know. Friends are still friends after law school, so staying in touch with law school friends should be pleasant rather than a chore. Keeping track of names and contact information in a document (*i.e.*, your business plan) will make it easier to stay in touch. And you may be surprised in just a few years by how many people you meet in the legal and business community. Include the associates who have moved on to other things. Go ahead and list the partners you work for in your contacts, too. When you move up the ranks enough at the firm to have client contact, congratulate yourself and work hard to meet the client's needs. Add him or her to your contact list. A satisfied client will speak well of you to your partners and other potential clients who may want to hire you someday. The reality is, if your goal is to make partner, you will have to be able to do just that eventually—bring in business. You cannot bring in business if you do not know people in the legal community and if they do not know you.

As you become more senior, you may want to separate out what I call (1) close contacts—people you could seek and even receive business from, (2) personal contacts—friends in the profession, and (3) professional contacts—people who are good to know for various reasons, such as referrals or specialized knowledge in a certain area. Using these three different categories also makes me feel more comfortable that I am not simply viewing others as a means to an end but rather as individuals.

PROFESSIONAL DEVELOPMENT

List the interesting legal matters (past and present) that keep you busy and help to develop your skills. It's important to keep track so you can speak up confidently when the partner asks, "Have you ever done a *Daubert* motion?" and you respond, "Sure, I worked on one last year with so-and-so." If you do not keep track of such things, you will forget in a year or two just how brilliant you were at the *Daubert* hearing. Also, this section is a nice reality check on the goals that you listed in the prior section. For example, if your goal is to get more deposition experience, are any of your current matters going to provide that experience? If not, can you take on another matter that will? If the firm is slow right now, what about a pro bono case that will provide the deposition experience? Or, if your goal is simply to avoid the next round of layoffs, what are you doing to make yourself indispensable? If your group is slow, have you thought about asking if you can pick up assignments in a different practice area?

For example, in my first business plan, I included the relatively obvious step of talking to the partners I work with about how to advance within the firm. Not exactly rocket science, but I probably would not have taken the time to focus on those conversations if I had not created a business plan. Is that salesmanship? Maybe. But I know that I needed to begin these conversations with the partners, and the conversations would not have happened unless I had made them happen. And not one of the partners told me, "Just keep doing great work and you will make partner." Instead, they pointed out areas where I would need more experience, the kinds of matters I should work on, and even other partners I should work with.

MARKETING

In some ways, marketing is the easiest effort you can make as an associate, because typically at our level, it does not mean bringing in business—although it's great if that happens. Whenever you are in the public eye as a lawyer, you are marketing the firm. Speaking engagements, articles, bar activities, and pro bono activities all contribute toward your marketing efforts. Find something you enjoy doing in the community as a lawyer and go for it. And make sure the partners you work with—and the firm in general—know about your activities.

As time passes, you may set a goal to ask a client for whom you have done great work, "Is there anything else the firm can help you with?" You should discuss your plan for such a conversation with the partners you work with before it happens. Client relationships can be surprisingly complicated and dynamic, and the last thing you want to do is commit a breach of etiquette in this area. Your firm culture may mean that those conversations do not happen until after you become a partner. In that situation, you should still be laying the groundwork so that it is clear to the partners that you have developed the kind of relationships that lead to business for the firm.

CONCLUSION

Believe it or not, your business plan, once you have invested the time to create it, will become a friend. Every time you update it, which you should do at least every three months, you are reminded of things you have done well in the past. It memorializes your successes. It clarifies what you have achieved in your current position and benchmarks your professional progress going forward. It reminds you to send a card to a friend. Most importantly, it counteracts the tendency that all associates have to focus on the work at hand at the expense of their long-term goals. For me, a business plan forced me to accept responsibility for my career. What my mentor told me in 2007, when the economic picture looked a lot different, still rings true—your career belongs to you. If you do not think about your career, plan for your career, and take the steps to achieve your career goals, no one else will.

Mentoring

The Dark Side of the Mentoring Relationship
By Kathleen B. Havener

Sitting in a doctor's office waiting for an early morning appointment (essential, of course, because if she didn't make it to work by nine, her senior partner would start combing the office in search of her with fire flaring from his nostrils), a young female partner at Big Law Firm—we call her Carrie—thumbed through the only available reading material, an old women's magazine. The magazine fell open to a well-worn article about codependency. "How sad," Carrie thought. "How can anyone let herself get tangled up in a relationship like that?" She had heard of codependency and thought of it as something other people have problems with.

Quickly skimming the list of symptoms, however, Carrie raised her head with a lightning bolt of shock. She had every one of them! Not with a spouse, a child, a parent, or even an old boyfriend. The object of Carrie's codependency was her long-term mentor—her trusted senior partner.

She had to admit it. She was in an unhealthy relationship with her senior partner, exclusively involving work. How could it have happened? Carrie is an independent, strong-willed, mature, well-educated, and accomplished lawyer. But she is in a deep hole with this guy and she doesn't know how to crawl out. She suddenly felt sicker than when she entered the doctor's waiting room.

Carrie's senior partner is a fine fellow and a great lawyer. Working with him has made her a much better lawyer. She trusts him. Carrie correctly sees him as her strongest advocate at Big Law Firm. He has been her mentor. But over the course of the five years she has worked with him, she has allowed herself to fall into an unhealthy relationship with him.

From the **Woman Advocate**/Summer 2006/ABA/Section of Litigation

We think Carrie's situation is not unusual. Here's the list of symptoms Carrie read:

- Your good feelings about yourself stem from receiving that person's approval.
- Your mental attention is focused on solving that person's problems.
- Your mental attention is focused on pleasing that person.
- Your mental attention is focused on protecting that person.
- Your self-esteem is bolstered by solving that person's problems.
- Your self-esteem is bolstered by relieving that person's anxiety.
- Your own hobbies and interests are put aside in favor of meeting that person's expectations.
- How you feel depends on how that person feels. If that person is in a good mood, you're fine. If that person got up on the wrong side of bed, you're walking on eggshells.
- You are not aware of what you want. Your attention is focused on giving that person what he or she wants.
- Your expectations of the future are linked to that person.
- Your fear of displeasing the other person determines what you say or do.
- Your fear of invoking that person's anger determines what you say or do.
- You use meeting that person's expectations as a way of feeling safe.
- You sacrifice your own opinions and defer to that person's opinions.
- The quality of your life is in direct relation to the attitude of that person toward you.

Do you recognize your own relationship with superiors at your own organization in this list? If you have a mentor in your law firm or other organization, you must monitor yourself and test your relationships with your mentor against the backdrop of what you consider to be healthy in any relationship. It is inevitable that your mentor is senior to you and—to some extent—is in a position to wield economic power over you. This person can impact your future in your organization. If you have allowed yourself to fall into an unhealthy pattern of dealing with your superior, your life will not right itself until you have found a way to make that relationship healthy again.

It is critical to note that you cannot control anyone's conduct other than your own. So healing the relationship will take courage and creativity. It will take time. You may need help addressing the situation—

and if you do, you should get it. Don't expect your mentor to recognize the problem and help you to change it. Often, women in this situation simply leave their firms only to fall into another similar relationship somewhere else. We don't think that is a solution to anything.

We don't know how to solve the problem. But we know it exists and that it can strangle an otherwise flourishing career. If you recognize yourself when you read the symptoms listed above, you need to stop taking your temperature on someone else's forehead and take charge of your own career.

A Mentoring Checklist to Help Make the Mentoring Relationship Productive

By Amy Messigian, Anne Marie Seibel, and Lu Ann White

When you begin your legal career, there are so many unknowns that it is often difficult to identify what questions you should be asking. A productive mentoring relationship allows new attorneys to overcome obstacles and improves their likelihood of success in the profession, as well as in a particular office or firm. Mentoring can help encourage and prepare a new lawyer to stay in the profession. For women lawyers, a mentoring relationship may be particularly desirable to help them become more comfortable and adept in their offices, communities, and areas of practice. Such relationships are beneficial to both the mentor and the mentee because they help each expand his or her perspective and improve the quality of what a lawyer has to offer professionally.

Mentoring relationships can take many forms and may cross areas of practice, age, and different walks of life. Mentoring is not just for law firms, and not just for lawyers in large firms. A lawyer can serve as a mentor to a lawyer in another office, practice area, or community. A mentor can be from the same firm or office as the mentee or from outside the mentee's office. A mentor can be much more experienced in the law or have only a few more years of experience. In this global, technological age, a virtual mentor is even a possibility.

If an office or a firm does not have a mentoring program, a potential mentee or mentor can arrange her own mentor relationship. It is also worth inquiring into whether a local or special interest bar association has a mentor-matching program available.

To encourage positive and successful mentoring relationships, we offer a checklist for mentors and mentees of potential topics to discuss, as well as general suggestions for making the relationship successful, pleasant, and worthwhile. The topics may or may not be relevant depending on the relationship and the individuals involved; however, many of the topics will apply regardless of whether the mentoring relationship is pursuant to a formal program or a more informal one. Although the checklist and suggestions are more specific to a law firm setting rather than another type of practice, such as a government agency or corporate office, readers can tailor the topics and suggestions to apply to their own situations and needs. The suggestions, we hope, will aid in developing a productive mentoring experience.

From the **Woman Advocate**/Winter 2008/ABA/Section of Litigation

CHECKLIST OF TOPICS FOR MENTOR AND MENTEE

Office Protocol and Basics of Practice. What are the policies regarding timekeeping, work hours, billing, vacation time, reporting to staff or management, expenses, technology, and employee benefits?

Mentorship. Is your firm's program formal or informal? If it is formal, are there written procedures or guidelines to follow for the mentoring program?

Understanding the Firm Structure. What is the management structure of the firm? What are the significant committees, and who serves on them? Do any firm committees include associate members? Are there any informal networks within the firm or any other means of getting to know the other lawyers?

Advancement. What does it take to make partner? Are a certain number of hours required? Is client development emphasized? At what level are you expected to start bringing in clients? What are the unwritten expectations for advancement?

Court and Bar Admissions. How and when does one become admitted to a particular court? What are the requirements regarding registration, yearly reporting, change of address, fees, and continuing legal education?

Bar Associations. What bar associations are active in your area? What are their purposes, and how does one join? What groups exist for young lawyers? Is anyone else at the firm involved? What women's bar associations or interest groups are available?

CLE and Bar Activity Allowances. Is there an allowance for CLE or bar activities? How do you apply for permission to attend? What are the limits on the type of activity, location, or cost?

Performance Evaluations. What are the review procedures? Is there a review committee, or are reviews conducted informally? If there is a committee, who is on it? What are the review and evaluation criteria? How often are associates reviewed? Is there a self-review process?

Training and Development. Is there a formal associate training program? Do the firm's practice groups hold regular meetings that associates can attend?

Firm History. From the time the firm was formed, what has been its history, and who are the named partners of the firm? What has the history of women been at the firm?

Administrative Staff. How should an associate interact with office staff? What is appropriate in terms of conduct, protocol, and communications? What should be delegated to a secretary or paralegal? Who does what within the firm?

Community. What recommendations can you give to a lawyer new to the area in terms of local amenities, facilities, events, entertainment, dining, banking, schools, neighborhoods, health-care providers, child care, and so on?

Sociopolitical Groups. Is involvement in community groups encouraged or discouraged? Are certain types of involvement more favored in the office than others? What is the protocol for discussing involvement with a political group, and what is the level of acceptance? What activities have young professionals' boards? What groups have connections with your firm? Who else at the firm shares common interests?

Pro Bono Activities. What are firm policies on counting work as billable? What limits do you have on the type of work you can accept? How do you secure approval to do work?

Marketing. Is there a marketing budget set aside for an associate's use? What activities are recommended? How is one included in marketing events?

Networking Opportunities. What other opportunities exist for introducing the new associate to other lawyers, including other women lawyers?

Professionalism. How is the associate expected to treat clients, staff, senior lawyers, opposing counsel, judges, court personnel, and clients? What turnaround is expected for phone calls and email? How formal should email communications be?

Dress and Grooming. Does the office have a dress code? What is appropriate attire for attending court or meetings? What constitutes "business casual"? Are there guidelines regarding skirt length? Is wearing jewelry discouraged? What sort of jewelry is appropriate?

Conduct Issues. What behavior is expected during office hours? During off-hours? What conduct is expected in relation to members of the staff or other lawyers? Is there a fraternization policy? What should a lawyer do if an intraoffice relationship develops?

Issues Specific to Substantive Law Areas. What are the procedures and protocol for work in particular practice areas? Who is in charge of each practice area? To whom does the lawyer report? What is a reasonable amount of time to spend on work such as motions, pleadings, or research?

Ethical Issues. What is the conflicts clearance procedure? Are certain partners designated firm counsel? Who should one contact with concerns about an ethics issue?

Important Clients. Who are the firm's significant clients, and when is it appropriate to make direct contact with such clients?

Research. What free resources are available for legal research? Which websites do you find most helpful at the local, state, regional, and national levels?

Personal Life Issues. How do other female lawyers manage work-life balance? Does the mentee have any particular family or child-care issues or concerns?

Gender Issues. Are there any concerns regarding sexual harassment, discriminatory comments, or conduct? What are ways of dealing with gender disparity in the office?

Recruiting. What are the expectations for the mentee's role in recruiting? Should she limit involvement in activities or costs for same?

Practice Development. What work opportunities are available now? Where do you see trends in the law? What types of experiences does the mentee want?

The Mentoring Relationship. What do both sides expect out of the relationship? How often should you meet?

SUGGESTIONS FOR MENTORS TO MAKE THE RELATIONSHIP SUCCESSFUL

Listen. Don't just talk and talk. Listen to the mentee to find out what she wants to know, needs to learn, and is understanding. Plus, you might learn something from the mentee and develop a new friendship in the meantime.

Break the Ice. Encourage participation and bring the mentee along to a luncheon or an event to break the ice and get the mentee started on her own.

Schedule a Time to Meet. Meet for coffee, lunch, or after work, or at a convenient time during the workday. If you schedule a time, then even if you have to cancel, you will be more likely to reschedule a time to get together. In an informal setting, scheduling a time may not always be necessary, but it will help to make sure that concerns and questions are being addressed. Mentees may be uncomfortable asking a mentor to schedule a time to meet, so feel free to ask the mentee about scheduling a time. When you meet, if appropriate, schedule a follow-up meeting at the conclusion of a meeting or discussion. Perhaps scheduling at least a monthly meeting to discuss general issues is a good way to get the process started.

Discuss Expectations, Interests, and Concerns. Discuss what the mentee wants to learn or is interested in learning, and what you can offer. You may be able to introduce the mentee to others to mentor on other topics or areas not in your area or realm of information or experience. Revisit the expectations when you meet again.

Assess the Progress of the Mentoring Relationship. Revisit the expectations when you meet again. Assess how the mentoring process is working, whether progress is being made, whether areas need to be addressed, and whether the relationship should be ended.

Use Your Time Efficiently. In assessing how the mentoring process is working, be mindful of the amount of time you are spending in the relationship. If contacts, calls, email, and drop-in visits are becoming unwanted and overly time consuming, address it; indicate which times are available and which are not. Take control. If contacts outside of scheduled meetings are undesirable, set the parameters.

Virtual Mentoring May Be a Good Fit. Think outside the box. Mentoring with someone outside of your office or even your community or state, or continent, is a possibility. You may practice in an area in which someone in another office or a satellite office, or in a completely unrelated office, may be in need of assistance.

Give Constructive Feedback. Feedback is important particularly for practice areas and substantive law matters, and for noticeable problem areas in need of work or attention or of concern. It is difficult for many lawyers to provide feedback, especially when the mentoring is in an informal situation. Giving feedback can also be difficult if a problem area concerns the mentee's dress, grooming, or inappropriate behavior. However, feedback is important. Constructive, positive feedback is best. If you hear or have positive comments about the mentee or her work, pass them on to her.

You Don't Have to Be a Mentor for All Areas. You may not be the right person to mentor on a topic, practice area, or different activities. Feel free to refer the mentee to someone else who is knowledgeable and may be of assistance. Make the introduction for the mentee. Know who the mentee is working with and the kind of work the mentee is doing, and attempt to learn whether the mentee is progressing appropriately in her area of practice.

Be Willing to Mentor Male and Female Lawyers. New lawyers, whether male or female, will be dealing with male and female lawyers and clients. They can learn a lot from you.

You Don't Have to Be a Seasoned Lawyer to Be a Mentor. You may be able to be a mentor to a newer lawyer even though you have not practiced very long. You certainly will have learned a lot already about the practice area, the office, the legal community, and your office's expectations.

Don't Ever Stop Being Willing to Mentor. Your experiences and insights are valuable and can help someone else in the profession. If someone you mentor leaves your office or leaves the practice, it does not mean that you wasted your time. Many influences and circumstances no doubt affected your mentee's decision to leave her position or the practice, and she will take the benefits of your mentoring with her when she leaves.

Find Another Mentor If the Mentoring Is Not Working. If it seems that your mentee just does not understand you, or that you two just do not click or get along, then pursue having someone else be the mentor, and be willing to act as a mentor to another.

HOW MENTEES CAN MAKE THE RELATIONSHIP SUCCESSFUL

Be Proactive. If there is no mentoring program, initiate inquiries and contacts to find a mentor. Once you have a mentor, initiate contacts with your mentor about questions, concerns, workload, assignments, and other matters.

Schedule Times to Meet. Schedule a time to talk with your mentor, perhaps over lunch or coffee. If the mentor does not come to you, go to the mentor. At the first meeting, schedule the next meeting. Questions about specific problems, workload, and issues that arise in between meetings may necessitate more frequent conversations. So as not to become a burden, trying to limit conversations to once a week or once every two weeks may help the mentor maintain some control over the interruptions.

Ask Questions. If your mentor does not know the answer, find out from your mentor whom you need to contact. Ask your mentor to introduce you. If you find yourself having many questions, make a list and ask whether your mentor can meet you for coffee or lunch—that way you can ask all your questions in one sitting and show an appreciation of the mentor for her time.

Listen. Your mentor has experience of all kinds in the practice of law from which you can learn. You can learn about many aspects by listening and by being open to insight, perceptions, tips, and suggestions beyond what you may be focusing on or asking.

Be Available. Be available to meet with or talk with your mentor. Understand that your mentor is busy, so making the mentoring time productive and efficient is important.

Be Appreciative. Let your mentor know that you appreciate her willingness to take a break out of her schedule, share her expertise, and serve as a sounding board for you.

Explore Suggestions for Other Contacts. If your mentor does not work in your specialty area, or even in your office or firm, ask for suggestions on finding someone who may be able to serve as a mentor or contact for that kind of work. Your mentor may be able to help you make those connections, but you need to ask.

Follow Up. Take to heart any suggestions from your mentor for improvement.

Inform Your Mentor. Tell your mentor about the type of work you are doing and are interested in doing. Tell your mentor what you want from the mentor relationship, the types of questions and concerns you have, and the things you want to learn.

Develop Your Own Board of Directors. Ask your mentor to help you identify good individuals from whom to seek guidance and with whom you can develop relationships. The personal board of directors helps serve as eyes and ears for the mentee and provides advice and support from various different perspectives at the law firm, office, or company.

Be Open. Accept and seek mentorship from lawyers of all levels of experience and from mentors who are different from you.

Seek Alternative Mentors. If your current mentorship relationship is not working, pursue a change in mentors or seek the advice of an additional, informal mentor. Address any problems regarding lack of interest from your mentor or personal differences, if possible, taking into account any office politics.

Learn to Be a Mentor. It will not be long until you know more than the new associate down the hall. So, learn from your mentor and pass it on.

Accelerating Career Development Through Multiple Mentoring Opportunities
By Nan E. Joesten

Those of us who have been blessed with the opportunity for education remember clearly those teachers who helped change the course of our lives with their wisdom, wit, and sincere interest in us, their students. The same can be said for our progress in the legal profession. There are numerous lawyers whom we hold in high esteem due to their generosity of time, advice, and encouragement along the way. This is the essence of mentoring: According to *Merriam-Webster's Dictionary*, a mentor is a "trusted counselor or guide," a tutor or coach. Hearkening back to the classics, Mentor was a friend of Odysseus, entrusted with the education of Odysseus's son, Telemachus, when Odysseus went off to fight in the Trojan War. While the subject of increasing focus in the legal profession, mentoring is hardly new—Aristotle once mentored Alexander the Great.

The goal of mentoring is to enhance professional development through effective personal relationships. Mentoring is critical in the legal profession, where the start-up curve is steep and experience and judgment play such a critical part in one's ability to be a great lawyer. And it's widely accepted that mentoring brings with it a plethora of benefits in terms of accelerating the progress of new lawyers, expanding the comfort level of lawyers in trying out or applying their growing skills to the challenges of their clients, and improving the retention of lawyers in the profession. There are also potential rewards for the lawyer serving as a mentor: personal satisfaction, increased loyalty from grateful junior colleagues, appreciation from peers, greater influence within the organization. All of these can have a positive and direct impact on the bottom line.

CHALLENGES TO MENTORING

So why aren't law departments and law firms flush with stories of mentoring success? Perhaps in part because it is difficult for lawyers to carve time out of our inevitably hectic schedules to find the opportunity to act as mentors, and some lawyers make better mentors than others. Mentoring has typically been thought of as a one-on-one relationship, most often between a junior lawyer and a more experienced lawyer. While we often hope these informal relationships develop naturally over the

From the **Woman Advocate**/Summer 2006/ABA/Section of Litigation

course of cases or transactions, many organizations have formal mentoring programs where junior and senior lawyers are assigned to one another in a mentee-mentor relationship for some period of time. Often the junior lawyers have input in the selection of a mentor, which can improve the odds of a successful experience, but not always. When schedules pick up, or the relationship never really takes off, the junior lawyer must cast about for other options. In a scenario where the junior lawyer is also a woman or diverse lawyer or both, the risk of being left on the outside looking in can be magnified.

MULTIPLE MENTORING

One solution to the dilemma of not having any (or enough) natural mentors or not having a designated mentoring relationship be productive is to create more opportunities for mentoring. The problem is a shortage of good mentors, especially in organizations where senior women or diverse lawyers are in short supply. Developing those coveted mentoring opportunities using the traditional one-to-one model can be difficult because the most obvious way to increase mentoring is to expand the number of one-on-one mentoring relationships in which the most effective mentors engage, which time pressures frequently preclude.

Multiple mentoring is an alternative that addresses the pressing need for mentees to have exposure to mentors, where an organization has more of the former than the latter. Admittedly, multiple mentoring doesn't offer the benefit of one-on-one mentoring in attempting to address directly one mentee's needs without a preset agenda. Still, it is a model that creates opportunities for several relationships to grow while emphasizing teaching and leveraging the strengths of expertise.

MENTORING CIRCLES

Mentoring circles are one style of multiple mentoring that can be readily adapted to a law firm or law department setting. In a mentoring circle, a group of mentees typically meet with one mentor. This obviously helps address a scenario where there is an imbalance in the number of mentors and mentees, but the benefits are much broader than that. The experienced mentor is expected to lead gently the group and offer guidance and advice on both organizational matters and fundamental core competencies of practicing law. A good mentor should also be able to encourage the circle in combining their individual experiences and enthusiasm to help everyone in the group progress in their legal careers and comfort within the organization. The participants in the circle benefit from learning a variety of perspectives or approaches to issues rather than only the mentor's point of view.

TEAM OR GROUP MENTORING

Team mentoring is another variant of multiple mentoring. With team mentoring, the group does not designate a formal mentor; instead, the team members look to each other for mentoring support and guidance. As with circle mentoring, team or group mentoring offers the advantage of having numerous participants gain from the experiences of others in the group, rather than limiting the exchange of ideas and perspectives to a one-to-one. In a law firm or legal department setting, this encourages mentoring to occur among lawyers of varying seniority and experiences and has the added benefit of allowing the more senior lawyers to learn directly from entry-level lawyers about the problems and challenges within the organization and the practice of law. This type of reverse mentoring within the team can be extremely valuable in helping to keep the organization's leaders or rainmakers in touch with the experiences of more junior lawyers.

SETTING EXPECTATIONS

Multiple mentoring arrangements offer the inherent benefits of increased opportunities to build the natural relationships that can themselves be the jumping-off point for informal mentoring outside of a planned relationship. Still, there are direct benefits to be reaped by participating in a planned circle or team mentoring experience. But as with any undertaking, the success of any multiple mentoring endeavor begins with an assessment of the expectations of all the participants: What does each person hope to accomplish from the process? What particular issues will the group focus on? How will the group deal with any barriers to effectiveness that emerge during the course of the group's sessions? What does each person expect to contribute to the process? What does each person expect of the other group members? How will the group assess if the process is beneficial?

CREATING THE GROUND RULES

Once the individual members each have considered these topics, it is time for the group to come together to reach agreement on their fundamental ground rules. For nearly any mentoring experiences to be successful, participants need to feel that the group is a safe space for sharing ideas, where one's participation and input do not result in any negative repercussions in assignments, performance reviews, and the like. A guarantee of confidentiality is essential, and multiple mentoring groups typically operate under "Vegas Rules"—what happens in the mentoring sessions, stays in those sessions. An effective mentoring experience requires the participants to trust one another, and maintaining confidences is paramount to developing that trust.

Likewise, the group must make a commitment to regular attendance at the agreed-upon meeting times and venues. The group can decide for itself whether sessions are most productive when held in the office during business hours, over lattes at the local coffee shop, or perhaps in the privacy of someone's home over a shared meal. No matter where and how the group decides to gather, it's important to honor the schedule and participate regularly.

OFF AND RUNNING

The initial gathering should allow for a review of individual expectations for the group and agreement on the group's goals and ground rules. Once under way, participants should be committed to following up on previous discussions where appropriate, reporting back on new experiences or learnings, or evaluating the relative impact of new strategies that a group member might have tried based on previous mentoring. As the group becomes more comfortable with one another, intermediate evaluations may be helpful to identify whether objectives are being met, what has worked best, and how the process can be further improved with a midcourse correction.

While no substitute for informal mentoring, established multiple mentoring opportunities can help bridge that gap for organizations that are short on effective mentors and long on lawyers seeking critical mentoring support. So what are you waiting for? Give it a try and see how the effectiveness of your organization, and the satisfaction of your younger lawyers, can be multiplied.

Where Have All the Role Models Gone?

By Coke Stewart

Today there's much talk about dissatisfied lawyers in large law firms. Maybe lawyers were always grumbling, but most agree that the grumbling is getting louder. Last year, the Litigation Section created a task force called "Raise the Bar" to increase satisfaction for lawyers of all ages. We've considered everything from law-firm finances to the effect of technology on our practice, mentoring the next generation, partner-associate relations, and work-life balance.

Through my work on this project, I've been thinking about what makes great lawyers and great law firms. Maybe you can't help harkening back to the good old days—real or imagined. What I think of is the ethical lawyer, the Atticus Finches of the world. These days, Finches appear hard to find. However, the real problem may not be lack of role models, but the lack of opportunities to interact with the role models who work quietly around us every day.

Firms have gotten so big that lawyers don't recognize other lawyers in their own office, never mind in their firm. Thus lawyers have few role models and fall into the dissatisfaction everyone loves to cite. One solution is to reconnect with your colleagues—partners and associates.

Your firm should make sure that every lawyer meets every other lawyer in the office. At my old law firm, which had more than 100 attorneys and professionals scattered over several floors, each new hire was shown around the firm by another lawyer and introduced to *every* lawyer, paralegal secretary, and staff person. Believe me it took awhile, but it was amazing to see how well everyone responded to it. The firm took other measures as well. All the lawyers met monthly over lunch to listen to colleagues speak about interesting cases or firm management issues. At these lunches new lawyers were again introduced to the firm. Associates also met monthly. It was often a gripe session, but the associates bonded through these regular meetings. Finally, the firm published a face book with all of the attorneys' names, photographs, law schools, and other basic information. Nowadays most firms think having bios and photos on the internet is enough. It isn't.

My old firm was largely successful in making sure everyone knew each other. Although years have passed and many of the firm's lawyers have gone their separate ways, a strong bond remains. Alums from the firm still meet each other for happy hours—and refer business.

From the **Litigation Ethics**/Spring 2006/ABA/Section of Litigation

Law firm leaders should also make a special effort to interact with younger lawyers. It's not enough to know the few associates and young partners you work with regularly. Law firm leaders often make themselves available to summer associates. Once these associates accept their offers however, leaders move on to "more pressing matters." Nothing is more pressing for law firm leaders than knowing the attorneys they are trying to lead. Fortunately, it's not so hard. Law firm leaders can schedule regular get-togethers with small groups of attorneys. Five or six people is ideal. Take a few associates to lunch. Meet with the senior associates in their practice group. Take some junior partners to a baseball game. Have drinks in the corner office. Just make sure every young lawyer gets invited to one of these gatherings each year. No one wants to be snubbed.

Once lawyers in large law firms know each other better, some of the dissatisfaction will melt away. Attorneys will become more committed to their work and their firm. The best outcome may be that partners and associates will know each other well enough to recognize that a few role models are lurking out there after all.

Introduction

By C. Pierce Campbell

Good legal writing skills are critical to the success of any lawyer. Many cases are won or lost long before any oral argument before the tribunal, if there is any oral argument at all. Historically, legal writing was only considered adequate if it was convoluted, confusing, repetitive, and included some Latin phrases for good measure. For many centuries, lawyers wrote in a way that could only be understood by other lawyers, and even that was not a certainty. Thankfully, for lawyers and non-lawyers alike, that mindset has started to change.

The new key rule for legal writers is to keep the writing simple. This can be quite a challenge when one considers the many purposes served by legal writing. Any good brief or memorandum includes persuasive, narrative, and expository writing—three styles, each with its own purpose. The bulk of legal writing is designed for a reader mostly, or totally, unfamiliar with the case. The author must tell the story of the case, explain any complex factual or legal issues involved, and persuade the reader to adopt the author's position on the matter. All of this must be accomplished in as concise a manner as possible. This is a tall order.

The following collection of articles provides lawyers with many suggestions for improving their writing. Becoming a stronger legal writer takes conscious effort, practice, and hard work. Editing pays off and should include more than checking for typos and misspellings.

C. Pierce Campbell is an attorney with Turner Padget Graham & Laney in Florence, South Carolina, whose practice focuses on commercial and probate litigation. Mr. Campbell is active in the ABA Section of Litigation leadership, including serving as a Co-Chair of First Chair Press during the creation of this book.

Often it can be beneficial for a non-lawyer staff member to read the final product with an eye for comprehension. The ability to be understood by a non-lawyer should be the goal. Sometimes, a lawyer must write differently than he always has, even if that means more work is necessary.

An attorney's primary job is to successfully advance the client's position. This is increasingly accomplished by writing alone. Hopefully, a few tips included here will help the reader improve his writing skills and advance the causes of his clients, all the while growing the lawyer's professional reputation.

WRITING

Clarity and Persuasion

48 Litigation Writing Rules
By Peter R. Silverman

I've compiled the following rules through the years while working with associates on litigation writing.

THE FIRST RULE

1. Rules are meant to be broken. Do it only knowingly and for a purpose.

GRAMMAR AND WORD CHOICE

2. Don't insert "of" after "all"; it's an unnecessary junk word almost all [of] the time.
3. "In order to" has two too many words. Use "to."
4. Learn the difference between that and which and between than and from. "That" is different from "which," which is a difference that you should master.
5. In addition to the aforementioned rules, avoid "hereto," "wherefore," "hereinbefore," and any other word that ancient lawyers devised by gluing together normal words to create monster words.

This article is reprinted with permission from the Ohio Lawyer, May/June 2005 issue. It appeared later in: **The Woman Advocate, Fall 2005, ABA Section of Litigation**

6. In the hands of a gifted writer, a hackneyed phrase can ring the bell. When it comes to the rest of us, we're all thumbs when we use them. Avoid hackneyed phrases like the plague.

7. Use "only" immediately before or after only the word or phrase it's meant to modify. (Do this only if you want to say only what you mean.)

8. More generally, be aware of all misplaced modifiers. Just ask the mock turtle.

9. Use the possessive to avoid unnecessary words. While staying sensitive to nuance, become the rules' master rather than master of the rules.

10. The fact is that "the fact is" or its variations are unnecessary clutter words.

11. It is often a sign of laziness to begin a sentence with "it is."

12. However much you want to start a sentence with "however," don't do it unless you mean "no matter how." Yeah, this is elitist, but it's a good tool that will help with rule 26.

13. In the event that you're tempted to use "in the event that" rather than "if," don't. It's pompous.

14. Before using "prior to," try to find a less pretentious one-word substitute.

15. Subsequent to reading "subsequent to," I usually have to think whether it means "before" or "after." Use "after" or "later."

16. Except for citation form, don't use Latin, *e.g.,* "*e.g.,*" "*i.e.,*" "supra," "infra," or "inter alia." Use English; *e.g.,* "for example." If you don't know a Latin word's or an abbreviation's English equivalent, definitely never use it. "Etc." is an exception, but that's because normal Americans use it, and it works better than "and so forth."

17. Use "plaintiff," "appellee," or the like only when you have a difficult time remembering the parties' actual names.

18. Your using the possessive with gerunds is elitist but will help avoid mush writing.

19. Having made that point, make sure to follow "ing" clauses at the beginning of a sentence with the proper subject. (Having finished this peeve, I hope you'll notice I erred by example.)

20. "Instant" refers best to oatmeal. When discussing the case you're litigating, try "our case" or "this case" or, if that doesn't work, the "present case."

21. Don't nounify verbs or verbify nouns. I don't like the way it impacts me.

STYLE

22. Don't Capitalize Words That Don't Need To Be Capitalized. Capitalize only proper nouns or defined terms.

23. Always use the active voice; the passive voice should not be used by you, even in certificates of service. Speaking of which, I want to retch when I read that something was served this 4th day of March in the year 2004. Try, "On March 4, 2004, I served. . . ."

24. Use scoring, italics, bolding, and exclamation points sparingly. They are **_used too often_** as a substitute for making a point clearly!

25. Don't put time or parenthetical clauses, when you need to use them, at the middle or end of the sentence. When you need to use them, put them at the beginning of the sentence.

26. Improve your writing by striking 50 percent of your uses of "but," "however," and "although" from the start of your sentences.

27. Improve your writing by striking 50 percent of your commas. Use more short sentences. But not too many.

28. Great writers can be sarcastic, bombastic, humorous, angry, aggrieved, or bitter *and* use these tones to make their point more persuasively than they could with straightforward narrative. Most of us aren't great writers. Resist the temptation until you become one.

29. If you want to sound like a sophisticated corporate or real estate lawyer, stay away from litigation and get in the practice of marking up 50-year-old forms and using the earlier of long sentences or multiple clauses, whichever is later, and repeating and using over and over synonymous pairs of words and phrases that are duplicative and redundant. Use phrases, such as "witnesseth" and "our hands subscribeth," that no one has a clue what they mean and, in settlement agreements, start some of the agreement's numbered paragraphs with the phrase "the parties agree" or "the parties understand," but don't use those phrases in front of the agreement's paragraphs that the parties don't agree on or don't understand. Ignore rule 5. By the way, you'll have a leg up in doing all of this if you were swaddled too tightly at birth.

30. You are hereby notified that I prefer to be notified without trumpet fanfare announcing that the notice follows. Just say it.

ORGANIZATION

31. If you can't write a convincing topic paragraph for a section, break up the section into coherent parts that can be described in a topic paragraph and a succinct heading. You don't need to keep

69

the topic paragraph in the document, but you need to be able to write it. Paragraphs should express one idea, even if it means a one-sentence paragraph. I don't like long paragraphs. Do you? By the time I get to the end of a long paragraph, I can't remember the point the writer was trying to make at the beginning of the paragraph. Can you?

32. The reason men don't like to ask for directions is that we don't like admitting we're lost. Don't put your brief reader in that dilemma. Right from the start, give clear directions as to where you're going. Directions should refer to landmarks, which are headings and sections. Real men like directions; they just don't like asking for them.

33. Pay attention to whether you want your headings phrased neutrally, to disarm the reader, or slanted, to move the reader along. Choose the more persuasive strategy. Either way, a reader should be able to read only your headings and understand your argument.

34. I'll criticize you for incoherent, complex, or too few headings, but never will I criticize you for too many single-topic, clear headings.

35. Half the time the problem with a bad sentence is that it's surrounded by an incoherent paragraph. Rewrite the whole thing.

36. When you're done rewriting a brief (or even an article or other writing), go back and review the headings to make sure they're still appropriate for what follows.

37. Think through your arguments before writing. Then write clearly and don't skip any of the argument's logical steps. This forces you to rethink. Repeat—think, write, rethink, rewrite—again and again until every square of the Rubik's Cube is in place. I don't want to see the brief before then.

38. Any idiot can present facts in a straightforward, chronological narrative. Be an idiot.

INTEGRITY/PERSUASIVENESS

39. Be detached enough from your clever words, phrases, sentences, and arguments to know when they distract or detract more than persuade or add. Don't name the cow.

40. Unless a case's point is idiot proof, don't cite it without a parenthetical explanation. I don't want to drop the brief to read the case to figure out why you cited it, and the judge won't want to either.

41. Never, ever stretch the point of a case or the gist of deposition testimony without giving the reader fair warning as part of the citation or summary. If I read something and find you've tried to sneak by a stretched citation or summary, I won't trust any of your other citations or summaries and neither will the judge.

42. Quotations are much better than paraphrases. When used in context (see rule 40), quotations let readers know you're not trying to spin.

43. It's important to note that, if you have to tell a reader that it's important to note something, then you probably haven't laid the proper foundation for the reader to reach that inference without your prompt. Readers appreciate being persuaded rather than lectured to. Ditto "it is certainly the case," "clearly," and the like.

44. Emotion is good but must be earned. We cry at the end of a good movie, not at the opening.

45. Don't start writing until you've figured out why we should win and until you've figured out the difference between which arguments are jabs and which are knockout punches. Knockout punches rarely connect the first time you throw them. Throw them well and often.

46. Express the guts of the case in the brief's first few sentences. Tie the guts back into the brief time and time again.

47. Persuasive legal writing, at its best, is persuasive storytelling. The writer masters the facts and the law and blends them seamlessly into a consistent, comprehensive, and compelling story. The reader is swept along, responding to each step of the tale with a heartfelt nod of the head: "Yes, yes, yes, this is the way it is." This requires hard work—organizing and reorganizing, adding and winnowing, writing and rewriting—until the pages sing. I don't want to see the brief before then.

THE FINAL RULE

48. When you work with me, be as constructively critical of my writing as I am of yours. That helps me grow and serves the cause of advancing our clients' interests with all the talent and skill we can muster.

If You've Got It, Flaunt It: Persuasive Brief Writing
By Evelyn Storch

Most arguments are won (or lost) not at oral argument but on the papers submitted. Judges and their law clerks review papers and routinely decide the issues, at least preliminarily, in advance of the return date. In addition, more courts now do not request or even permit oral argument as a matter of course. Accordingly, briefs are an increasingly critical tool in a lawyer's arsenal. They must shape the debate, focus the court's attention, and guide the judge to the "right" point of view—yours. These goals can be achieved by determining the focal point of your application, organizing your arguments around that central theme, and writing simply, succinctly, directly, and forcefully. Here are tips for doing just that.

PUT ALL YOUR EGGS IN ONE BASKET
(OR TWO OR THREE)

A scattershot approach rarely is successful. The more distinct points you argue, the less attention each one gets. To be an effective brief writer, you must determine your goal for the particular application, devise an approach to achieve it, and include in your brief only those points that directly advance that goal. Anything else you include is a distraction and counterproductive.

No lawyer worth her salt would go to trial without a central theme, which she would reinforce at every opportunity. Brief writing is no different. Ask yourself what relief you want, what facts are necessary for the court to consider to give that relief (including any adverse facts that may be critical to the decision and that you must concede), and what arguments support your claim for relief. Discard everything else. It is difficult advice to follow but well worth it. A winning tangential point still is tangential. It will not get you the result you want, so why divert the court's attention?

IT'S WHAT'S UP FRONT THAT COUNTS

A brief should have a preliminary statement. The preliminary statement should be short (preferably a page or two) but should include all the essential points you make in the brief (if you adopt my prior advice, this is not so difficult). Indeed, the court should have to read no further than the preliminary statement to understand your position and to feel comfortable ruling your way.

From the **Woman Advocate**/Fall 2005/ABA/Section of Litigation

Although concise, the preliminary statement should be passionate. Yes, the brief is going to a judge, not a jury. But judges are people too. They expect the advocate to believe in her cause and to demonstrate that belief. This is the place you can exercise your right brain and be creative. Analogize. Use literary references. Take the high ground. Show the judge that an injustice has occurred or will occur absent relief and that the relief you want is the "right thing to do," if not the *only* thing to do under the circumstances. Such an approach gives you a leg up on victory from the outset and, at the very least, will encourage the court to review the remainder of the arguments through the prism you have furnished.

SIZE MATTERS

Consistent with my theme that brevity, clarity, and focus are the key ingredients to success, this point will be short. It is called a *brief* for a reason. Listen to the advice its name provides.

ON A CLEAR DAY, YOU CAN SEE FOREVER

Clarity is key. If you do not state clearly what you want and why you are entitled to get it, you are more likely not to get it. Got it? You must choose the arguments to be made to ensure that your point is clearly stated, supported, and reinforced. Clarity is achieved through structure, organization, and word usage.

Titles focus both the brief writer and the court. Every brief of five pages or more should have a formal structure with titles and subtitles. The titles should summarize the argument that follows. The following are examples of titles designed for an appellate brief.

> The Trial Court Erred by Not Requiring Party X to Perform Her Obligations Under the Settlement Agreement, as Enforced by Two Courts, or to Deposit into a Conforming Trust an Amount Equal to the Value of the Properties She Promised to Transfer to the Conforming Trust.
>
> Alternatively, the Trial Court Erred by Not Ordering Rescission of the Settlement Agreement Performed on Only One Side.

The first example is long, to be sure, but even without background facts, the nature of the dispute is readily discernible, and the "right" outcome is underscored. When detailed titles are used, the table of contents serves as a summary of the brief and an outline to which the court can refer in formulating its opinion. Thus, time spent drafting effective titles is time well invested.

Although structure and organization go hand in hand, each has a distinct purpose. Structure lets the court know where the brief is going and provides guideposts for the journey. Good brief organization lays the foundation, builds the argument, and leads the court to the brief writer's desired (and, hopefully, inescapable) conclusion. Rarely, if ever, is there one right way to organize a brief. One should not be a slave to chronology. Rather, a brief should take into account the rules of primacy and recency: The reader or listener remembers best, and is influenced most, by what she reads or hears first and last. Start strong and finish stronger.

A brief is formal writing and should be treated as such. But formality does not mean stilted language nor does it require legalese. The most persuasive arguments are those stated simply. The logic of a simple, declarative sentence seems irrefutable. The logic of a convoluted argument seems inscrutable. Be direct. Be precise. You will persuade.

YOU CAN (SHOULD) JUDGE A BOOK BY ITS COVER

Everything counts. Appearance counts. Grammar counts. Spelling counts. Typos count. Know the basics. If they are not second nature to you, learn them. Study punctuation; it makes a difference. Commas are not a matter of style. As an appellate judge recently said at a bench-bar conference, a sloppy appearance may indicate to the court that you do slipshod work. At the very least, avoidable mistakes distract. At worst, they undermine your credibility, and credibility is your most important asset. Safeguard it jealously in every brief you write and in every argument you make.

YOU'RE IN GOOD HANDS

I asked a good friend, a once and future judge, for a brief-writing tip from a judge's perspective. She said a brief should tell the court it's safe to rule your client's way. In other words, you must reassure the court that the facts and the law fully support your position. Put yourself in the judge's shoes. If you were not the advocate but the decision maker, would you feel confident that you could adopt the position being advocated?

That sentiment was echoed in a recent bench-bar conference at which a jurist told the audience that the best arguments, especially to higher courts, are for "tweaking," not for sea change. If you are arguing for a change in the law and it is within the court's power to effect such change—or, better yet, for a logical extension of a doctrine—identify your argument as such and support it with good and sufficient policy reasons on why the change or extension should be made.

COME IN LIKE A LION, BUT DON'T GO OUT LIKE A LAMB

A dynamic beginning is essential. A forceful closing is crucial. The conclusion should reinforce the preliminary statement and, for that matter, the brief as a whole, without seeming repetitive. The job is to emphasize and not simply to repeat.

Once again, it's time for the right brain workout. Find a creative way to restate the rule of law you want to establish. Use a thesaurus. Raise a rhetorical question. State your most salient point and demonstrate how it inexorably leads to your conclusion. How can the court refuse you?

Write your brief with the four C's—clearly, concisely, credibly, and compellingly—and soon you will be calling your client with good news.

An In-Depth Look at the Legal Argument

Writing a Winning Legal Argument: What TO Do and What Not TO Do

By Lawrence D. Rosenberg

INTRODUCTION

Writing a winning legal argument can often be the most important single element in a case. In this era of fewer and fewer jury trials, the prevalence of summary judgment, and endgame strategies more often focusing on appellate courts, a lawyer's skill in writing a winning legal argument—whether before a trial judge or on appeal—may well dictate whether the client wins or loses. That is not to say that all of the other facets of litigation, including discovery, oral argument, trial presentation, etc., are unimportant, but in some cases writing a winning legal argument may be the most crucial.

Fortunately, writing an excellent legal argument is not extremely difficult. While it takes care, focus and a good amount of hard work, it is certainly possible to write a winning legal argument by following the key, straightforward principles of effective written advocacy. This article sets forth a number of approaches, strategies and tips for developing and writing winning legal arguments. It looks at several important steps in preparing to write a compelling legal argument and then examines the key "do"s and "don't"s of brief writing. Along the way, it includes a number of examples of effective and ineffective written advocacy.

THE KEY STEPS IN PREPARING FOR WRITING A WINNING LEGAL ARGUMENT

Writing a winning legal argument takes a significant amount of preparation. While it is difficult to write anything very well without a lot of thought, it is particularly hard to write a focused, compelling legal ar-

From the **Appellate Practice Journal**/Summer 2007/ABA/Section of Litigation

gument without having first considered most of the likely content of the document. The following are the most important, critical steps in preparing to write an outstanding and persuasive legal argument.

Analyze the case. First, while this probably goes without saying, it is essential when considering a written legal argument to begin by analyzing and thinking about the case. Even before reading documents and deposition transcripts or researching legal issues, it is important to spend some time (often several hours or perhaps even a day or two) reviewing the complaint, any answer, any memoranda evaluating the claims in the case, or any other fundamental pleadings or analyses to understand what the important issues are in the case and what kinds of arguments have the potential to convince a judge or panel of judges regarding the issue(s) about which you are contemplating writing an argument. Certainly, if you are planning on writing a dispositive motion or an appeal brief, it is necessary to have carefully thought about the case before doing anything else. But even if you are writing a motion to exclude the testimony of an expert, or to compel discovery, it is very helpful to look at the case as a whole, determine the key issues in the case, and develop a sense for how the argument you are considering will fit arguments have the potential to convince a judge or panel of judges regarding the issue(s) about which you are contemplating writing an argument. Certainly, if you are planning on writing a dispositive motion or an appeal brief, it is necessary to have carefully thought about the case before doing anything else. But even if you are writing a motion to exclude the testimony of an expert, or to compel discovery, it is very helpful to look at the case as a whole, determine the key issues in the case, and develop a sense for how the argument you are considering will fit into the rest of the case. At this point, it is also helpful to make a very preliminary list of the issues that you are beginning to consider for your argument.

Examine the relevant parts of the record. The next step in preparing to write a legal argument is to review thoroughly the parts of the record relevant to the argument that you are considering. In determining the content of your argument, it is very important to review all of the materials that contain factual information that may affect the argument. Therefore, if you are writing a motion to compel discovery, after having analyzed the case, you would need to examine all of the discovery requests and responses in the case, any relevant documents produced in the case, and any relevant deposition testimony. If you are writing a summary judgment brief, you would need to review all of the written discovery requests and responses in the case, all relevant produced documents and deposition testimony, and all of the prior pleadings and motions in the case; of course, you would also need to review any prior decisions by the court in your case. If you are writing an appeal brief, you would also need to examine the entire trial transcript (if there is one) and all relevant exhibits admitted at trial as well as all pretrial and post trial briefs and rulings from the trial court. While such review can be time consuming, it really is essential to preparing a written argument that will persuade a judge or appellate panel that will either have first hand knowledge of the details of the record of the case or at least access to the entire record and law clerks who are likely to examine the parts of the record that they feel are relevant to your argument.

Preliminarily identify the issue or issues that you will address in your argument. Once you have analyzed the case and reviewed the relevant parts of the record, you should begin to get a pretty good idea of the issue or issues that you will address in your argument. To be sure, it may be easier to identify the issue if you are preparing a discovery or evidentiary motion. But you should attempt to identify the issues you will address even if you are preparing a summary judgment motion or an appeal brief. While you may abandon certain issues and adopt other issues as the writing process progresses, you want to have as good an idea as possible of the main issues before you undertake extensive research or spend a lot of time drafting. At this point, it is helpful to draft a one or two sentence statement of each issue that you are considering.

Research the law pertaining to the issues you have identified. Once you have preliminarily identified the issues that you think you are likely to raise, the next step is to comprehensively research the law pertaining to those issues. This part of the process may be undertaken by the lawyer ultimately responsible for the written argument under consideration or it may be undertaken by several lawyers working with or under the guidance of the responsible lawyer. In all events, it is critical that the key issues are very carefully examined. The most helpful authorities will be statutes or cases that directly govern the issues about which you are concerned. If there is not a statute or case that directly controls, the next best authority may be a controlling case that addresses a different but analogous issue or has pertinent and helpful language, a non-controlling factually similar case from a lower court or different jurisdiction, or an administrative regulation that speaks to the relevant issue. Other helpful authorities may be non-controlling cases that address different but analogous issues, legislative history, treatises, law review articles, dictionaries, and other sources that can help develop your argument. When undertaking your primary research, it is important to make sure that you plan to rely, not merely on helpful language in a case or the legal rule that a case sets forth, but also upon how that language or rule was specifically applied to the facts in the case. Ultimately, the most persuasive authorities are those that articulate or adopt the legal rule that you advocate and then apply it to similar facts and reach the result that you advocate should be reached in your case. To be sure, there may be instances, such as in interpretation of a statute, where sources like legislative history or dictionaries may be more prominent than most cases would be in supporting your argument. But for the most part, it is the similarity of the application and outcome of the rule you advocate that will persuade judges to rule in your favor.

When undertaking your primary research, it is important not to rely on a single research method, such as computer searches. While it is possible that you may find most of the key authorities regarding your issue by performing only a single search method, it is also quite possible that you may miss one or more of the most pertinent authorities. It is usually ideal to begin your research by examining a treatise or a law review or similar article that addresses the issue that you are researching. Such an examination will likely lead you to many of the authorities that you need. It is also beneficial to examine the relevant practice digest(s) that include the issue you are researching. For statutory research, it is usually helpful to consult the annotated version of the statute at issue. After you have reviewed such sources, it usually makes sense to supplement your research with computer searches. Unfortunately, it is far too common for a lawyer to miss important authorities by relying solely on either book research or computer research.

Complete your secondary research. Once you have carefully researched the primary issues in the case or with which you are concerned, it is often helpful to complete research on secondary issues. These might include the applicable standard of review on appeal or for summary judgment, general statements about the desirability of resolving certain issues by way of legal motion, and analogous areas of the law upon which you may wish to rely. While it is possible to complete such research at a later stage of the writing process, I have found that completing as much of the research as possible before undertaking any extensive drafting usually makes the drafting process go more smoothly.

Select the issues you that you will present. After having completed your research, it is a good idea to revisit your preliminary list of issues and refine that list. You may abandon one or more issues that are unlikely to be the basis for a persuasive legal argument. You may add one or more issues that your research has led you to consider. Think very carefully about these issues because they will serve as the foundation for your legal argument. You should also revise your prior descriptions of each issue that you had previously considered and draft one or two sentences defining each new issue that you intend to present. You may very well edit or alter your definition or abandon an issue at a later stage of the drafting process, but it is beneficial to have a clear idea of the composition of your issues before you begin to draft your outline. You should also be very careful about the number of issues you select. As a general rule, presenting more than three issues in any brief runs the risk of signaling to the court that none of your issues has merit. While in an exceptional case, I have seen four or even five issues persuasively presented on an appeal, I have also seen many cases in which one or two legitimate issues were lost in a sea of several other weak or frivolous issues.

Draft a focused outline. In my view, one of the most critical steps in writing a winning legal argument is carefully developing a focused outline of your brief or other document. I typically recommend using the outlining process to develop the theme or themes of your written argument, to highlight the most important facts that you want to set forth in your document, the issues that you want to address, and the primary components of the arguments that you want to present. Therefore, it is usually helpful to include in your outline a description of the introduction and theme to your argument, the most important facts that you want to include in your written presentation, the point headings and subheadings for the argument section of your brief or document, the key cases and other authorities upon which you plan to rely (and ideally a one sentence description of each critical point from each authority), and at least a brief description of how you plan to apply the authorities to each issue that you plan to address. While there is no magic formula for how long such an outline should be, and it will vary depending on the length of your written presentation, an outline of 1–2 pages will often suffice for a single issue motion like a straightforward motion to compel, but an outline of 3–4 pages may be more appropriate for a summary judgment motion or an appellate brief. Occasionally, outlines of 5–6 pages may be warranted in a particularly complicated matter. Once you get much beyond that, however, your outline begins to resemble a first draft more than a true outline. If there are more than one lawyer working on the case, it is very helpful to circulate your outline and get feedback on it before beginning to draft your brief or document in earnest. Particularly, if there are more senior lawyers working on the case, circulating an outline is an excellent opportunity to make sure that everyone is reasonably in agreement as to the approach to the brief before you have spent many hours drafting an argument that others may believe is unlikely to be persuasive.

GENERAL CONVENTIONS FOR EXCELLENT LEGAL WRITING

Before suggesting specific approaches to the different sections of a brief or similar legal document, it is important to discuss certain general conventions for excellent legal writing.

1. **Always employ respectful and appropriate language.** While this point should be obvious, I have observed a significant amount of legal writing (including from experienced attorneys) that does not evidence the appropriate respect and decorum necessary for formal writing that is intended to persuade a judge or panel of judges. Of course, you should never submit something like the document in *Figure 1*.

Figure 1

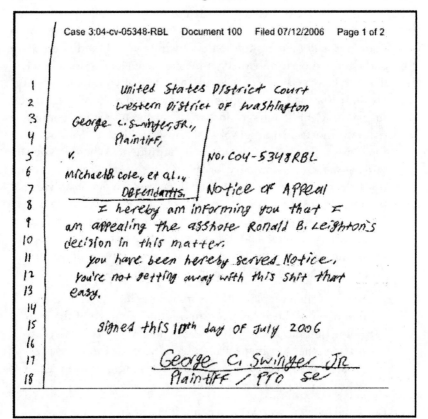

But overblown rhetoric, the use of *ad hominem* attacks on opposing counsel or the opposing party, excessive and unjustified indignation, or merely insulting or snippy comments are just as ineffective. A winning legal argument is virtually always comprised of temperate, respectful language that has persuasive value based on its content rather than its tone.

2. **Use simple, clear language and relatively short sentences.** Almost all good writing uses straightforward and understandable language. Clear and direct language is even more important for excellent legal writing. While some lawyers feel that it is impressive or somehow more persuasive to use jargon, large uncommon words, or convoluted phrases, such devices are usually unhelpful and off-putting. One of my colleagues suggested long ago that it is most advantageous to use language that any high school graduate would readily understand and to avoid language that invites reference to a dictionary or thesaurus. Similarly, it is best to avoid long, complicated, and/or run-on sentences. A complex thought can usually best be expressed through a series of short, declarative sentences, rather than a run-on sentence with multiple clauses. Even though it may be tempting to demonstrate your broad vocabulary and ability to perform word gymnastics, such tactics are much less likely to be effective than they are to irritate or confuse the reader.

3. **Develop focused paragraphs with appropriate topic sentences.** Just as unclear language and run-on sentences may confuse a reader, unfocused paragraphs or those lacking a clear point or topic are unlikely to advance your argument. Whether you are writing a factual summary or describing controlling precedent, use a clear topic sentence and then develop each paragraph so that it logically flows from your topic sentence. If you wish to transition to another point or thought, it is generally best to begin a new paragraph. With that said, it can be effective to list a few supporting points within a single paragraph by using transitions such as "first," and "second." For example:

> The cases cited by plaintiff are unavailing for several reasons. First, none of those cases addresses the language of the controlling statute. Rather, those cases all involve common-law doctrines that are inapplicable here. Second, those cases all predate the Supreme Court's recent decisions interpreting the controlling statute, and are therefore unreliable.

But in all events, keep your writing focused and clear.

4. **Avoid footnotes in most circumstances.** Certain legal writing teachers claim that it is helpful to use footnotes for citations and less important factual or legal points. My experience and understanding is that that vast majority of judges, and likely the vast majority of the best practicing legal writers, disagree and find footnotes almost always more distracting than they are worth. It is virtually always easier to read a citation in the text of a document than to search the bottom of a page (or worse, in the case of endnotes, the last few pages of the document). And if a factual point or legal argument is not significant enough to be in the text of your brief, you should question whether it should be omitted entirely. To be sure, many excellent legal writers have different perspectives on this issue, and some regularly employ footnotes in certain circumstances. In my view, the *only* circumstances in which you should consider using a footnote are (i) when it would be distracting to state a necessary but substantively insignificant point—something such as "Intervenor incorporates and adopts the Statement of the Case set forth in Petitioner's Brief" at the beginning of a Supplemental Statement of the Case; (ii) where you wish to include the citation of many cases from non-controlling jurisdictions, such as where you want to show that all or many of the federal appellate courts agree with your position and you want to cite them following an *Accord* or *See also* signal; or (iii) where you feel compelled to include a point that is particularly tangential and distracting, such as a case's lengthy prior or subsequent history or the history of amendments to a statute. Accordingly, footnotes should virtually never be used to include facts relevant to your case or subsidiary legal arguments. Simply put, if the factual point or legal argument is not important enough to appear in the text, you should almost always delete it from your document.

5. **Do not under any circumstance misrepresent or overclaim any fact or legal authority.** A critical component of the persuasive value of a written argument is the credibility of the author. Any misrepresentation or inaccurate portrayal of a fact or authority in your document is likely to destroy that credibility. As one well-respected advocate put it:

> The four outstanding don't"s for brief-writers, in my judgment, are (a) inexcusable inaccuracy; (b) unsupported hyperbole; (c) unwarranted screaming; and (d) personalities and scandalous matter. They are don'ts, not only from the point

of view of one's own professional standards and self-respect, but also from the narrow aspect of intelligent self-interest; every one of these faults is bound to backfire—and most unpleasantly.[1]

If you always fairly and accurately describe the facts of your case and the authorities you rely upon (and avoid intemperate rhetoric as previously suggested), you will not have to worry that you may lose as a result of your own missteps rather than the substance of your arguments.

6. **Consider using helpful demonstrative aids.** A picture can be worth a thousand words (and will sometimes save that many words). While many excellent legal writers would never think to use demonstrative aids in a brief (particularly an appellate brief), a timeline, chart, diagram, table or even a picture can sometimes add immeasurably to the persuasiveness and clarity of an argument. For example, intellectual property lawyers have used such devices to great effect in trial court briefs, and in appellate briefs in patent cases in the U.S. Court of Appeals for the Federal Circuit. But such demonstratives can be usefully employed in many other cases. Timelines are almost always useful in cases with complicated facts, and other demonstratives can be used where likely to be effective. Don't overdo it, however. A picture book rarely makes an effective legal brief. But if carefully chosen, a limited number of demonstratives can enliven and enhance many legal arguments. The following is a (somewhat altered) example from a recent brief:

> It is undisputed that Plaintiff's claims are for breach of an "express contract" between Plaintiff and the United States. Therefore, to establish a sovereign immunity defense, the Government must point to "unambiguous evidence" that Congress has by statute "withdrawn" Tucker Act jurisdiction for Plaintiff's claims. But the Government has not even attempted to do so. Indeed, the Government does not cite any purported statutory basis for its sovereign immunity defense. And there is none. There is nothing that even arguably limits Tucker Act jurisdiction over Plaintiff's claims

---

[1] Frederick Bernays Wiener, *Effective Appellate Advocacy* 149 (ABA Publishing, Rev. ed. 2004).

in the enabling legislation for the UPC, 10 U.S.C. § 7426, the legislation authorizing the sale of the Government's interest in the Elk Hills Reserve, 10 U.S.C. § 7420 note sec. 3412, or the legislation authorizing the Secretary of Energy to enter into contracts, 42 U.S.C. § 7256. To the contrary, the statute authorizing the sale of the Government's interest in Elk Hills specifically states that "[n]othing in this subtitle shall be construed to adversely affect the ownership interest of any other entity having any right, title, and interest in" the Reserve. Pub. L. No. 104-106, § 3413(c), 110 Stat. at 634-35. See graphic below:

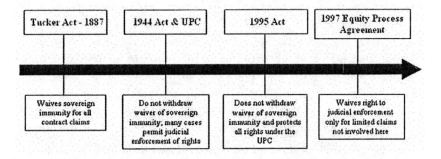

Accordingly, there is simply nothing that limits the United States' waiver of sovereign immunity with respect to Plaintiff's claims, and thus nothing that limits this Court's Tucker Act jurisdiction over those claims.

7. **Review the rules of the court in which your case is pending.** It is, of course, necessary that you know the basic federal or state rules of procedure that apply in your case. Those will contain many of the rules governing your brief or document and what may or may not be required or appropriate to include. But many state and federal courts themselves have their own nuances with respect to the rules of procedure. It is therefore critical that you also know those "local" and/or "chambers" rules and tailor your written argument to conform to them. It is difficult to prevail on your brilliant legal argument if your brief gets "bounced" by the Clerk's Office.

8. **Edit carefully.** Always carefully edit your drafts. While theoretically possible, it is unlikely that you will get it exactly right the first time. Some writers go through a dozen or more drafts in the

course of writing a legal argument; others may only work through a few. But virtually all good legal writers go through each draft in a focused effort to improve, tighten and polish their arguments. The editing process should include a rigorous assessment of your brief's structure, persuasiveness, language and syntax. As part of this process, you should also proofread very carefully. Always run a computer spell check, but also examine grammar, syntax and spelling yourself. You should also always check and double check to make sure that you have included all portions of your document that are required by the rules of the court in which your case is pending (*e.g.*, statement of facts or jurisdiction, summary of argument, statement of related cases, etc.).

> It is also helpful during the editing process to have other lawyers read a draft of your brief, particularly those who have not worked closely with you on the case. In a large law firm or government office, it may be fairly easy to have a colleague review your draft. In other settings, it may be more difficult. But your argument will almost always improve when others with a fresh perspective have considered it. I recall an instance many years ago when I was working on a Supreme Court brief with several colleagues. One of our colleagues who had not worked on the brief reviewed a draft and convinced the rest of us entirely to restructure the brief in a way that ultimately made it much more readable and persuasive.

PUTTING TOGETHER A WINNING LEGAL ARGUMENT

Bearing in mind the general conventions of excellent legal writing and having completed your research, analysis, outline, and other preparations, it is time to start drafting your brief or legal document. Let's examine each of the components of a winning brief, motion or similar persuasive legal document.

Statement of the Issues Presented

In an appellate brief, you will usually be required to include a formal statement of the issues or questions presented and it will normally be the first substantive portion of your brief. Most trial court rules do not require a formal statement of the issues for either motions or briefs. While I don't think that you need to include a formal statement of the issues in a trial court brief, I do think it is essential to include a clear description of the issues in the introduction or preliminary statement to a trial court brief. It is critical within the first one or two paragraphs to clearly set forth for a trial court what the issue(s) are and what relief you seek. Your statement should incorporate the following principles:

- **Clearly and accurately state each issue.** It is essential both for your credibility and for the persuasive value of your argument to rigorously define the issue(s) that you will present.
- **Use language that is likely to elicit a favorable response.** Your advocacy begins with the definition of the issue(s) that you are presenting to the court. You should define each issue such that the court may be persuaded in some fashion by the definition alone. For example, it is more effective to frame an issue as: "Whether the agency reasonably denied relief where the requested relief would have been inconsistent with decades of agency precedent and would have resulted in an unwarranted windfall for the petitioner," than merely as "Whether the agency erred in denying relief."
- **Frame the issue(s) with whatever background material is necessary.** In a trial court brief, it is often most effective to provide a paragraph or so of context before defining the issue for the court. While the practice has not always been followed in appellate courts, it is now becoming more common to do the same thing in appellate and U.S. Supreme Court briefs. A good recent example of this is as follows:

A divided panel of the Court of Appeals for the Third Circuit held that a district court **must** first conclusively determine if it has personal jurisdiction over the defendant before it may dismiss the suit on the ground of forum non conveniens. The court acknowledged that its holding was inconsistent with the interests of judicial economy, recognized that its decision in the case deepened an already-existing 4–2 split among the circuits, and invited this Court's review.

The question presented is:

Whether a district court **must** first conclusively establish jurisdiction before dismissing a suit on the ground of forum non conveniens?

Unfortunately, the opposing brief neither provided any context nor accurately stated the question. That brief stated:

The question presented is:

Whether a district court **should** establish jurisdiction before dismissing a suit on grounds of forum non conveniens?

A hypothetical case. To illustrate some of the principles of excellent brief writing, consider the following hypothetical case. Your client, Pharma, a major U.S. pharmaceutical company, makes Happynol, a "nextgen" antidepressant. A well-known pharmaceutical "entrepreneur," Dr. Evil, has been importing and selling a very similar drug, Euphorizem, that is made outside the U.S. and allegedly uses a different, but remarkably effective, active ingredient. Both drugs are patented—Happynol in the U.S., Euphorizem in the EU. Both drugs are sold at high prices. Consumer plaintiffs have brought suit alleging that Pharma and Dr. Evil have conspired to fix prices in violation of the Sherman Act and that plaintiffs have suffered cognizable damages under the Clayton Act.

The issue presented. Suppose that the district court had granted summary judgment on the ground that no reasonable jury could find that there had been direct dealings between Pharma and Dr. Evil sufficient to establish a price-fixing conspiracy and emphasized that there was no evidence in the record that Pharma and Dr. Evil had directly communicated with each other. On appeal, you could phrase the issue presented as: "Are plaintiffs correct that there is sufficient evidence in the record such that a reasonable jury could find that there existed a conspiracy by defendants to fix prices?" Such a statement, however, fails to mention the district court's ruling in your client's favor or the lack of evidence in the record that the defendants had directly communicated with each other and casts the issue in the best light for plaintiffs. A more effective statement would be: "Whether the district court erroneously determined that plaintiffs had failed to proffer sufficient evidence that a reasonable jury could have found that Pharma and Dr. Evil, who never directly communicated with each other, nevertheless conspired to fix prices." Some advocates strenuously oppose beginning a statement of the issue or question presented with the word "whether"; a good alternative to consider here would be to start with "Did the district court erroneously determine. . . ."

Statement of the Case and Facts

The statement of the case and facts is not merely a necessary part of your brief, it is an excellent opportunity for advocacy.

The statement of facts is as important as any portion of the brief. The statement should be written, rewritten, and then rewritten again before being placed in final form. The statement is designed to inform. But a good statement does more; it engages the reader's interest, making the judge look forward to working on the case. The statement of facts tells the story of your case. This does not give you a license to embellish or to throw in irrelevant but juicy facts to liven up the plot. Stick to the essentials. But remember, it is not unconstitutional to be interesting.[2]

There are several specific things that you can do to make a statement of the facts compelling and persuasive.

- **Follow chronological order.** Many poor statements of facts result from the common mistake of structuring the statement by topic or witness. While such a structure can seem logical and may even shorten the statement a bit, it does not result in a compelling story. You should start from the beginning and craft the statement as a narrative, building each new fact upon those already described. Typically, you can break up the statement into the background facts and the procedural history of the case. If you do so, you can create a compelling chronological description of everything relevant that has happened both before and after the case was filed.

- **Adhere to a chronological structure even if you have to include a separate Statement of the Case.** In many appellate courts, you are required to have a separate "Statement of the Case" that must precede the "Statement of Facts." If so, my recommendation is not to abandon a chronological structure. Rather, you can draft a pointed one to two paragraph statement that relays the critical procedural events of the case, but does not attempt to address them in detail. Leave the detail for the procedural history section of your Statement of the Facts. Thus, an effective Statement of the Case could read like this:

Pharma makes many drugs that have improved the lives of millions of consumers. Pharma's research into new and improved drugs costs hundreds of millions of dollars per year. Prices for drugs with significantly improved efficacy necessarily reflect those costs.

In March 2005, plaintiffs, a class of consumers of Happynol and Euphorizem filed suit claiming that Pharma and Dr. Evil conspired to fix the prices of these drugs. After expedited discovery, in February 2006, Pharma and Dr. Evil moved for summary judgment on grounds that (1)

---

[2] Ruggero J. Aldisert, *Winning on Appeal: Better Briefs and Oral Argument* 163 (National Institute for Trial Advocacy 2d ed., 2003); *see also* Justice Robert H. Jackson, *Advocacy Before the Supreme Court*, 37 A.B.A. J. 801, 803 (1951) ("It may sound paradoxical, but most contentions of law are won or lost on the facts. The facts often incline a judge to one side or the other.").

there is no evidence of any communications between Pharma and Dr. Evil that could have given rise to a conspiracy to fix prices, and (2) Pharma and Dr. Evil lack market power because of the availability alternative products. On September 15, 2006, the district court granted summary judgment on the ground that plaintiffs have not proffered any evidence of communications between Pharma and Dr. Evil that could have given rise to a conspiracy to fix prices; the court did not reach the market power issue. On December 10, 2006, plaintiffs filed a timely notice of appeal.

- **Tell a compelling story.** A corollary to structuring your statement chronologically is that you should tell a complete and compelling story in your statement of facts.

A lawyer engaged in stating facts is telling a story, a story the court should accept and understand as it reads along, without having to supplement your narrative by its own independent efforts. Or, to use a different metaphor, the lawyer stating the facts is painting a picture—and those who look at that picture should not be troubled by the details of how the artist mixed his colors. To the extent that the reader may want to check the facts of the story, or the art-lover those of the picture, the record references supply the necessary assurance that what has been depicted is real and not imaginary.[3]

The idea is to relate the facts in such a way as to tell a coherent story that casts your client's actions in a positive light and will lead the court to adopt your client's perspective on the salient details. You should select the facts that advance the story in a meaningful way and avoid facts that are unimportant, distracting or, unless central to the case, would not reflect well on your client's actions. You should also be sure that no important details or events are omitted. Your statement should give the reader all of the key details needed to understand what happened and to conclude that your client acted in a reasonable manner. It is critical that, on the whole, your story makes sense and depicts the actions of your client as fair and sensible.

Lawyers often question whether they should reveal "bad facts" in their statement of the facts and attempt to address them, even where the opposing party has not yet relied on them. That is a difficult issue and entire books have been written on the subject. My advice is that if a bad fact is so central to a case that it is sure to be relied on by the opposition and it is sure to get the attention of the court, it probably does make

---

[3] Wiener at 35.

sense to address it as part of the story you are telling. But it is not beneficial to pay too much attention to that fact unless and until your opponent does. Thus, in our hypothetical, if there is evidence in the record that Pharma and Dr. Evil both attended the same pharmaceutical convention a month before their new anti-depressants came on the market, it could be addressed as follows:

> None of Pharma's employees ever discussed Happynol or Euphorizem with Dr. Evil. Dr. Evil has never been seen in the presence of any of Pharma's employees, and his business, personal and cell phone records show that he has never called any of Pharma's employees. Two of Parma's executives, Dr. Strange and Dr. Love did attend Medcon 2004 in Las Vegas, but they left the same day that Dr. Evil arrived, did not attend any of the same meetings or events, and were not seen together by anyone; neither their hotel nor cell phones were used to communicate with Dr. Evil.

If the "bad fact" is not central to the case, I would recommend not addressing it at all until and unless your opponent has raised it. Otherwise, it will appear as if you believe that it is important and are "sponsoring" that fact.[4]

- **Be rigorously accurate.** It bears repeating that it is critical to be completely accurate in your description of the facts. To be sure, you want to emphasize and highlight the facts that support your story and reflect well on your client's actions. But you cannot in any sense play "fast and loose" with the facts. It is also important to cite the record to support each fact that you introduce. When you are writing an appellate brief, you should try to cite to the trial court's decision if you can for most facts because your panel and their law clerks will certainly read the trial court's decision and will assume that the trial court's description of the facts is accurate. You should try to keep citations relatively unobtrusive by abbreviating where possible. And, as previously discussed, you should not place your citations in footnotes, which are quite distracting.
- **Avoid any argument or editorializing.** You will have plenty of opportunity to argue the case. The statement of facts is not the place to do it. Rather, the statement should not include any argument or editorializing about the facts. Your credibility as an advocate and the seriousness with which a court regards your state-

---

[4] *See generally*, Robert H. Klonoff & Paul L. Colby, *Winning Jury Trials: Trial Tactics and Sponsorship Strategy* (Lexis Law Publishing, 2d ed. 2003).

ment of facts will all be enhanced by delivering a pristine statement that includes facts and only facts. Thus, a sentence such as
"Happynol was developed over a five-year period and is more effective than previous-generation anti-depressants" is much more
effective than: "Plaintiffs ignore that Happynol was created by the
hard work of brilliant scientists over a five-year period and is truly
a 'wonder drug,' giving new hope to thousands of people who had
previously been overcome by despair."

- **Carefully and completely set forth the procedural history.** Finally,
be sure to include all elements of the procedural history that are
pertinent and helpful. Even if an event seems tangential to your argument, such as transfer of the case or removal to federal court in
the distant past, it is usually helpful to give the court all of the background that the court may wish to know. The last thing you want
to do is to confuse the court by omitting a detail that you know
about and think is insignificant, but which a judge or law clerk
wants to learn. If there has been a prior decision in the case, seriously consider quoting helpful statements from such a decision.
Trial judges rarely are offended if you quote their earlier decisions
or those of their colleagues. Appellate judges are more likely to rely
on statements expressly made by trial judges than on your paraphrasing. You should rely as much as you can on the language of
any prior decisions.

Introduction/Summary of the Argument

The introduction and/or summary of the argument are also quite important components of your brief. For most trial court motions and
briefs, a formal summary of the argument is not required. But an Introduction or Preliminary Statement section can and should be used to accomplish the same things as a more formal summary: introducing the
theme of your argument, clearly identifying the issue(s) presented, and
summarizing your argument as to each issue that you have raised.
Thus, in trial court briefs and motions, it is important to carefully write
your Introduction or Preliminary Statement to accomplish all of those
objectives. Again, there is no magic formula for length or detail. A good
general rule of thumb is that your Introduction should rarely, if ever, be
longer than 10% of the total length of your brief—2 pages maximum for
a 20 page brief, 5 pages for a 50 page brief. A good model is to include
one or two paragraphs setting forth the theme and defining the issue(s)
that you are addressing and then one paragraph summarizing your argument for each issue that you raise.

In appellate briefs, the summary of argument will also state your theme, make clear the issues you are raising, and summarize your argument as to each issue. But there is one nuance to consider. It has become more acceptable in appellate briefs to include a short introduction prior to or in lieu of a statement of the case that sets forth the theme of your argument and very briefly describes the background of the case. An example based on our hypothetical could be:

> Anti-depressants have improved the quality of life for millions of people. Pharma has spent millions of dollars and years of research developing its "nextgen" anti-depressant Happynol, which is more effective for more people than most prior drugs. Naturally, Pharma's substantial costs are reflected in Happynol's price. Dr. Evil markets a similar nextgen anti-depressant, Euphorizem. None of Pharma's employees have ever discussed the price or marketing of Happynol or Euphorizem with Dr. Evil, and there is no evidence in the record that suggests otherwise. Furthermore, even though these new drugs are innovative, there are numerous other drugs available that can provide effective relief for most people suffering from depression.
>
> Plaintiffs urge that they have paid artificially high prices for Happynol and Euphorizem and allege a conspiracy to fix prices for those drugs. The district court rejected plaintiffs' unjustified assertions because there is no evidence in the record from which a reasonable jury could conclude that Pharma and Dr. Evil ever communicated about, let alone conspired about, the prices or marketing of Happynol or Euphorizem. In addition, although the district court did not reach the issue, Pharma is also entitled to judgment as a matter of law that defendants do not possess sufficient market power to restrain trade. For both of these reasons, the district court's grant of summary judgment should be affirmed and plaintiffs' attempt to obtain an unwarranted windfall should be rejected.

There are several important guideposts for writing an excellent introduction or summary of argument:

- **It is important to draft a powerful opening paragraph or paragraphs.** As the example above demonstrates, it is essential to orient the court very quickly as to the theme of your argument, the key issues, and the outcome you seek.

The introduction of your summary—the exordium in the schema of the rhetoricians—must let the reader know, in a few sentences, the scope, theme content, and outcome of the brief. It sets the stage for the discussion to follow. It dispatches your argument to the reader at once in succinct, concise, and minimal terms. It describes the equitable heart of the appeal.[5]

The beginning of your introduction or summary has to grab the court and concisely articulate why you should win.

- **You should summarize all of your key arguments.** Many ineffective summaries or introductions are either too spartan or ramble and fail to actually summarize the argument. When describing your argument on each issue you should include each necessary component of that argument.

The summary is critical because it gives the reader a concise preview of the argument. The summary should be crafted so as to allow the judge to construct a practical outline of a memorandum. Alas, this often does not occur, because the brief writer either has not prepared a summary or has slapped one together without the thought necessary to create a statement that is both comprehensive and concise.[6]

As will be discussed in the argument section, your summary paragraph for an issue should include a topic sentence that defines the issue, a sentence or two that describes the governing legal rule, a sentence or two that shows how that rule applies to your case, and at least a sentence that describes the outcome you seek with respect to that issue.

- **You may include citations, but keep them concise.** While an introduction or summary is not the place for a lengthy discussion of the law, it may be appropriate to include a small number of particularly important citations. For example, you may wish to refer to a controlling case that is directly on point or to a controlling case that has adopted the precise legal rule that you advocate. But don't overdo it. It is rarely effective to cite more than a few cases in an introduction or summary and it can get unwieldy very easily.

An example of a summary paragraph based on our hypothetical is:

The district court's ruling should also be affirmed on the alternative ground that plaintiffs have failed to prove that Pharma and Dr. Evil had market power sufficient to restrain trade. A showing of market power must include a definition of the relevant market and proof that the market lacks sufficient substitutes to offset any

---

[5] Aldisert at 184.
[6] Aldisert at 183.

attempt to artificially raise prices; in other words a plaintiff must analyze and offer proof regarding the "cross-elasticity of demand" for the products at issue. *Todd v. Exxon Corp.*, 275 F.3d 191, 200 (2d Cir. 2001). Plaintiffs here have failed to provide a coherent definition of the relevant market, referring only in general terms to "nextgen" anti-depressants. They have failed to proffer any evidence that other anti-depressants are not economic and therapeutic substitutes for Happynol and Euphorizem. Indeed, plaintiffs' experts have not even attempted to account for Happynol's recent loss of market share or for studies indicating that a majority of consumers are not willing to pay significantly higher prices for somewhat more potent anti-depressants. Defendants lack market power, and thus could not possibly have restrained trade.

The Argument

The argument is the heart of your brief or motion. It is obviously critical and it is likely to be the portion of your document on which you will spend the most time drafting and redrafting. While constructing an excellent argument section of a brief may appear daunting, there are several fundamental principles to follow.

- **Use argumentative point headings.** The point headings in your argument present an opportunity to persuade and focus the court. They should always be argumentative.

Headings should always be argumentative rather than topical or even assertive. For instance, say "This suit is barred by laches because brought twenty-five years after the issuance of the original certificate" rather than "This suit is barred by laches." The first gives the argument in a nutshell, the second does not—though certainly the second assertive heading is infinitely more effective than the merely topical "The question of laches."[7]

This rule applies even to subheadings describing the governing legal rule. It is remarkable to me when I see an otherwise excellent brief with a subheading that says "The law regarding laches" or "The standard for summary judgment." It is much more effective to say "Laches bars a suit when the plaintiff has unjustifiably delayed in asserting a claim" or "Summary judgment is appropriate when no reasonable jury could find that the defendants conspired to fix prices."

---

[7] Wiener at 54.

In our hypothetical, it would be much better to say:

"II. The District Court Correctly Concluded That Pharma And Dr. Evil Possess No Market Power Because There Are Many Economic Substitutes For Happynol and Euphorizem That Relieve Depression,"

than to say "II. Defendants Have No Market Power." Moreover, as these examples show, it is important to have point headings that, while concise, actually state your argument in a persuasive manner.

- **Make your best argument first in most circumstances.** If you have carefully selected your issues, you will likely have three or fewer issues to present to the court. In the event that you have more than one issue, it usually is most effective to present your strongest argument first. You want to lead with the argument that is most likely to grab the attention of and persuade the court. Certainly, if you feel like you have a slam dunk winner, lead with that argument. The only exception to this rule is where you have a procedural argument that you feel really has to be made first, even if it is perhaps a bit weaker than your best substantive argument. It does look rather obvious to make a jurisdictional or standing argument at the end of your brief. With that said, I have seen briefs (and even written some) that have made a jurisdictional argument such as mootness at the end of the argument, particularly where a substantive argument was very strong and where the client would prefer to win on the substantive argument, but where the procedural argument was also strong and obvious.
- **Use the "IRAC" structure for each issue.** We are not talking about the war in the Middle East here. It is generally very effective to use the Issue-Rule-Analysis-Conclusion structure for each issue that you address in your argument. Under this convention, include at least one sentence that states and defines the issue you are addressing, a paragraph or more setting forth the governing legal rule. It will often make sense to divide a main section of the argument into a subpoint that sets forth and describes the legal rule and a subpoint that applies that rule to the issue involved. The reason that this structure is usually the most effective to employ is that it is the most logical way to construct a legal argument. Identifying the issue at the outset orients the reader and sets the stage for your analysis. Defining and explaining the legal rule gives the court the criteria for decision and in many ways limits the possible analyti-

cal outcomes with respect to a given issue. Applying the rule to the issue provides the logical impetus for the court to rule in your favor. And explaining the outcome that you contend the law compels makes plain the result that you urge the court to order. Many legal writers discuss the key facts regarding an issue and then set forth the legal rule. While in very unusual circumstances such an approach can be effective, it usually is not. It is much more analytically compelling to establish the rule of decision first and then to apply that rule to the case and its key facts than to list a number of facts and expect the court to draw the proper conclusions from the legal rule that you subsequently set forth. And it is unnecessarily repetitive to describe the salient facts, set forth the legal rule and then apply that legal rule to the facts that you will have to re-describe, at least in part.

When establishing the legal rule, it is also helpful to start with general statements of the legal rule from cases and then demonstrate how that stated rule has been applied to the facts of the most relevant cases. While statements of the law are important, it is how those statements have been applied in analogous circumstances that will most effectively persuade a court.

- **Make your best affirmative case before responding to your opponent's actual or anticipated argument.** While employing the IRAC methodology, it is important to state your affirmative case first.

Always write your brief in such a way as to set out and make the most of your affirmative case. This admonition is perhaps most to be borne in mind when you are appellee or respondent; don't content yourself, in that situation, with a point-by-point reply to appellant or petitioner. Accentuate the affirmative features of your case and don't let the other side write your brief or even shape it.[8]

There are several ways to implement this precept. If your opponent disagrees with your statement of the governing rule, it is most effective to set forth and describe the legal rule you advocate (including showing how that rule has been applied in the most relevant cases), and then to respond to your opponent's argument. It is more persuasive to establish the legal rule as the point of comparison before attempting to demonstrate the flaws in your opponent's proposed rule. Similarly, if your op-

---

[8] Wiener at 98.

ponent disagrees with your application of the governing rule, it is most effective to fully set forth your application and then to critique your opponent's attempted application.

There are also likely to be many circumstances where your opponent makes an argument that neither directly conflicts with your statement of the governing rule nor your application, but nonetheless counsels for a different outcome. In such circumstances, it may be effective to subdivide your argument on the issue with a subpoint as to the governing law, as subpoint as to its application, and a third subpoint that directly responds to your opponent's arguments that are not in direct conflict with your statement of the law or you application of it. You could use a point heading such as: "C. Plaintiffs' Contrary Arguments About Market Power Are Unsupported and Erroneous."

- **Rely most heavily on cases that apply the rule you advocate in circumstances analogous to those in your case.** As has been noted previously, the most persuasive cases are usually those that set forth or adopt the legal rule that you advocate and then applies that rule in analogous circumstances in the same way that you advocate the rule should apply in your case. It may be helpful to cite or quote cases that set forth the legal rule that you advocate but that apply that rule in different circumstances or cases that apply a different rule in a way that supports your argument. But if possible, you want to rely primarily on those cases that are as similar in all respects as possible to your case. In defining the legal rule that you advocate, you want to show how that rule was applied in those cases. And in applying that rule, you want to compare the application in those cases to your case.
- **Address controlling or significant contrary authority.** In most circumstances, you opponent will cite (or will be likely to cite) one or more cases that are troublesome for you. If a case is controlling and clearly undermines your argument, you have an ethical obligation to address it. Often such a case can be distinguished or can be shown to no longer be effective, or at least can be plausibly argued to have been wrongly decided. If a case is not controlling, but undermines your argument and has been or is certain to be cited by your opponent, it likely will make sense to address it, particularly if you have a good answer. If a case is not controlling, only arguably undermines your argument, and has not been or may not be cited by your opponent, it is usually best to avoid it unless your opponent cites it (in which case you can address it in reply, or at

oral argument or in a letter to the court if you have no right of reply and there will be no argument).

- **Avoid string cites, unnecessary citations, and long block quotes.** It is very important to use legal authority to its best effect. If you are stating an obvious or well-settled proposition, cite only to one or at most two cases; the court will realize that the proposition is well supported and will only be irritated and/or distracted by numerous citations. If you are citing several cases for a single, less well-established point, you should include either a sentence or more discussion of each case in the text, or at least a parenthetical containing a helpful quote and/or showing why the case is useful. In almost all circumstances, a case citation without discussion of the case or a parenthetical is useless.

String cites of numerous cases for a proposition should virtually never be used. The only exception to this rule is where you want to show that several other jurisdictions agree with the novel or less well-established point that you are making. Such a string cite should either come at the end of a paragraph or placed in a footnote. Long block quotes should never be used. While I don't agree with some practitioners that block quotes should never be used, they should only be employed when they are used infrequently, are very helpful, and are limited to about 5-10 lines in length. I have seen several awful briefs that contained block quotes several pages in length. That is a recipe for argument suicide.

An example of a poor argument section. Using our hypothetical, one could conceive of an argument such as this:

Plaintiffs' assertion that defendants possess market power does not take into account the realities of competition and interchangeable or substitute products. *United States v. E.I. du Pont de Nemours & Co.*, 351 U.S. 377 (1956); accord *Balaklaw v. Lovell*, 14 F.3d 793, 799 (2d Cir. 1994). Just because Happynol is more expensive, does not necessarily mean that it so unique that has its own distinct market or that it truly possesses a significant market share. *See Global*, 960 F. Supp. at 705; *Shaw v. Rolex Watch, USA, Inc.*, 673 F. Supp. 674, 679 (S.D.N.Y. 1987). Plaintiffs do not account for the public recognition of older drugs similar to Happynol as well as evidence that most consumers are unwilling to pay substantially more for a somewhat more effective antidepressant. *See Brown Shoe Co. v. United States*, 370 U.S. 294, 325 (1962). Just like other federal courts have granted summary judgment to plaintiffs under similar circumstances, so was it appropriate here. *See, e.g., Bogan v. Hodgkins*, 166 F.3d 509, 516 (2d Cir. 1999).

This example conflates the legal rule and the application of that rule, does not discuss the application of the legal rule in analogous circumstances, and only superficially applies the legal rule.

An example of a much better argument section. The following is greatly improved:

> Plaintiffs have failed to show that defendants have sufficient market power to restrain trade. The alleged product market "must bear a rational relation to the methodology courts prescribe to define a market for antitrust purposes—analysis of the interchangeability of use or the cross-elasticity of demand." *Todd v. Exxon Corp.*, 275 F.3d 191, 200 (2d Cir. 2001). Thus, plaintiffs must include all reasonably interchangeable or substitutable products, *United States v. E.I. du Pont de Nemours & Co.*, 351 U.S. 377 (1956), taking into account "the realities of competition." *Grinnell Corp.*, 384 U.S. at 572-73. Accordingly, a relevant market is determined not only by the prices of its products but also by their use and other qualities. *See AD/SAT v. Associated Press*, 181 F.3d 216, 227 (2d Cir. 1999). A relevant market definition must account for industry or public recognition; the products' peculiar characteristics and uses; unique production facilities; distinct customers; distinct prices; sensitivity to price changes; and specialized vendors. *See Brown Shoe Co. v. United States*, 370 U.S. 294, 325 (1962). A product that is unique in some ways does not necessarily fall into a market by itself. *See Global*, 960 F. Supp. at 705. Rather, "it is the use or uses to which the commodity is put that control." *E. I. du Pont de Nemours & Co.*, 351 U.S. at 396.

Thus, an antitrust plaintiff's failure to account for interchangeable substitutes requires dismissal of or summary judgment against the plaintiff's claim. For example, in *Bogan v. Hodgkins*, 166 F.3d 509, 516 (2d Cir. 1999), the court affirmed a grant of summary judgment to defendant where plaintiffs confined their definition of the relevant market to experienced National Mutual Life insurance agents without considering the cross-elasticity of demand with regard to other sales agents in New York, and failed to produce factual evidence distinguishing potential substitutes in the insurance companies market.

Plaintiffs here have plainly failed to properly define the relevant product market. Their expert, Dr. Know-It-All, never provided any specific evidence as to why joynols, which are widely-accepted therapeutic substitutes for Happynol, are not reasonably interchangeable on the bases of price, use and other therapeutic qualities. Although he recognized that many therapeutic alternatives overlap one another with respect to efficacy, tolerance, range, as well as price, Expert Rep. at p.6, failed to make any mention of the potential clinical interchangeability of therapeutic substitutes for Happynol and Euphorizem. That is directly contrary to the expert testimony below of psychiatrists and managed care organizations, which consider them to be essentially fungible. Instead, Dr. Know-It-All looked only at price competition, even though "significant price differences do not always indicate distinct markets." *AD/SAT*, 181 F.3d at 228. Dr. Know-It-All also could not explain why many studies documented the robust competition between Happynol and other joynols and Happynol's recent decline in market share. Thus, Dr. Know-It-All failed to take into account the "realities of competition" as he was required to do. *See Brown Shoe Co.*, 370 U.S. at 325-26 (emphasizing that it is "unrealistic" to divide markets on price alone). In this case, as did the plaintiffs in *Bogan*, plaintiffs have made the critical mistake of proffering flawed market-definition analysis that fails to account for reasonably interchangeable substitutes for Happynol and Euphorizem. *See Bogan*, 166 F.3d at 516. Therefore, plaintiffs' proposed market definition is incorrect and insufficient as a matter of law, and this Court should affirm the grant of summary judgment for that reason.

- **Do not construct reply briefs that are overly defensive.** The subject of writing compelling reply briefs could justify a book of its own. My limited advice is to write reply briefs that generally comply with the principles for opening briefs. The structure I recommend is to use your introduction/summary of argument to summarize the key arguments that you made in your opening brief and either briefly address the most important of you opponent's arguments (if you have the room and it's justified) or simply state that your opponent's contrary arguments are unpersuasive.

In the substantive sections of the reply, briefly restate your specific argument from the opening brief and then address your opponent's responses one by one. Follow the general structure of *your* opening brief, not your opponent's brief, and use responsive, but argumentative headings. For example: "Defendant's definition of market power is wrong because it entirely relies on far-fetched substitutes and ignores more important economic considerations such as product features and price maintenance." Be sure to address the primary authorities cited by your opponent and explain why your authorities are more persuasive. You may also be able to fold in affirmative points that you made in your opening brief as responses to your opponent's arguments. For example: "Defendant's argument ignores the principal component of market power: 'the ability to maintain prices higher than those charged for potential substitutes.' *Brown Shoe*, 370 U.S. at 324."

Finally, do not feel compelled to address every point raised by your opponent, however minor. You must address all of the significant arguments and authorities and correct any material misstatements of fact or mischaracterizations of the record. But you need not address points that are trivial, clearly inappropriate, or facially implausible.

The Conclusion

Your conclusion should be succinct and should state clearly the relief you seek. For example: "For the foregoing reasons, this Court should reverse the district court's grant of summary judgment and remand for a trial on the merits."

CONCLUSION

Writing a winning legal argument just takes applying the principles we have discussed, focus, hard work, and a bit of experience. With significant effort, you can write excellent briefs and motions that have a great chance to persuade any judge or panel. Good luck and go get 'em!

(I would like to thank Victoria Dorfman, Thomas Donlon, Todd Holleman, and my Appellate Practice Committee Co-Chair Paul Watford, for their significant contributions to this article. I would also like to thank my colleagues at Jones Day, most notably Donald Ayer, Glen Nager, Robert Klonoff, and Gregory Castanias, for influencing my approaches to these subjects.)

Quick Tips for Successful Writing

Young Lawyer's Spotlight Ramblings on Writing: "Like A Lawyer" Not

By Rick Alimonti

Like many newly-minted lawyers, I emerged from Law School back in 1989 with an acquired style of writing that I assumed represented the way a lawyer was supposed to write and "sound." I was never specifically taught this manner of writing, but somehow by virtue of reading numerous decisions, briefs, and other "legal documents," I came to believe that, by virtue of convoluted, repetitious, and antiquated language, a document should announce at a glance that it had been written by a lawyer and should, therefore in all fairness, only be read [and understood] by a lawyer. In short, law school, through some form of osmosis (or infection) taught me how to write badly. Thankfully, there is a growing appreciation for legal documents written in simple English.

I offer a few subjective suggestions on preventing prosaic prose and writing reader-friendly briefs, memoranda, and pleadings. They are presented in no particular order and range from the grammatical to the stylistic—some even touching upon the ethical. In other words, it's basically a rant.

1. **Keep Sentences Short When Possible.** The longer a sentence, the more opportunity for confusion. The general order of a sentence should be subject, predicate, object. Nonetheless, sometimes long sentences can work, and I find that as my writing has matured, I have tended toward longer sentences. However, proceed with caution. The longer the sentence, the more room for confusion. Pronouns are a good example: "The Captain took control of the aircraft from the First Officer after he observed the failure of the landing gear to lock." Who is "he"?

From the **Aviation Litigation Quarterly**/Spring 2008/ABA/Section of Litigation

2. **No Read-Me-Twice Sentences.** We have all read briefs, decisions, and articles in which we had no choice but to go back, re-read, and parse a sentence to understand what the heck the author is trying to say. If a sentence needs to be read twice to be understood, it is defective. Throw it away, and start over.

3. **Death to Lawyerisms!** You know the terms, "aforementioned," "heretofore," etc. These terms and others like them do little more than add a note of arrogance and self-importance to our writing. Lawyers also like to say in several words (or a bigger words) what could [and should] be said in one small word:
   - "on the subject of" or "with respect to"; write "about."
   - "the individual"; write "he" or "she" or just use the name. Even "person" sounds better and saves three syllables.
   - "Annexed hereto as Exhibit "A"; what's wrong with simply "Exhibit "A" "? Do you think the court or your adversary is going to think there is some secret Exhibit "A" annexed "thereto" and not "hereto"?
   - "enclosed please find"; does anyone talk like this? How about, "I enclose"?
   - Similarly, "As and For a First Affirmative Defense." How about "First Affirmative Defense"? Would you ever say "as and for my shopping list" or "as and for my invoice for services"?
   - And don't get me started on the needlessly verbose repeat and reallege paragraphs splattered throughout the typical pleading! Find a simple way to say you meant what you said before in fifteen words or less.
   - These are just a few examples; you get the idea.

4. **Combine Like Parties into Groups.** If simple shorthand references can eliminate awkward and bulky references to multiple parties, use them, *e.g.*, "the manufacturing defendants," "the hull insurers," "the property-damage plaintiffs." Remember, not to depersonalize **your client** by using terms like "defendants" or "appellants."

5. **Make Skillful Use of Headings and Subheadings.** Your point headings and subheadings are the signposts along the highway of your argument. They serve many useful functions: they create an outline of your brief, allowing the reader to more easily bounce around; they organize the argument (this is an aid both to writing and reading); they break the monotony of endless text; and they signal the reader that one line of reasoning is complete and another one is about to begin.

Because these subheadings will become marquees of the brief, avoid bland markers like "The Standard for Summary Judgment" and "The Grounds for Declaratory Relief." Rather, write "Defendant Ambassador Air is Entitled to Judgment as a Matter of Law Because . . . " and "Ambassador Air is Entitled to Declaratory Relief Because there is a Genuine Case and Controversy."

6. **Topic Paragraphs; Topic Sentences.** Each section and subsection in a brief should include a topic paragraph that sets up the paragraphs to follow in the larger picture of your case. Similarly, each paragraph should begin with a topic sentence that assists in the transition from the previous thought and theme. Sometimes, this transition can be initiated at the end of the proceeding paragraph, hopefully presaging what is to follow and building up a sense of anticipation in the reader.

7. **Avoid the Passive Tense.** Sometimes the passive test can be used to break a chain of similar sentences beginning with the same subject. In general, it ekes of desire to avoid responsibility or to distance a subject from its actions. "Mistakes were made!" Need I say more?

8. **Do Not Use Weasel Footnotes.** The scenario is this; a party elects to bury its responses to the adversary's strongest arguments by relegating them to the footnote; as if doing so suggests that the opposing argument was so weak as not to deserve recognition in the text. However, the footnote in fact forces the reader to break her train of thought and focus exclusively on the note. This, ironically, highlights the weakest parts of your argument.

   Rather, I advocate the footnotes be used for "piling on" or delivering the *coup de grace*. For example, having thoroughly taken apart plaintiff's theory of the case in the text, a footnote might be a great place to point out that plaintiff has nonetheless failed to prove the very theory he has posited. It is also a good place to point out an inconsistency in the adversary's position that does not fit the flow of the main body of the text.

9. **Be Forthright with Opposing Authority.** Candor, Candor, Candor! Related to the previous comment, deal realistically and candidly with opposing authority. While there is no need to fall on your sword, failure to deal candidly and credibly with opposing authority will undermine your credibility with the court. Much as it is better to address weakness on direct examination of your

own witness, opposing authority should be addressed and de-fused before your opponent can highlight it in opposition or reply. This is a judgment call; if you feel your responsive argu-ment is so strong that the blow can best be reserved for reply, hang onto it. If you need to deal with something that is genuinely bad for you, get it behind you early and honestly.

10. **Educate While You Argue.** Only by being forthright with op-posing authority, can your brief be both persuasive and educa-tional to the court. This is where real craftsmanship comes in. The best briefs, in this author's opinion, manage to walk a fine line on which they make a compelling argument yet educate the court along the way. Naturally, the stronger your argument, the easier this is to accomplish.

11. **Write Compelling Facts.** It's easy to approach your facts as something to "get out of the way" before the real arguments. This is a mistake, and a proper exposition of the facts should lead the court in your direction before it even gets to the legal arguments. Ideally, the facts should cry out for a favorable ruling, leaving the court looking to the argument only for the legal justification to rule in your client's favor.

12. **Establish a Theme.** Develop one or two themes to your argu-ment, and keep coming back to them.

13. **Don't Forget the Big Picture.** Particularly when writing opposi-tion and reply briefs, it is easy to become lost in the minutia of opposing authority while ignoring broader arguments. Some years ago, a junior associate presented a reply brief to me that carefully distinguished each of the plaintiff's cases but never pointed out that plaintiff had no supporting authority whatso-ever. Rather, every case cited by our adversary ruled favorably to us with the "opposing" language derived from "what if" dicta. Certainly, the fact that the plaintiffs could cite not one case with a holding favorable to them was worthy of specific mention. This is an extreme example, but always looks for common threads to bind your opposition into a cohesive argument. Spotting trends and repeated flaws in an adversary's argument can also help you avoid the monotony of seriatim analysis of a litany of cases. If several opposing authorities share a common flaw and can be swept away in a sentence or two, sweep away.

14. **Don't be Cute or Flippant.** We have all dealt with sloppy, rude, and obstreperous adversaries. It can be so tempting to fight fire

with fire. There is room for only one jerk in litigation; let it be your adversary. I have never regretted maintaining the moral high-ground in litigation. Eventually, when it comes time to make the critical motion or application, how much better is it to be in the position of the party that has afforded his adversary every chance to save himself. There are few things less interesting to a court than having to adjudicate the classic excretory contest between two unreasonable lawyers. Gladly take a few harmless lumps along the way in the form of enduring evasive tactics. When the time comes to lower the boom, you need only cite the record you have built—one showing your continuing patience and your adversaries continued abuses.

Similarly, avoid innuendo, let alone insulting remarks, in your legal writing. If your adversary has been foolish enough to create a record of unprofessional conduct, delight in the lengths of rope with which your adversary has elected to hang himself.

15. **Avoid Ascribing Improper Motives to Your Adversary.** Most of the time, when an attorney ascribes a motive to another attorney or party, it amounts to little more than an accusation. It can be so tempting to ascribe a motive to a pattern of behavior, *e.g.*, "counsel for plaintiff is trying to delay the completion of discovery, harass the defendants, and run up expenses." I always cringe when someone advises the court of my intentions, and I am similarly reluctant to suggest the intentions of others. Face it; you simply cannot know what motivates another. You can point out to the court a pattern of behavior that suggests a particular motive; you certainly can point out the effect of that behavior. Lead the court down the path and let it ascribe the motives.

16. **Use a Reader/Buddy.** When you think you have a finished product, have a colleague read your work—preferably one not familiar with the case. It is amazing what insight the uninitiated can bring to your writing.

17. **Include the Question in Discovery Responses.** Okay, so this is really not a writing point, but it is a pet peeve. ALWAYS include the question or request in a discovery response, and try to convince your adversary to do the same. It makes reading them so much easier—even with respect to your own responses when you review them months or years after serving them. Most importantly, all discovery is potentially an exhibit to the court; give the judge a document that is user-friendly.

I could probably continue this list at much greater length. I hope a few of these suggestions are helpful. So much of what we do in law is writing and research. Crafting a well-written and well-constructed argument can be very satisfying. Now get in there, and convince the partner to let you argue it!

TRIAL PRACTICE

Introduction

By David W. Sterling

As a litigator, you should always focus on what will happen when you finally get your case to trial. But to be consistently successful, a good trial attorney does most of the work long before he or she enters the courtroom. Trial practice involves detailed preparation during the days, weeks, months, and sometimes years between filing your first pleading and the eventual trial date to ensure you have all the tools in place to effectively advocate for your client. It often involves filing and orally arguing pretrial motions, working with opposing counsel, and understanding your judge to keep you from being caught off guard in the courtroom.

Many books and resources are available that walk you through each specific facet of the trial process, from filing or answering the complaint through verdict and post-trial motions. The following compilation offers additional general advice on trial practice from successful litigators and seasoned judges. The tips and advice you find here will help you become more prepared and composed when it matters most—when presenting your case or argument in the courtroom.

Preparation is the key to a successful trial practice and this section starts with two great articles on this subject, including checklists and timelines that will help you throughout the litigation process. You will also find articles in this section discussing private securities class actions, ethics, courtroom demeanor, and closing arguments. Several arti-

---

David W. Sterling is a partner at Cox, Sterling & McClure in North Little Rock, Arkansas where he practices general business and commercial litigation. He is a past member of the ABA House of Delegates and currently serves as Co-Chair of the Section of Litigation's First Chair Press.

cles include anecdotes, war stories, and tips from experienced litigators and lessons they have learned in trial and working with difficult opposing counsel. Other articles provide tips from judges on what they expect and how to put your best foot forward in advocating for your client while maintaining your good reputation and respect from your colleagues in the bar and on the bench.

Of course, your courtroom successes must often be protected, so it is imperative that you make and preserve your record at trial, always with an eye toward a subsequent appeal. Accordingly, this section also presents several articles dealing with appeals that provide a preview to what needs to be in the trial record and tips on oral argument that are universally applicable to both trial and appellate advocacy.

Unfortunately for many trial lawyers who love trial practice, the vast majority of cases never make it to trial. Due to the ever-growing expense of litigation and uncertainty of trial outcomes, most cases are eventually settled, and a large percentage are won or lost through pre-trial motions. Therefore, the conclusion of this section includes articles discussing successful motions practice skills to help you either prepare or withstand a dispositive motion, well-position your case for pre-trial resolution, and further strengthen your case for trial.

TRIAL PRACTICE

Trial Preparation

The Trial Lawyer's Motto: Be Over-Prepared
A "How To" Guide To Trial Preparation For The New (And Experienced) Trial Lawyer And Her/His Invaluable Support Staff

By Reena M. Sandoval and Jane K. Manning

Have you ever had one of those dreams in which you are giving a speech in a crowded forum and you realize you are completely nude, or taking a life-altering exam and you realize you forgot to study, or . . . standing in front of a judge on the first day of trial and realize you forgot to prepare? Of course, we do not wish this level of anxiety on anyone and so, with the goal of alleviating some of the stress that trial preparation can cause, we have put together this article as a reference guide for attorneys who have not yet experienced the trial process and as a reminder for those who have.[1] Whatever stage you are at in your practice, whether it be partner, associate, or paralegal, we hope that this article can be of assistance to you.

WHAT'S YOUR MOTTO?

Procrastination may get you a little more sleep in the morning but it does not make for good trial preparation. While many lawyers work best under pressure, the last-minute lawyer may think twice about that method come the eve of trial. The key to effective trial preparation is just

---

From the **Trial Practice Newsletter**/Spring 2005/ABA/Section of Litigation
[1] This guide is an accumulation of information obtained by the authors from personal trial preparation experience as well as the innumerable sage colleagues and mentors with whom our paths have crossed. We thank you all.

that—preparation. Do not be afraid to over prepare. Trial preparation is the critical difference between making a clear, confident and winning case and watching your case slip away from you midtrial. The unavoidable reality is that trial preparation takes a lot of time, but the more productive you are in the weeks leading up to trial, the less anxiety you will feel when it comes time to enter the courtroom. While it is easy to think of trial preparation in general terms, it is often a matter of tying up the little details early that can make all the difference. Trial preparation can seem quite daunting, especially to a solo or small firm practitioner whose resources are limited. If you feel overwhelmed by the enormity of it all, remember this calming advice from a partner at our current firm with almost forty years of trial experience: "How do you eat an elephant?" The answer: "One bite at a time."

Preparedness begins with familiarity with the basics. First and foremost, be familiar with your litigation files. Litigation files are commonly organized into three categories: Court Documents, Attorney's Records and Evidence. Most firms have their own organizational system, but the following are some general guidelines. The Court Documents file includes pleadings, discovery, motions and responses, orders and subpoenas, and the like. The Attorney's Records file often includes a chronological litigation history, legal research and other miscellaneous documents. The Evidence file may include bills, invoices, statements, receipts, correspondence and so forth between parties and from third parties; business records and public records; photographs; diagrams; maps and charts; expert files; and other things of a tangible and evidentiary nature. *Nota bene:* By its very nature, this file contains documents that may become exhibits at trial; consider early on whether an expert may be needed to decipher them, and whether you will need that expert to testify at trial or only to consult with counsel.

In its broadest sense, trial preparation begins as soon as a complaint is filed. Information that may be of use at trial comes early when counsel begins to formulate in her/his mind the facts of the case and potential arguments that can be made.[2] Some of the more useful documents generated in this early stage may include: original notes generated from client interviews, investigative reports, information from experts, written discovery and information obtained through subpoenas. There are jurisdictions that even allow for limited pre-complaint depositions to

---

[2] In fact, in many if not most jurisdictions, a complaint must have some basis in fact, confirmed by the attorney and attested to by the attorney's signing or filing of the complaint. Failure to do adequate pre-filing investigation can, in some jurisdictions, subject the attorney to discipline and/or sanctions.

determine the factual basis for filing a complaint, another potential source of information.

Whether taken pre-filing or during discovery, deposition transcripts are a very significant source of information and should be viewed and pursued as a building block toward the trial. What a bounty of information they hold! Take time to summarize each deposition transcript in detail, including page and line references. While this may seem a tedious task, it will not only save you the energy of having to re-read all of the transcripts as trial approaches, your summary will prove a valuable reference tool for other lawyers and paralegals helping you to prepare. As should be evident, one of the overarching themes of this article is to do things early no matter how big or small the task may be. Know every fact and read every word. To convey the importance of this mantra the following is a single, yet invaluable, experience. While showing a partner the exhibits that had been preliminarily identified for trial, he pointed something out that was entirely overlooked—a fax line. Reading the fax line for the context of the document was not the issue. The important aspect of the fax line was that it decisively contradicted a vital statement made by a witness at his deposition on a key issue for the trial. Again, know every fact and read every word. This will provide you with many more of those glorious "Aha!" moments that motivate us as the trial approaches.

CREATE A PLAN & ASSEMBLE THE TROOPS

In addition to beginning the document identification process early, you must create a plan for moving forward. The ability to think logistically and with a focus on the end result is paramount. It is worth taking the time to consider a number of factors before beginning the trial preparation process, so that as trial approaches, you ensure that each step is aligned with your overall game plan. Of the many factors that you will contend with, one universal consideration is cost. Part of increasing your time efficiency is knowing when to stop the clock on a project. This may prove a real challenge to the new lawyer whose drive for perfection could arguably turn a two-day research project into weeks. You may, for example, find that as the trial gets closer additional depositions or research may be helpful, but if the costs of doing so outweigh the probative value on the key issues in the case, it may be excessive for both you and the client. If you are not privy to the cost concerns of your client, do not be afraid to raise the issue with the partner in charge of the matter or with your client directly if appropriate (*i.e.*, "I would like to do X, but want to address the financial feasibility of doing so before I proceed.") They will most likely appreciate your concern for the big picture.

Another question to ask yourself is "why am I doing this?" Think strategically, keeping in mind that one pitfall to avoid is over trying your case. At trial, you will need to present a clear story with an identifiable theme or themes, or you will risk confusing or losing the attention of your jury. The last thing you want to do is bury important facts in a miasma of details that do little to advance your basic proposition. It may be helpful to think in terms of whether *not* pursuing a certain avenue of discovery will put you at risk of missing something important. If in doubt, again ask the other lawyers on your case and ask your client. After all, you are first learning the facts; your client lived them, making your client an invaluable resource in helping to focus your discovery.

There are also non-monetary costs that can be reduced or eliminated through the delegation of tasks to others. Remember that your support staff is an important resource; rely on them. Once a trial team is assembled, it is necessary to coordinate the roles that each person will play and to make certain that everyone understands their role within the group. This means not only dividing the labor among lawyers, but also utilizing your paralegals and making sure everyone understands the key themes and objectives, as well as the ultimate facts that you will need to prevail at trial. People who can identify their role within the larger framework and are accountable to a team perform better than those who are left to perform isolated, piecemeal tasks without any notion of what the issues are or what the lawyers are hoping to prove or dispute. Even looking for a needle in the haystack can be done if the support staff is told early that it is a needle they are looking for.

Most importantly, meet often and be proactive in checking in with your team, seeking regular updates on their progress (this should include communication with any outside investigators, experts, or vendors you have engaged). It is useful to create a task list to which everyone has access and can see where they should be in the trial preparation process. This does not mean that you need to micromanage every task, but you should maintain a sense for what progress is being made. Use your team meetings to allow for input from your support staff. Many new lawyers are humbled to find out that the paralegal knows far more about trial preparation, both in general and in terms of firm logistics.

CHART YOUR COURSE: ESTABLISH A TIMELINE AND FOLLOW THROUGH

Building a timeline creates an important tool that can provide guidance to everyone on the team. The following timeline may be a helpful guide.[3] Be aware that the issues raised here are not exclusive and that other issues may be more of a priority for your case (*e.g.*, the local rules of your judge or jurisdiction may prescribe an alternative timetable for filings). While many preparations can be done far in advance, given the nature of the flow of information and the full schedules that envelope the life of a trial lawyer, the bulk of pre-trial preparation is usually done within six weeks of trial. Combined with your other caseload, not to mention professional and personal commitments, your trial preparation can quickly become overwhelming if you do not have a clear game plan.

Throughout your practice, take the time to watch other attorneys at work. Go sit in a courtroom for an afternoon. If you know who the judge presiding over your trial will be, check the court's calendar and try to observe a day or two of trial, so that you can get a feel for how your particular judge likes to run her/his courtroom proceedings. You can learn a lot about how to properly prepare (and learn from some of the common mistakes made) by watching other litigators at work as well as how the judge reacts to them. Not only that, it's free entertainment—often better, and *real*, in contrast to law-related television dramas. If you simply do not have time to sit through a trial, a quicker alternative is to read the transcript of a great trial.

Months before trial start thinking about the documents you are accumulating in your case. As you are reading through the various pleadings and discovery, it is worth separating and organizing documents that may be useful during trial, and once again coordination with your paralegal team will be important in this regard. For example, "hot docs" folders and "witness pockets" can be created once you recognize facts and people that could be of importance later on.

As you forage through the documents and discuss them with your client, you will need to determine whether an expert is necessary, either to help you decipher certain evidence or to testify at trial. Early on, the expert should have a clear view of their role in the proceedings and, if they are generating any documents to assist you at trial, communication of exactly what you will need is imperative.

As touched on above, an expert will need to know whether they will be serving as your consultant only, whether they will be testifying at trial, and whether they will be required to produce an expert report and/or sit for an expert deposition. Keep an expert witness pocket, and check the rules regarding what kinds of expert materials you may need

---

[3] As with many of the topics discussed in this article, litigation support software is available that will provide this service.

to disclose later in discovery, as well as what documents might assist you at trial if your adversary questions an expert's qualifications or credentials. If your expert will be testifying, find out whether she/he will have use for demonstrative trial exhibits. Some experts can generate their own demonstratives, while others may prefer for you to hire an outside graphics firm to do so. Allocate time for this: your expert will need time to formulate her/his opinion, you will need to discuss what kind of demonstratives will be useful, coordinate with a graphics firm in advance to make sure that everyone is on the same page, and then carefully double check your demonstratives for accuracy.

Also, if you or your adversary were not required to make an election at the pleading stage, take this time to analyze whether you want to proceed with a bench or jury trial.[4] This will affect how you prepare in the upcoming months and weeks. If you proceed by bench trial, it may be necessary to prepare for the Court, in addition to a pre-trial order, a pre-trial memorandum of law (usually submitted shortly before trial) outlining your legal arguments in a clear and concise manner.[5] The court might also require a pre-marked list or book of trial exhibits. Be sure to check your local rules and the judge's requirements. If in doubt, ask the judge during a pre-hearing conference.

If you are considering hiring a jury consultant, you should do so now if not earlier. While not every lawyer, or every case, requires a jury consultant, the more time you give your consultant to learn about your case and canvass the jury pool, the more effective they will be during voire dire. Good jury consultants also can assist you with preparation of demonstratives aimed toward the particular jury, and with advice on everything from counsel and client dress to deportment at trial.

4–6 weeks before trial is a good point at which to review the pleadings and to begin (or, even better, continue) to refine and focus your strategy and arguments. If it is still permitted, now is the time to file any additional or amended pleadings. Also, use this time to review all discovery, as documents crucial to your case may have been previously overlooked or their significance not perceived earlier on. As with the filing of pleadings, if the supplementation of discovery is still permitted, use it to address any unresolved discovery issues.

---

[4] While this article briefly touches on the option of a bench trial, the majority of information is targeted to the preparation for a jury trial.

[5] Be aware that some judges may require a pre-trial memorandum of law even if the case proceeds by jury trial. This may be apparent by reading the judge's pretrial procedures or may be raised at a pre-trial conference with the judge.

From the review of pleadings and discovery stems the potential need to file pre-trial motions, for example, *in limine* motions to preclude the improper use of evidence at trial. During this time you should have received from the judge presiding over your case a list of her/his pre-trial procedures—which absolutely must be followed. So be sure to refer, and adhere to, those procedures, as well as the court's local rules, before you file. Keep in mind that many courts require that *in limine* motions be filed closer to trial, but this should not preclude you from preparing your arguments now.

The judge's practices may require a pre-trial order and pre-trial memorandum of law, to be submitted jointly or separately. If relevant, use this time to confer with all parties regarding what facts they will stipulate to, transcript designations they wish to make, and how exhibits should be marked. While a standard procedure as to marking exhibits is generally adhered to, if you are engaged in a multi-party case that involves several claims or defenses, you may want to consider marking your exhibits specific to your client. If needed, consider requesting an all-party conference with the court to discuss any such pre-trial concerns.

Each judge and courtroom are unique, and because you will be spending quite a bit of time in front of the judge and in the courtroom, it is a good idea to study and research the conditions of the courtroom beforehand, *especially* if it is your first trial. Knowing your judge is very important, so ask your colleagues questions concerning the reputation that your judge has, both generally and with respect to issues relevant to your case, and, as we suggested above, try to observe your judge in her/his courtroom if possible.

Do not neglect that subpoenas should be served on any witnesses you wish to call at trial. Serving subpoenas at this stage will allow your witnesses to secure their schedule and ensure their availability to attend trial. It also will afford you time for judicial assistance with recalcitrant witnesses or an order for a trial deposition if the witness genuinely cannot attend at trial.

3–4 weeks before trial it is key to get a handle on your paperwork. The month before trial is when it all heats up. Be sure you are in frequent communication with your support staff and use their knowledge and skills as much as you can. One good way to stay organized is to create a trial notebook with the help of your paralegal staff. This will be an incredibly useful tool to have and, because of its importance, is discussed more fully in the following section.

Organizing documents in folders (*e.g.*, "exhibit" and "witness" folders) can also prove to be useful at this stage. Personally, we prefer to color code the folder categories for easy reference, but to each, her/his own. This undertaking is actually a re-organization of documents that you have already identified as important. Witness folders can include potential exhibits you intend to show the witness and any statements the witness has previously made (*e.g.*, deposition transcripts, reports and statements to police investigators or self-regulatory bodies). Transcript folders should include, not surprisingly, transcripts from depositions, hearings, on-the-record interviews and other proceedings. While you will need to have access to at least two copies of a full size transcript in the courtroom (one to show the witness and one to give to the judge), it is generally easier to work with miniscripts at trial, so, for convenience, you may want to keep miniscripts in your working file. They are not only easier to handle, most often they include a computer-generated word index that may save you valuable time and possible embarrassment at trial. This is also the perfect time to begin drafting your direct and cross-examination outlines, with exhibit and transcript references.

Consider what, if any, exhibits you would like enhanced for trial. If you expect to use demonstratives at trial, it might be a good idea to order them now. For some, it may seem early to be thinking about this detail, but it is not a detail that you want to be worrying about on the eve of trial. We have heard too many horror stories about inaccurate facts or depictions of facts, or printer mishaps, to stay this task. As we mentioned above, this task may take even longer if you are creating documents to assist your expert(s) in explaining their opinions. You also need to ask yourself (or your jury consultant) what kinds of demonstratives will make the best impression on your jury. Do you want blowups? Highlighted words or phrases? Pictures? Charts? Overlays?

Setting aside admissibility issues, you need to decide how to display your demonstratives and whether or not your courtroom has the space and/or facilities to accommodate your choices. For instance, will the entire crushed car fit in the courtroom during your product defect or personal injury case? How, most certainly in this case, will you transport your demonstratives to the courtroom, and will the judge allow you to leave them in the courtroom overnight? Discover what methods of display are available in the courtroom and, alternatively, what you will have to purchase. Does the court have an easel? A video player? Will your demonstratives be on computer disc and, if so, are the judge and jurors wired in with their own screens or will you need a projector and large monitor? Perhaps most importantly, make sure that the judge will allow your demonstrative. If you are using a computer or videotape, will the judge require you to produce it to the other side in advance so that they can examine it, have an expert examine it (for authenticity or otherwise), and/or to make counter designations (as in the case of videotape excerpts)? By addressing these questions early, you give yourself a safety cushion and save yourself from unnecessary stress later on.

Another optional tool that can be prepared at this stage is a trial chart that indicates the various elements of claims and defenses. It should be continued for each element of your required, and your opponent's anticipated, proof. As the trial unfolds, it will assist you in identifying where your (and your opponent's) proof is strong and where it is weak. By all means, continue to amend this chart and make sure your list of necessary evidence is complete before you enter the courtroom. Imagine the situation where an incomplete chart leaves you closing your case having forgotten to, for example, read the key portion of a deposition transcript establishing a small but vital element of your claim (or you read a document but forgot to move for its admission into evidence). You do not want to take the chance that the judge will allow you to re-open your case once defense counsel moves for a dismissal or a directed verdict.

Approximately one month before trial, you also want to prepare jury instructions. It is perhaps the best opportunity for you to put your, at this point, vast knowledge of the case to use. Assuming the court requires or allows the submission of proposed jury instructions by the parties, use it to your full advantage. Consider the issues you want the jury to focus on. For example, if you are defending a claim of unauthorized trading by a stockbroker client, but discovery revealed that the plaintiff had authorized a third person to make at least some decisions as to his account, you will want to include instructions as to the law of agency in support of your defense.

The preparation of jury instructions can be a long and arduous task, especially if this is your first trial. If you are proceeding under a joint defense agreement or there are multiple plaintiffs'/defendants' counsel, you may want to consider sharing the workload but never at the expense of your client. At this point, you should have exchanged ideas with all relevant counsel and decided whether you will be submitting jury instructions jointly or separately.

2–3 weeks before trial is the perfect time to revisit the theory of your case. Here, the focus is on broad themes that you will cover throughout the trial. This will help you focus on your jury selection strategy. Consider your case from the jurors' perspective and begin formulating your voire dire, or questions you would like the court to propound in judge-conducted voire dire. What do you want in a jury? If you have not yet given thought to hiring a jury consultant, now may be your last opportunity to do so.

This is also the time to prepare opening and closing statements and direct and cross examinations, and to contact the witnesses you intend to call to schedule them for trial preparation if appropriate. It is crucial to maintain constant communication with your witnesses in these remaining weeks.

1–2 weeks before trial, you will likely have done so already, but if you have not, you may want to discuss potential stipulations with the other parties. You should also take time to prepare your client for testimony and consider her or his courtroom presence. Even if your client will not be testifying, physical appearance is often crucial for the jury, from attire to facial expressions and other external reactions. All factors must be considered and in line with the story that you are telling. Maintain contact with witnesses and, where appropriate, prepare them for testimony (*e.g.*, your expert witnesses). It is also important to contact the court to re-confirm the trial date. This may seem like an inane detail, but it can help to eliminate surprises and hopefully help you sleep better at night.

The week before trial, picture your trial already in progress and determine what else must be completed. Meanwhile, continue to prepare your client while focusing and refining your case. The importance of keeping in touch with your witnesses cannot be overstated. You do not want to find out at the last minute that your key witness is a no-show. Revisit the order of witnesses in light of the preparation you have been doing and let witnesses know a general timeframe when they will be needed at trial. Find out whether the court will require witnesses to be in the courtroom all day or will allow them to be on telephone standby.

A useful tool that can be prepared at the last minute is an "exhibit chart." This chart is for use at trial to indicate whether or not the exhibit was shown to a particular witness, whether it was moved into evidence, if it was objected to and what the objection was, and if and when it was admitted. This will be a useful reference at the end of each trial day as well as when preparing mid-trial and end-of-trial motions. Revisit your cross-examination preparations as well as your opening and closing statements. Take the time to rehearse and practice but be careful to build in some flexibility. You may not get a ruling on *in limine* motions until the day before, or the morning of, trial. We have heard of at least one instance in which a defense lawyer objected to entire key points in the plaintiff lawyer's opening statement based on *in limine* rulings the judge made the afternoon before. The objections were sustained, plaintiff's lawyer's opening was eviscerated, and the jury, not knowing why the judge kept precluding (read as: reprimanding) the plaintiff's lawyer, started to show signs of displeasure with the plaintiff's attorney. The case settled after opening statements.

Strange as it may sound while you are already entrenched in so much detail—do not forget the mundane. Under what can be tremendous pressure and long-hours for counsel in the weeks leading up to a trial, you must remember the little details—like your wardrobe. First impressions are crucial!

THE ULTIMATE HANDBOOK: A TRIAL NOTEBOOK

The trial notebook is going to be one of the most important tools at your disposal during trial and deserves a separate section to explain. The skeleton of your notebook can be built at any time but, as mentioned above, a good rule of thumb is to have it as complete as possible up to three to four weeks before trial. It can be maintained in paper form, electronically, or both, but its usefulness is dependent on the facts that you have access to it at all times and that it is divided into sections that parallel the trial process. Again, use a configuration that works for you, and modify the substance of each section to suit your style and the nature of your case, but the following is a commonly used organizational structure:

(a) **Facts:** Include in this section a contact sheet for all parties and counsel, a chronology of events, summaries of reports, including police and investigators' reports, and perhaps a summary of pleadings if desired;

(b) **Pleadings:** This section is for amended pleadings (make sure they are in order), pretrial orders, and a copy of any applicable statutes (if there are statutory claims);

(c) **Discovery:** Any interrogatories and answers, document demands and responses, and requests to admit facts and responses are included here. Also add your deposition summaries and any additional discovery;

(d) **Motions:** All past motions, responses and orders, the pretrial memoranda and orders are kept here. You may also wish to create a separate section for anticipated trial motions;

(e) **Charts:** Three key charts should be included here—(1) a trial chart, with elements of claims, defenses, and proof (see discussion above); (2) a witness list, with appropriate contact information; and (3) an exhibit chart, which indicates whether or not an exhibit has been objected to, moved, and admitted into evidence, and if so, when;

(f) **Jury:** Another chart that is useful, but usually kept separate from the others, is a jury chart form and challenges record. Included with the jury chart are juror profile outlines, requested voire dire questions to submit to the judge, a checklist of voire dire questions and a copy of applicable jury selection statutes and rules;

(g) **Openings:** Include an outline of your planned opening statement, along with a blank page to take notes on your opponents opening statement;

(h) **Plaintiff:** If you are the plaintiff, create an outline for each direct examination. If you are the defendant, do the same for each anticipated cross examination;

(i) **Defendant:** If you are the plaintiff, create an outline of each anticipated cross examination. If you are the defendant, do the same for each direct examination;

(j) **Closings:** Like the opening statement, it is good to have an outline of your planned closing. There should also be a number of blank pages to write notes on potential closing arguments and those that you anticipate from your opponent. If you are the plaintiff, you should also have a planned rebuttal argument;

(k) **Instructions:** Include both your and your opponent's proposed jury instructions; and

(l) **Law:** Relevant rules of evidence for both state and federal courts, along with key statutes and cases, should be included in this section.

(m) **Trial notebook:** It should include everything you need to have handy at trial, with the exception of exhibits, witness folders and transcripts. For each of these items, we recommend you maintain them separately and keep multiple copies.

EARN YOUR MERIT BADGE

Now that you are fully prepared, if not over prepared, you are ready to face the courtroom. Or are you? Have you coordinated the logistics of transporting all your preparations to the courtroom? As silly as it sounds, make sure you know how you will transport yourself and your trial team, to make sure everyone is where they are supposed to be, when they are supposed to be. Being late on your first day of trial is not a good way to impress the judge, your partners, or your client. Have you stocked everyone's litigation bags with all the necessary supplies—like paper, pens, highlighters, post-its, staplers, staples, and so forth? If you can delegate, do it—you have enough on your plate—but always have your finger on the pulse of what is going on.

As mentioned throughout this article, being prepared includes knowing your facts inside and out and never failing to ask questions. While we may all be familiar with the saying: "There are no dumb questions," trial lawyer Henry G. Miller brilliantly added, "Well, almost none. There are, however, dumb lawyers. Who are they? Lawyers who don't ask questions."[6] Be sure that throughout the preparation process you have not ignored any troublesome facts. If you do not address it, your opponent will. It is an almost 100% guarantee that any fact ignored will come back to bite you, one way or another.

Remember, when working with a support staff, you are ultimately responsible. If a box of transcripts does not arrive in the courtroom with the other exhibits, blaming the person to whom *you* delegated the task is *not* an appropriate response.

By now your anxiety level is at an all time high, so do your best to resist the urge to go ballistic when things fail to run smoothly. They *will* fail to run smoothly at some point. Even a well prepared lawyer cannot anticipate everything. But they can respond more quickly and effectively, creating the appearance that everything is under control. Calmly make arrangements for the situation to be remedied (as most situations can be) and continue focusing on the trial ahead, with confidence in your preparedness. What follows is a step-by-step timeline for trial preparation.

---

[6] Miller, Henry G., *On Trial: Lessons from a Lifetime In the Courtroom* (2001).

CREATE A TIMELINE[7]

Throughout your practice:
- Watch live trials and other attorneys for Do's and Don'ts
- If no time, read the transcript of a great trial

Months before trial:
- Organize pleadings/discovery documents for use at trial (*e.g.*, "witness pockets")
- Contact experts, informing them of their role
- Consider whether to use a jury consultant
- Consider bench or jury trial, if the option is still available

4–6 weeks before trial:
- Review the pleadings
- If still permitted, file any additional pleadings
- Review discovery
- If permitted, supplement discovery
- Formulate, and perhaps file *in limine* motions, in accordance with local rules
- Begin preparing or serving trial witness subpoenas
- Know your judge and conditions of the courtroom
- Confer with counsel regarding pre-trial issues; if needed, seek court conference

3–4 weeks before trial:
- Create a trial notebook
- Prepare jury instructions
- Prepare exhibit folders
- Prepare witness folders
- Prepare exhibit binder for the judge, if required
- Consider demonstratives and other courtroom exhibits

2–3 weeks before trial:
- Revisit the theory of your case
- Revisit jury instructions and clean up
- Prepare voire dire
- Prepare opening and closing statements

---

[7] As previously mentioned, this guide is merely a suggested means of organizing your pre-trial paperwork. If you are not first chair on this trial, be sure to check with the lead attorney and make sure that whatever organizational style you choose will be helpful to her/him.

- Prepare direct and cross examinations
- Consider serving trial witness subpoenas, if you have not already done so
- Contact trial witnesses and schedule prep sessions, if appropriate
- Create a list of facts that you would be willing to stipulate

1–2 weeks before trial:
- Discuss and finalize potential stipulations with the other parties
- Prepare bench memorandum for the court, if required
- Prepare client for testimony and courtroom presence
- Maintain contact with witnesses and prepare them for testimony, if appropriate
- Contact court and confirm trial date

The week before the trial:
- Keep in touch with witnesses; continue to prepare them, if appropriate
- Revisit the order of witnesses
- Continue preparation of your client
- Refine the exhibits list
- Revisit cross-examinations, opening and closing statements; rehearse
- Confirm all transportation and logistical arrangements
- Double check all supplies

Final Trial Preparation
By Hon. Christopher T. Whitten

Two months away from the next big trial? Panic! After allowing yourself that self-indulgence for a good half hour, it's time to roll up your sleeves and get to work. Make a plan of things to do for the next eight weeks. Below are five suggestions.

JURY INSTRUCTIONS AND BENCH BRIEF

Everything a good trial lawyer does, from day one through the verdict, is framed by one set of papers: the jury instructions. Knowing this, you, being a good trial lawyer, drafted a set of instructions when you opened the file. Those instructions helped you draft your complaint or answer; they framed your disclosure statements and guided your discovery requests and responses; and they steered your thoughts in preparing or responding to dispositive motions.

Now that discovery is closed, reexamine and update your initial draft jury instructions. Perhaps some of your claims or defenses have fallen by the wayside over time. Maybe you realize now that the facts that your client told you were "for sure" have not come to be and at least one of your initial theories on the case is not supportable. Whatever the case, it's a great starting point for your two-month sprint to trial if you reconsider which instructions the court should read to the jury.

Your local standard instructions are a great starting place for this. (Often no more is needed.)[1] If these do not fit right, turn to case law or Restatements[2] to draft your own. If this becomes necessary, do not just

---

From the **Committee on Pretrial Practice & Discovery** / Fall 2007 / ABA / Section of Litigation

Hon. Christopher T. Whitten is a judge on the Arizona Superior Court in Maricopa County, Phoenix, Arizona. The views expressed are those of the author and do not represent those of the Arizona Superior Court.

[1] For a good discussion of the trend toward using these standardized instructions, see *Construction of Statutes or Rules Making Mandatory the Use of Pattern or Uniform Approved Jury Instructions*, 49 A.L.R.3d 128.

[2] An example of an area of law not normally covered by standard instructions and where courts have been persuaded to adopt instructions based on the Restatements (Second) of Torts is "loss of chance" medical malpractice claims. Thompson v. Sun City Cmty. Hosp., Inc., 141 Ariz. 597, 688 P.2d 605 (1984); De Burkarte v. Louvar, 393 N.W.2d 131 (Iowa 1986); Sherer v. James, 334 S.E.2d 283 (S.C. Ct. App. 1985).

cite the applicable case or Restatement section in a footnote; make a copy of the appropriate authority for the judge and provide it with the instruction. If the issue is complex, consider writing a separate brief addressing it.

Even if this is your umpteenth trial on the same topic, do not give in to the temptation to just pull the instructions from an earlier trial and change the caption. Starting from scratch will have two benefits: It will ensure that the instructions you request fit your specific case, and it will help you prepare the framework for the work you will do in the coming weeks. Just as creating an outline for your civil procedure class in law school often was when the information was committed to memory, the writing of jury instructions is often the best thing you can do to commit to memory the framework of your upcoming trial.

The office printer should barely be unjammed from printing your jury instructions as you start drafting a bench brief. It is astounding how few lawyers provide the trial judge with this valuable tool. Remember that the judge has little to no knowledge of the specific facts of your case and may sometimes be dealing with an area of law unfamiliar to him or her. Even if you argued substantive motions before this same judge a few months ago, do not assume anything.

Keep your bench brief as succinct as possible. A few paragraphs should be all you need to describe the factual background well enough to provide the judge a general orientation. In all but the most basic negligence case, and maybe even then, a list of the elements the plaintiff must prove and the standard of that proof should follow. A short discussion of any defenses might be next. Finally, a list of witnesses along with a brief description of what each is expected to say would certainly help the judge follow your case. Although some judges may have clerks who will prepare a bench brief for them, most will not. If you do not do it, it likely will not be done (unless your opponent does one).

MOTIONS IN LIMINE
Quality, Not Quantity

Properly used, motions in limine are welcomed by most judges as a chance to make sometimes difficult evidentiary rulings with some time to think or the opportunity to avoid a mistrial after weeks of work. With improperly used motions in limine, you risk annoying the judge before you even park your car on the first day of trial.

The rules of procedure in most jurisdictions make no mention of motions in limine. Historically, the first common-law mention of this type of motion was in 1933, when an appellate court found that such motions were an improper usurpation of judicial authority.[3] How far we have come.[4] The vast majority of jurisdictions, if not all, now allow the trial judge, in his discretion, to use motions in limine to screen out prejudicial and inadmissible evidence prior to its being offered in the jury's presence.

These motions can be put into two broad categories: motions to exclude the opponent's evidence and affirmative motions seeking a determination that your evidence is admissible. Regardless of the type, the motions that tend to be successful are those that do not require weighing of evidence. For example, a motion seeking to preclude evidence as too prejudicial will likely require the judge to hear evidence before he or she can rule; whereas a motion to preclude evidence that a party is insured will be readily decided before trial.

When contemplating whether to file a motion in limine, make sure, above all else, that it is an issue on which you are right. Losing a motion in limine to preclude evidence on the merits has two effects: It affirmatively allows the other side to introduce evidence that it might have thought twice about offering absent the ruling and have the confidence to discuss it in its opening statement; and it might, in some cases, reduce your credibility with the court. After all, before you start voir dire, you will have come to the judge with an assertion that he or she has found unfounded in law or fact.

SURROGATE JURY

You have convinced yourself, your secretary, the other lawyers you have bought lunch for, and your spouse that you have a great theme and that your expert witness will wipe the floor with your opponent's. Their feedback—largely backslaps and "you can't lose"—has been too deceptively helpful. Now put your theme, key witnesses, and theories to a real test: some form of trial simulation.[5] These range from focus groups and Internet jury studies to full-blown mock trials with multiple panels giving separate verdicts and feedback.

---

[3] Bradford v. Birmingham Elec. Co., 227 Ala. 285, 149 So. 729 (1933).

[4] "Although the Federal Rules of Evidence do not explicitly authorize *in limine* rulings, the practice has developed pursuant to the district court's inherent authority to manage the course of trials." Luce v. United States, 469 U.S. 38, 41 n.4 (1984).

[5] For an excellent discussion of the validity of simulated trials, see David L. Breau & Brian Brook, *"Mock" Mock Juries: A Field Experiment on the Ecological Validity of Jury Simulations*, 31 Law & Psychol. Rev. 77 (2007).

There are generally two reasons that a good lawyer opts not to present a case to a surrogate jury: the time and expense involved, and fear that the results or the information submitted will become known to the other side.

To address the first concern, the time and cost involved in obtaining the benefits of a surrogate jury can, indeed, be substantial. Good information, however, can also be obtained for an investment of less than a couple of thousand dollars and a day of work. Especially with the Internet, companies that provide low-cost surrogate jury services are rampant.[6] Incredibly, the costs of presenting a case over the Internet to 100 jurors, obtaining not only their verdicts but also their responses to an extensive list of subjective questions about the credibility of witnesses and their case theories, can be as low as $600.[7]

The second reason that some attorneys do not use surrogate juries is the fear that, having presented their trial theme and strategy, the opposition will somehow discover these things and thereby obtain a huge advantage at trial. Universally, information gathered in conducting some form of surrogate jury research has been found to be not discoverable. The courts that have addressed this issue have found that this type of information is not likely to lead to the discovery of admissible evidence or that it is protected by the work-product privilege.[8] Be careful, however, if you involve your expert witnesses in mock trials, because anything the expert witness does to prepare may become discoverable.[9]

PREPARING FOR VOIR DIRE

The purpose of voir dire has been articulated as follows:

> [to] probe each prospective juror's state of mind to enable the trial judge to determine actual bias and to allow counsel to assess suspected bias or prejudice. Thus, a voir dire examination must be conducted in a manner that allows the parties to effectively and

---

[6] Nancy S. Marder, *Cyberjuries: A New Role as Online Mock Juries,* 38 U. Tol. L. Rev. 239 (2006).

[7] One of the pioneers in the field of Internet mock juries, ejury.com, has prices starting at $600, with an average cost of $1,500. The time spent submitting a good summary argument through that service, with well-worded subjective questions, is the biggest factor in obtaining useful results.

[8] *See generally Discovering Trial Consultant Work Product: A New Way to Borrow an Adversary's Wits?,* Am. J. Trial Advoc. (Spring 1994).

[9] *See generally In re* Air Crash at Dubrovnik, Croatia on April 3, 1996, 2001 WL 777433 (D. Conn. 2001) (unpublished opinion).

intelligently exercise their right to peremptory challenges and challenges for cause.[10]

Far too often, even in more hotly contested trials, attorneys seem to forget that the jury's first impression of them will be formed during jury selection, not opening statements. An attorney may spend weeks fine-tuning an opening statement but conduct voir dire on a wing and a prayer, without much forethought.

Jury research shows that many jurors form their first impression about a case within minutes of entering the courtroom, and many develop some impression of who should win the case by the end of opening statements.[11] Although these first impressions can change,[12] it is an uphill battle you do not want to face.

The first thing to determine is your trial judge's attitude toward voir dire. Does the court allow the trial lawyer to ask questions of the jury? Is there a time limit imposed?[13] Are the attorneys limited in their questioning to following up on answers given to the court's questions? Because impressions are formed so quickly, you do not want to have the judge scolding you in voir dire.

The successful lawyer's trial theme will be introduced in voir dire. Clearly, extracting promises from potential jurors or arguing the case in voir dire will draw sustained objections, achieving the opposite of the intended result.[14] Instead, a lawyer with a trial theme of corporate respon-

---

[10] Darbin v. Nourse, 664 F.2d 1109, 1113 (9th Cir. 1991); *see also* Rosales-Lopez v. United States, 451 U.S. 182, 188, 101 S. Ct. 1629, 1634, 68 L. Ed. 2d 22 (1981) ("[L]ack of adequate voir dire impairs the defendant's right to exercise peremptory challenges where provided by statute or rule, as it is in the federal courts.").

[11] *See* Paula L. Hannaford et al., *The Timing of Opinion Formation by Jurors in Civil Cases: An Empirical Examination*, 67 Tenn. L. Rev. 627 (2000).

[12] *Id.* (suggesting that first impressions are not as firmly rooted as many believe).

[13] For a good argument against the imposition of time limits on voir dire, see Howard M. Snyder, *Time Warp: How Arbitrary Voir Dire Limits Harm the Jury System*, Ariz. Att'y (Oct. 2006).

[14] Sandidge v. Salen Offshore Drilling Co., 764 F.2d 252, 258 (5th Cir. 1985) (improper to ask whether anyone on jury panel would give more weight to evidence presented by videotaped deposition than to that presented by written deposition); Hinkle v. Hampton, 388 F.2d 141, 143 (10th Cir. 1968) (improper to question whether panel members had same confidence in osteopathic physicians and medical doctors and would give equal credence to member of either profession who testified); DeLaCruz v. Atchison, Topeka & S.F. Ry. Co., 405 F.2d 459, 462 (5th Cir. 1968) (improper to ask questions that are "subtle attempt on counsel's part to lay a foundation for his case"); Smith v. Tenet Healthsystem SL, Inc., 436 F.3d 879 (8th Cir. 2006) (similar).

sibility in a products liability case might question potential jurors about whether they have a problem applying the principle of "self-responsibility" to a corporation in the same way as they would to a person.

FINAL PREPARATION

The final steps discussed below are the type of housekeeping tasks that never seem to end as a trial approaches: building a trial notebook, ensuring service of trial subpoenas, filing exhibits with the clerk of the court, editing or summarizing deposition testimony to be presented at trial, and preparing important witnesses for trial.

Trial Notebook

Gathering and organizing your thoughts as you enter your final preparations for trial often mirrors the building of a good trial notebook. Both the sections in your trial notebook and your thoughts in final trial preparation should include jury instructions, closing arguments, cross-examination of the opposing witnesses (with citations to portions of the record or deposition needed to impeach), direct examination of your own witnesses, opening statements, jury selection, an anticipated schedule for each day of trial, a list of contact information for each witness, notes for anticipated arguments on important exhibits, and a section for notes to be taken during trial.

Again, just as the process of organizing and drafting an outline of your law school civil procedure class probably ingrained the material in your mind more than your later review of that outline, actually building your trial notebook yourself will better prepare you for trial.

Trial Subpoenas

Trial subpoenas should be served on all witnesses, not just those who are openly hostile. Such service can be as simple as a letter sent by mail two months before trial to all your nonhostile witnesses with an enclosed subpoena and an extra copy to sign and return acknowledging receipt, along with an explanation that the rules of procedure require the formality of service. This process will pay off the first time a witness "forgets" to appear and you need to prove that he or she is unavailable.

Marking Exhibits

In getting your trial exhibits to the clerk of the court, remember that a judge is likely to hear what his or her staff thinks of you as a lawyer and a person. If you arrive at 4:30 P.M. two days before trial, with loads of poorly organized exhibits and dump them on the judge's clerk, expect the judge to hear (sometimes loudly) a bad review. If you call and make an appointment that is convenient to the clerk, arrive on time and with a neatly organized set of exhibits, expect the reviews to be glowing.

Jurisdictions vary greatly in how exhibits will be marked. Find out well in advance—certainly by the final pretrial conference—what the practice is in your court. Will they be marked by the lawyers or the clerk? Will they be marked sequentially with no missing numbers allowed? Does this court mark plaintiff's exhibits with letters and defendant's exhibits with numbers? Find out before you waste time doing it the wrong way.

Editing Deposition Testimony

Perhaps the clearest way to ensure that a jury totally discounts the testimony of a witness presented by deposition is to read or play the entire deposition.[15] Start with the understanding that the jury may, at least subconsciously, view the testimony of a witness presented by deposition as so unimportant that the witness did not even have the courtesy to come to the courthouse and talk to the jurors in person. Add to that the inherent lack of spontaneity and excitement accompanying a deposition transcript being read or the kindergarten-nap-time feel of turning the lights down to watch a videotape of a deposition taken long ago. Finally, if you add two hours of questions and answers relevant only to discovery, not to any issue presented at trial, you will be fortunate if each juror has not mentally prepared next week's shopping list, doodled a fine art piece, and caught 40 winks without hearing the five minutes of important testimony the witness offered somewhere in the second hour of the deposition.

Instead, edit the transcript or videotape to its essence or offer a summary of the testimony by stipulation or by motion to the court if no stipulation is forthcoming.[16]

Preparing Witnesses

Finally, in the last few weeks before trial, prepare your important witnesses for trial. Give them copies of their deposition transcripts and

---

[15] David M. Balabanian, *Medium v. Tedium: Video Depositions Come of Age*, Litig., Vol. 7, No. 1 (Fall 1980).

[16] Rule 1006 of the Federal Rules of Evidence provides that "[t]he contents of voluminous writings, recordings, or photographs which cannot conveniently be examined in court may be presented in the form of a chart, summary, or calculation."

prior recorded statements. Call them to find out whether they have any questions. If they are nervous about testifying, offer to meet them at the courthouse before trial and show them where they will sit, where you will sit, and the like. If you are afraid that this will look bad if brought out by your opponent at trial, don't be. Remember that the people the jurors most identify with in the courtroom are usually the witnesses, not the attorneys or the judge. They would expect to be nervous themselves if they testified at trial. If your opponent brings out the fact that you tried to help ease this anxiety, you will more likely be seen as a compassionate hero rather than as someone trying to get an unfair advantage.[17]

Witness preparation is not a one-way street. It includes you, the trial lawyer, preparing yourself to present your witness to the jury. This entails much more than just getting the testimonial facts out of the witness's mouth. For these testimonial facts to have the desired effect, jurors must like and understand the witness. Jurors are partial toward witnesses with whom they have something in common.[18] It is your job, as a good trial lawyer, to personalize your witnesses so that jurors can more readily identify with them.

When you prepare witnesses, find out about them as people, not just fact reciters. Where were they born and raised? Where were they educated? What hobbies do they have? Was their first grandchild born last night? This information, although not technically relevant to any element of any claim or defense, may be important to a juror, at least on a subconscious level, in determining how much weight to give the facts the witness later testifies about.[19]

CONCLUSION

In the last two months before trial, the key is to be organized. The time spent quietly contemplating what you want to do during those eight

---

[17] If this happens, do not hesitate to ask the opponent's witnesses if they are nervous and if they would have appreciated being offered the opportunity to come down to the courthouse in the weeks before trial to see where everyone sits and what would be expected of them.

[18] Jeffrey T. Frederick, The Psychology of the American Jury (1988) (noting that jurors are more influenced by the testimony of a witness who is a member of the same political, religious, social, economic, employment-related, or demographic reference group that the jurors belong to).

[19] Caldwell, Perrin & Gross, *Primacy, Recency, Ethos, and Pathos: Integrating Principles of Communication into the Direct Examination*, 76 Notre Dame L. Rev. 423 (2001).

weeks is time well spent. Drafting jury instructions, writing a bench brief or motions in limine, presenting your themes to a mock jury, and preparing for voir dire are just some of the things good lawyers should do in this crunch time. Whether your list of things to do includes these suggestions or not, the key is to sit down, make some plan for the last couple of months, and then get to work.

In Support of the "To Do" List

By Hon. Samuel A. Thumma

Preparation is essential to a good outcome in any civil trial. Viewed pragmatically, trial preparation begins before the first pleading is filed and then never ends. Trial preparation time is always at a premium, and that is particularly true during the last 60 days before trial.

There are a large number of moving pieces in any civil trial, and as complexity increases, so does the number of those moving pieces. Keeping track of what there is to do and who is doing what by when is difficult in the best of circumstances and can be the critical difference in winning issues, claims, or even cases.

One mundane and frequently overlooked part of bringing order to the chaos of final trial preparation is the "to do" list, or agenda. In her thoughtful article in this edition of *Pretrial Practice & Discovery*, Rose Kulczycki provides insight into what should go on a "to do" list. Careful analysis of her article, in the context of the needs of a specific case, will be an enormous help in achieving organization when it is needed most. Rose makes a great case for why a useful "to do" list is, in many ways, an essential part of final trial preparation, particularly during the last 60 days before trial.

This article does not attempt to further amplify why such a list is essential as trial approaches; nor does it seek to summarize what is a somewhat surprising cottage industry of "to do" list resources, including a blog providing "to do" list guidance, literature, and even a directory for "to do" list parties and "slams."[1] Instead, this article addresses a few of the many benefits of creating and updating a "to do" list in a case long *before* final trial preparation. In doing so, the article briefly highlights just five reasons why having a helpful, vibrant, and continuously updated "to do" list can have many intended (and perhaps unintended) beneficial consequences.

From the **Committee on Pretrial Practice & Discovery** / Fall 2007 / ABA / Section of Litigation

Hon. Samuel A. Thumma is a judge on the Arizona Superior Court in Maricopa County, Phoenix, Arizona. The views expressed are those of the author and do not represent those of the Arizona Superior Court.

[1]*See* www.todolistblog.com (visited October 18, 2007).

ORGANIZATION

There are many steps in civil litigation, from pre-complaint investigation through post-trial motions and appeal. Sitting down, early on, in a case and roughing out a "to do" list of the anticipated steps can provide invaluable assistance in deciding how best to proceed; when tactically to press certain issues; and how to impose a logical order on discovery, motion practice, and case development in general.

Done correctly, a good "to do" list provides a general road map of what has been accomplished, what currently is contemplated, and what may be contemplated in the future. Such a list also can include what was once contemplated but then ruled out and the reasons why. Cases that are pending for extended periods involve lawyer turnover, turnover in client personnel, and dimming memories. Having a comprehensive, or even semi-comprehensive, "to do" list of what has been done and what is (or has been) contemplated can be immensely helpful in organizing activities years after the case was first filed.

SCHEDULING

Closely related to general case organization, a "to do" list can be a great help in addressing scheduling issues throughout a case. Scheduling issues will, at various points in a case, favor one side or the other. Moreover, counsel are required to address scheduling issues in advance of, and at, the Federal Rule of Civil Procedure 26(f) scheduling conference. Having a realistic "to do" list created sufficiently in advance of the Rule 26(f) conference can be a great aid in working through scheduling issues with the other side and then the court.

How, for example, can the parties expect to have the court accept that fact discovery will take three years unless they have some idea of what written and deposition discovery is necessary and anticipated? Similarly, how can one party claim that discovery can be completed in six months, unless that party has assessed what written and deposition discovery is required? In these and other ways, a thoughtful "to do" list at the beginning of the case is a very helpful scheduling reference.

BUDGETING

For decades, lawyers have avoided or ignored the "B" word. More and more frequently, however, clients of all types are vigorously requesting and demanding budgets providing some idea of how much litigation will cost for a variety of reasons, including planning and so that business options may be properly evaluated. Such budgets are requests by, and helpful to, private and public clients of all types, insurance carriers, and law firms for internal purposes.

Budgets can be extremely challenging for lawyers to prepare and are, to be sure, an inexact science. Clients, however, are less and less sympathetic to claims that budgets simply cannot be done with any certainty at all, particularly given that other professionals are able to provide budgets and do so with some frequency. The only way to begin to develop any realistic budget is to have a thoughtful and comprehensive "to do" list of what is contemplated and then assess costs for the various components of that list. From a budgeting perspective, a "to do" list may allow the client to decide that certain activities should be deferred, or not undertaken at all, and in any event to prioritize in a meaningful way various alternative courses of action with the advantage of a cost-benefit analysis.

Finally, a "to do" list may also help the lawyer and client consider alternative billing structures to enhance efficiency even further. For example, whether to enter into a blended rate structure may turn, for example, on specific actions contemplated or agreed upon. Again, a thoughtful "to do" list will help both client and lawyer to address such issues.

ACCOUNTABILITY

"To do" lists can enhance accountability in may ways, including both within a law firm and between the client and the firm. The "to do" list can be used to track who is responsible for doing what and by when. Such accountability avoids a situation where, for example, a critical dispositive motion and related deadline are identified, but where the person(s) responsible for drafting and finalizing the motion are not assigned.

A "to do" list can also be useful in establishing internal and external deadlines. Having a week for the client to review a draft may sound luxurious from the drafting law firm's perspective. But if that week coincides with the client's annual meeting or falls during the final days before the closing of a long-planned merger, it may create enormous headaches for the client. Again, a thoughtful "to do" list can help enhance communication and avoid such headaches.

CLIENT RELATIONS

Many things can impress clients, including clarity of thought and organization. Having a thoughtful "to do" list that is updated periodically can be an impressive tool in dealing with clients. Having one document that includes contemplated tasks, responsible personnel, internal and external deadlines, and other related information and that can be consulted quickly can help provide such organization, both for the routine and the unexpected client inquiry. Similarly, drafting such a list early on in a case can be a great way to show the client that the lawyer has thoughtfully considered where the case is going, has drawn up a general map for what may seem like a long journey, and has prepared a clear case strategy.

The mundane "to do" list has vital importance during the last 60 days before trial. On that there can be no debate. Such a list—setting forth in a thoughtful way the who, what, when, where, and how of pressing forward in litigation—can provide substantial benefits from a variety of other perspectives throughout the life of a case. A well-thought-out, frequently updated, and often consulted "to do" list will be an aid throughout any civil litigation—large or small—for the client and the lawyer alike.

General Advice

The Young Lawyer's Corner
Lessons Learned at My First Criminal Trial
By David M. Burkoff

As a second-year associate eager to get into court on any basis (except, maybe, as a defendant), I jumped at the chance to fill in for a senior lawyer at my firm who had a last-minute conflict and couldn't handle a client's felony arraignment. From what little we knew, the evidence against us was flimsy and we didn't expect the government's case to go anywhere. Certainly I could handle the arraignment, in the lowest-level trial court in our state, and then pass the case back to the partner for any more substantive work that might come along.

At least, that was the plan. The client had other ideas. After I managed to speak English and not drool on myself at the hearing, he proceeded to ask what, to him, was the key question at the time: were my rates lower than the partner's, and, if so, how much lower? My answer seemed to please him, unsurprisingly, and he asked me to handle his case going forward. He too thought the prosecution was going nowhere fast. Why not save a few dollars and let a junior lawyer take care of getting the matter dismissed?

After clearing this arrangement with the partner, I set to work. But I had already learned my first lesson from what would become the first case I took to trial: impressing the client is important, from day one. A client's very first impression of you tends to count disproportionately. (The same can be said about juries, which I learned more about later.) Indeed, with this particular client, my good work on the initial phases of his case, beginning with his arraignment, carried us through an eventual rough patch when he learned that I had never actually tried a case. (Our surprise was mutual—I didn't understand why he assumed I *would* have tried a case, just two years out of law school.) I quickly arranged a meeting for the two of us and the partner, and the client, upon reflection, decided that I had been doing a fine job and should remain as his designated trial counsel.

From the **Criminal Litigation Newsletter**/Fall 2006/ABA/Section of Litigation

Still, even though the client apparently was convinced that I could go it alone, I was keenly aware that I needed plenty of outside advice. This was lesson number two: however seasoned a lawyer you may be, two heads (or three, or a dozen) are invariably better than one when it comes to preparing for trial. Needless to say, this rule applies ten-fold to newly minted attorneys like me. I not only gave my opening and closing to more senior lawyers at my firm, I also practiced my examinations with other lawyers, complete with objections and arguments about the rules of evidence. (This is not to mention my interminable (I'm told) rehearsals before my fiancé and our dog, both non-lawyers.) I also consulted a lawyer who had recently tried a case in the same court for her advice on such basics as (a) the mechanics of the voir dire and (b) where to stand during the various phases of the trial.

During this process, I came to learn lesson number three: there's no such thing as too much preparation. Knowing every police report, every piece of evidence, backwards and forwards—and anticipating, as best I could, every objection—became my best weapon. As a lawyer in private practice, I had far more time to spend preparing my client's defense than the prosecutor had to prepare his case. Of course, this was no fault of the prosecutor's; he had many more pending cases than I did. But my hope was that this imbalance would cancel out the inescapable imbalance in our respective levels of experience. The prosecutor was also young, relatively, but I knew he had been on the job for at least a couple of years and had already cut his teeth at trial.

How did I know of the prosecutor's experience? Direct from the horse's mouth. Through friendly give-and-take in the months leading up to trial, I learned a little bit about him. Which leads to lesson number four: courtesy and civility towards the other side can go a long way. Among other things, since the vast majority of criminal cases (and civil, for that matter) are resolved by agreement rather than trial, a good working relationship with the prosecutor is crucial to getting the best possible deal for your client—*i.e.*, to being an effective advocate. Negotiation is not a mechanical process; at minimum, it requires parties to get along well enough to make calm, rational discussion of positions and interests possible. Some prosecutors might even cut your client a break because, on some subconscious level at least, they want to cut *you* a break. Friendly conversation with the other side might also reveal any number of useful pieces of information—the politics behind the prosecution, for example, or perhaps simply the weight of the prosecutor's workload. Both of these things might affect your approach to plea negotiations. Granted there are times when full-armor combat, so to speak, might best serve your client's interests, but, at all other times, why shut yourself off to helpful information by being unduly discourteous?

In my case, we ultimately couldn't get the matter dismissed, my client didn't want to plead to anything, and the prosecutor was determined to proceed. So we went to trial. Over the course of two exhausting days, I learned countless additional lessons. Chief among them, I suppose, is that mistakes are inevitable. Even the most experienced litigator doesn't do everything her hindsight later (sometimes seconds later) tells her she should have done. I made my share of mistakes, but I quickly mastered the art of just moving on. When a mistake is not serious and can't be quickly and painlessly remedied, the best course is usually to shrug it off, put it behind you, and continue forging ahead. In the end, although I hardly ran a clinic in trial lawyering, the jury came back after two hours of deliberating and read their verdict—not guilty. At that moment, I learned what might be the most significant lesson of all—that I'm in the right profession. The most exhilarating moment of my professional life thus far was when I stood with my client at counsel table, after a hard-fought trial, and heard those precious two words from the jury foreperson. I can't wait to do it all over again.

Young Lawyer's Advice to New Lawyers (And Important Reminders for the Rest of Us)

By James E. Scarboro

The legal profession is, of course, many things to many people. For those of us in private practice, it is partly a business. For all of us it is a trade and a craft. But the idea of profession conveys something more. It suggests a calling or a mission. Of course, it is necessary to put food on the table, and there is a deep pleasure to be gotten from performing one's work skillfully. Yet these are merely means to another end.

I don't know how many of you have thought about what that end is. None of us thinks about it very much. We are too busy with our professional and personal lives to step back and ask ourselves exactly what it is we are trying to accomplish. I have some suggestions about that, and I will say a little about those in this brief article. But the most important point I have to make is that only you can answer the question for yourself. Only you can decide what the legal profession means. And I do not think that I am making too much of my point to say that your decision will determine how the legal profession is regarded in your generation.

Some lawyers see law practice as an opportunity to accumulate personal wealth or power or acclaim. But these are mere private ambitions, and, standing alone, they have no public significance. Some see the legal system as the repository of our community's norms and values and the participants in that system as the guardians, for better or for worse, of those values. Others emphasize the importance of the legal system in bringing about social change or assisting minorities and the poor and the disadvantaged.

All of these purposes are important and pursuit of any of them would define a life worth living. But I think that the legal profession has a deeper mission—one that is at once so ordinary sounding and modest that it easily escapes our attention. Simply put, we are keepers of the peace. This is a deeply conservative project. It is the project that the Greek hero, Orestes, embarked upon when he submitted his defense— he had stolen a statue—to the judgment of a judicial tribunal, thus bringing to an end the cycle of revenge. It is the project which, if we successfully accomplish it, induces our fellow citizens all across the country year after year to entrust their disputes to courts of law rather than settling them in alleys or back rooms.

From the **Litigation Ethics**/Winter 2006/ABA/Section of Litigation

You are critical to this mission. The legal system cannot do its job unless it has integrity. The legal system cannot have integrity unless the lawyers and judges who practice in it are competent, honest, and hard working.

Let me give you a working definition of integrity. This is going to sound simple, but, believe me, it is not. It comes from the late Alfred Arraj, the chief judge of our federal trial court in Denver for many years and a much admired and loved judge. He once gave this advice to a group of young lawyers who would be practicing before him: "Be prepared, be candid with the court, and be courteous, especially to opposing counsel. If you will do these things, you will be successful in my courtroom." Now, Judge Arraj did not mean that you would always win. If you try cases, you are going to lose as well as win. What he was saying is that the legal system cannot have integrity unless he makes good decisions. He has a much better chance of making a good decision if the lawyers who practice before him are prepared and candid with the court. And, by the way, he would appreciate a little courtesy.

As you work your way into law practice, if you do appear before courts, you will find that judges are sometimes irritated with lawyers. There are all sorts of reasons why this might be true, but the most common reason is very simple. Judges are irritated when lawyers are unprepared because that makes their job more difficult. They are trying to arrive at a good decision and not make mistakes, but a lawyer who is ill-prepared and who is not candid makes their job more difficult.

Judge Arraj's prescription is not everything that can be said about integrity in the practice of law. I want to mention just one other ingredient—one that is particularly important to me. You will recall that, in the recent confirmation process, we learned that Chief Justice Roberts, while an appellate attorney in Washington, gave legal advice to an attorney about to argue a case in the United States Supreme Court on behalf of a group of gays and lesbians. Justice Roberts was well-equipped to advise the attorney. He had practiced many times before the court and presumably had good ideas about the best way to approach each justice. Roberts's supporters were upset to learn that he had given legal advice to a group with which, they assume, he had strong personal disagreements. They saw this as a kind of betrayal. This is a common confusion that lay people have about lawyers and judges. They think that lawyers are advocates for causes they personally believe in and that judges render decisions that enact their personal preferences. Of course this is not true. If it were, the legal system would have no more integrity than the ballot box and could not successfully accomplish its fundamental mission.

In fact, the exact opposite is true. Justice Roberts was displaying integrity when he gave advice to a group he personally disagreed with. Lawyers do this every day. Every day judges render decisions in favor of litigants of whom they might disapprove or at least with whom they disagree.

Some of you may recall the case of John Adams, our nation's second president, who, as a young man, was a very successful lawyer in Boston. He had a lucrative practice. In one of the Boston riots—I think it was the Boston Tea Party—British soldiers shot and killed several colonists. No lawyer in Boston would take their case. John Adams stepped forward to do so, knowing that the cause was deeply unpopular and that his reputation might be damaged. He also knew that it is a lawyer's solemn obligation to represent unpopular causes.

Closer to my home, we have the case of the late Ira Rothgerber, a distinguished Denver lawyer, who accepted an appointment from then Chief Judge William Lee Knous of our federal court to represent pro bono a University of Colorado professor accused of advocating Communism. These examples illuminate, for me, what integrity in the practice of law means.

So, I give you Judge Arraj's three prescriptions. When you appear in court, be prepared, be candid with the court, and be courteous, especially to opposing counsel. And I give you the examples of John Adams and Ira Rothgerber. Be prepared to take risks, to represent unpopular causes, to help the poor, the disadvantaged, those in prison. Often they will not be able to afford your services. If so, represent them for free, as much as you reasonably can.

If you will do these things, even to a modest degree, you will carry forward the very best of our traditions, and you will leave the legal profession, when the time to leave it comes, in excellent condition.

Tips for Working with "Difficult" Opposing Counsel
By David S. Coale

Litigation is adversarial, so some amount of "difficulty" with opposing counsel is inherent in any lawsuit, much less in a document-heavy and intense commercial dispute. And some opposing counsel are simply difficult people. But a few simple maxims, many with distinguished historical pedigrees, can help steer your relationship with opposing counsel in a positive direction:

1. "A rolling stone gathers no moss." Publilius Syrus, *Maxims* no. 524. Calls and letters that go unanswered for long periods of time can lead to irritation by your opponent and, if cited to a court in a discovery motion, can make you look unresponsive. To the extent possible, respond quickly to communications from your opposing counsel and keep the ball in his or her court.

2. "Separate the person from the problem." Roger Fisher and William Ury, *Getting to Yes* (1991). If your opposing counsel has a difficult client, or something about the case itself is particularly challenging, try to focus on your opposing counsel as a person and a professional rather than identifying him or her with the difficult situation.

3. "Let the other person save face." Dale Carnegie, *How to Win Friends and Influence People* (1936). Aggressively represent your client but allow your opponent the opportunity to effectively communicate with his or her client, without always seeking a "knockout blow" against everyone on the other side of the case, especially if there is an ongoing business relationship that is independent of the case.

4. "[T]he purpose of the Rules can be subverted when they are invoked by opposing parties as procedural weapons." Preamble, ABA *Model Rules of Professional Responsibility*. Minimize disputes about professional conduct if they are not truly important to the case.

5. "Be prepared." Motto, Boy Scouts of America. Before conferring about a matter with opposing counsel, understand the basic facts and consider your opponent's likely view of them. In going to court, focus on what the court will want to hear about the case rather than what you may want to say about your opponent.

From the **Commercial & Business Litigation**/Spring 2006/ABA/Section of Litigation

6. "A soft answer turneth away wrath, but grievous words stir up anger." Proverbs 15:1. Take a minute before sending an angry email or letter; consider letting the draft rest overnight for review the next morning.

7. "A communications disruption could mean only one thing: invasion." Governor Sio Bibble, *Star Wars I: The Phantom Menace*. Don't be like Governor Bibble. When communications are breaking down, especially if the breakdown has come from a long string of email or fax messages, give serious thought to just picking up the phone for a few minutes to identify the matters that are actually in dispute.

8. "And do as adversaries do in law—Strive mightily, but eat and drink as friends." William Shakespeare, *The Taming of the Shrew*. Act 1, Scene 2. Remember that the commercial litigation bar is not that large and that your adversary today may be your co-counsel tomorrow.

9. "The life of the law has not been logic; it has been experience." Oliver Wendell Holmes, Jr., *The Common Law* (1881). Consider the emotional and practical appeal of your positions and their logical structure.

10. "As advocate, a lawyer zealously asserts the client's position under the rules of the adversary system." Preamble, ABA *Model Rules of Professional Responsibility*. A lawyer should work with the opponent while also defending what matters to the client's case.

11. "Speak softly and carry a big stick." Theodore Roosevelt. Be courteous and professional, drawing upon confidence in your skills as a courtroom advocate.

Judge's Column
Basic Litigation Pointers and Courtroom Etiquette for Bankruptcy Lawyers
By Douglas O. Tice, Jr.

Bankruptcy litigation do's and don'ts is a frequent topic of law journal articles, CLE seminars, and bar meetings. Although the subject can be overdone, I have always found such presentations worthwhile and usually entertaining. Typically, it is the attorneys who need to hear these programs who are not present. Likewise, these same attorneys probably will not be reading the present article. So, I may be preaching to the choir here with this summary compendium of litigation tips collected during my twenty years on the bench. I do not claim originality, and readers who have an interest in the subject will probably have previously seen most of my examples. Some of them may seem ridiculously simplistic. Yet, I have seen lawyers stumble over nearly all of them and not just lawyers new to the bar.

Probably in most bankruptcy courts, as in the courts of the Eastern and Western Districts of Virginia, the number of lawyers appearing regularly at court hearings is relatively limited. A Richmond newspaper reporter once referred to this situation as the "clubby atmosphere" of our bankruptcy bar. As a result of this closeness, the presiding judges quickly become acquainted with bankruptcy lawyers and learn which ones do dependable work. An attorney's demeanor and performance before the court establishes his or her credibility (or lack thereof) and may have a substantial impact on a client's case. At a minimum, an attorney must develop and display a desire to be an effective advocate. It is urgent from the first appearance before a judge that an attorney demonstrate his or her knowledge of the law and other elements of professional competence. This may be done in a number of ways, some of which are mere common sense.

There is a common saying that trial work is preparation, preparation, preparation. Preparation may be divided into several areas of courtroom practice, and each area provides lawyers differing opportunities to demonstrate their essential characteristics and ultimate worth as practitioners.

From the **Bankruptcy Litigation**/Summer 2008/ABA/Section of Litigation
Hon. Douglas Tice became Chief Judge of the Eastern District of Virginia in 1999. He was appointed to the bankruptcy bench for the Richmond Division in September 1987 and reappointed in 2001.

BASIC ATTITUDE

Under the category of attitude, I consider the most fundamental rules of demeanor for lawyers appearing in any court. For an obvious example, arrive in court (*i.e.*, in the courtroom) on time. If you are unavoidably delayed, telephone the judge's chambers or other court staff and leave word of your anticipated arrival. Once there, do not leave the courtroom when your case is likely to be called. In my court, the latter happens almost on a regular basis.

Bring your current calendar information to court so that you may schedule future hearings without fear of a conflict in dates.

Dress appropriately and advise your clients and witnesses to do the same. It was a painful experience both for me and the attorney that I once admonished for appearing in court wearing an out-of-place neck tie. (The story later came back to me, apocryphally, that I had scolded him for wearing a "SpongeBob SquarePants" necktie.) In another case, an attorney attempted to disguise the absence of a tie with a crew neck sweater.

Be courteous not only to the judge but to opposing counsel, parties, and witnesses. Be particularly courteous to court personnel, who can be of great assistance to your bankruptcy practice. The judge usually learns which attorneys are discourteous, and it does not enhance their stature. Also, be careful what you say after the court has left the bench. Not only may the court reporter and court staff remain in court but the microphone transmitting to chambers remains on. A true story: A few years ago, following the conclusion of a relief from stay hearing, I was inclined to deny the motion but decided to give creditor's counsel an opportunity to persuade me otherwise by submitting a sketch order granting relief. After adjournment, that counsel made a comment in the courtroom to the effect that the judge expected him to do the judge's work. When I was told of this, I immediately reviewed my notes and the pleadings and prepared an order denying the motion.

Be aware you are in a court of record. It is important to avoid unnecessary talking (or mumbling) on the record. If you do not know the answer to a question by the judge and need to speak to your client or associate, ask the judge's permission. Put another way, while standing at the lectern do not turn away from the judge and talk to someone else without permission.

Make your presentations with confidence. If you do, the judge may have confidence in you. On a motions docket, when your case is called, address the court and present your motion. If your court requires use of a lectern, go directly to the lectern. Do not wait for the judge to ask why you are there. Always distinctly state your name (a common failing) and the name of your client for the record. If you are new to the court and have an unusual surname, it will be helpful to spell your name for the court reporter. And, to take a page from my father's book, stand up straight, and take your hands out of your pockets.

PREPARATION: BEFORE GOING TO COURT

It is essential that lawyers prepare themselves for trial work just as they must learn the law. Preparation for court appearances starts at least as early as law school and requires an appreciation for the nature of trial work, including proper demeanor. Also, because courtroom practice involves appearing in public, attorneys must train themselves in the rudiments of public speaking. Some come by this naturally; others have to work at it.

When you begin practice, seek out the best trial lawyers and observe their work in court. Consult learned books and articles on trying cases. Many of these are available, including an inexpensive new bankruptcy litigation manual recently issued by the American Bankruptcy Institute.

Learn to listen. Pay attention to opposing counsel and to witnesses. Pay particular attention to the judge's comments or questions as they may alert you to how you are doing and suggest other directions. They may also suggest it is time to sit down.

Bankruptcy practice includes all forms of appearances before the bankruptcy court. It requires extensive knowledge of the Bankruptcy Code and Federal Rules of Bankruptcy Procedure.

Also, you must know the local rules of practice in your court.

Many consumer bankruptcy lawyers who practice before me never litigate substantial matters. If you are not comfortable with this part of the practice, be sure and seek assistance when a creditor brings a dischargeability proceeding or similar serious matter against your client.

Know the local practice customs and any quirks or peculiarities of the judge. If you are appearing in a court for the first time, ask other attorneys about the judge's preferences and procedures.

Prior to any trial or evidentiary hearing consult opposing counsel and attempt to stipulate facts that are not in dispute. It goes without saying that you should attempt to resolve disputes by agreement and avoid the necessity of a hearing or trial. Promptly advise the court when a settlement has been reached.

Do not file motions for expedited hearings unless absolutely necessary. Advise court staff of the motion so that the judge may promptly rule and, when appropriate, schedule a hearing.

Familiarize yourself with and comply with the court's pretrial order, particularly as to filing deadlines for witness and exhibit lists and pretrial motions. File proper number of copies of pre-marked exhibits. Promptly review opposing counsel's list of exhibits and timely file any objections; failure to object will constitute a waiver of objections to exhibits. If you cannot fully comply with the pretrial order deadlines, file a motion to amend well before trial.

Know the law that governs your case and have a written game plan that lays out in detail the evidence required to prove the case. Plan your exhibits and witness examination accordingly.

In any substantial trial, consider preparing a trial notebook containing pleadings, exhibits, witness examinations, etc. In my court, we expect attorneys to provide at least three copies of each exhibit to the court. If there are more than a few exhibits, tab and place them in a binder. In appropriate cases submit a brief or trial memorandum prior to trial.

Prepare your witnesses for trials or depositions so that they know the questions you will ask. Coach them on how to answer questions truthfully, with short and simple answers; tell them to speak up so they can be heard by the court and reporter. Warn witnesses about objections. Caution them not to become advocates on the stand as it can reduce their credibility.

Know the Federal Rules of Evidence, particularly those that may be implicated in your matter. Know which questions are proper. The hearsay rule and its many exceptions are particularly important.

If there are serious evidentiary issues that may be raised with respect to evidence important to your case (or if you are aware that opposing counsel intends to use such evidence important to the opponent's case), consider filing a motion in limine in advance of trial so that the court may rule on admissibility prior to trial.

In preparing for trial, assume that opposing counsel may be smarter and working harder than you. Prepare your case accordingly.

LITIGATION—TRYING A CASE

For opening statements at trial, I prefer for attorneys to give a simple summary of their case and the result they seek. The opening should not be a recital of the evidence. However, some judges may prefer more extensive and substantive openings. Here is where the attorney must learn the judge's preferences.

Follow correct procedure to introduce exhibits that are not marked beforehand. (a. mark for identification; b. hand copy to opposing counsel; c. show to witness; d. ask witness to identify; e. offer in evidence.)

Have a list of all your exhibits. If they have not been admitted at the beginning of the trial, don't forget to offer them in evidence at the appropriate time, and be certain that the court makes a ruling on their admissibility.

Do not lead your witnesses on direct examination. Even if the other party fails to object, continually leading may unfavorably impress the judge. In an ABI panel presentation several years ago, one of the judge panelists said she was less inclined to allow leading questions by lawyers who were not well prepared. She stated also that leading questions tend to reduce the credibility of the witness.

On cross examination treat adverse witnesses respectfully, and always ask leading questions. It has often been said that a lawyer should never ask a question to which he or she does not know the answer. This is generally a good rule to follow although it must be considered in the context of your case. Also, carefully consider whether to cross examine at all. It is certainly not required and should usually be avoided unless you have something to gain. I have seen cross examination so poorly done that I found it necessary to caution the lawyer that the questions were reinforcing the position of the other party.

In making objections to opposing counsel's examination of witnesses or introduction of exhibits, you must stand and state the evidentiary basis for an objection with "reasonable specificity." If you fail to state a reasonable basis, you may not be able to raise the judge's overruling your objection as error on appeal.

Promptly object to the other side's questions; an objection does little good if the witness has already answered. Prior to trial, instruct your witnesses not to answer so quickly on cross examination that you do not have an opportunity to object. In general, object to admission of exhibits only where exclusion is of some importance. Frequent and inconsequential objections can be a distraction to the court and do not help your case.

During examination, if you wish to refer a witness to a particular place in an exhibit or elsewhere in the record, know exactly where it is located. If you need to approach a witness, request the court's permission.

You can argue your case from the exhibit. I have an aversion to listening to witnesses read from documents in evidence unless there is an important reason to do so. Maintain a poker face during trial and argument. Do not overreact, make faces, or shake your head at answers of witnesses, argument of opposing counsel, or, particularly, the rulings of the court. Instruct your client and witnesses to do the same. Rolling eyes, shaking or nodding heads do not help—they annoy the judge. To be more emphatic, as I once read in a top-ten list of litigation do's and don'ts, "no audible moaning if the judge rules against you."

POST-TRIAL PRACTICE

Be prepared to make oral closing argument. Here is where your trial game plan comes in handy. Summarize for the court the specific facts (and evidence) that support your position in the case. Argue the relevant law so as to show why the court should rule in your client's favor. Hand up to the judge copies of pertinent case decisions or applicable state statutes.

After lengthy trials or hearings, consider requesting the court's permission to submit a written brief or proposed findings of facts and conclusions of law. Promptly file post-trial briefs or other papers requested by the court. If you cannot meet the court's deadline, file a motion for extension.

Timely file notices of appeal. Consider the necessity for requesting stay pending appeal.

What Judges Want
By Mark A. Drummond

I want you to know that as a trial lawyer I violated most of the following rules—sometimes several of them in the same trial. But after trying cases for 20 years, and being a trial judge for six, I can reduce what judges want to a Top Ten list.

1. We Want the Exhibit

Since judges are individuals, each has idiosyncrasies. Some judges have so many idiosyncrasies they feel it necessary to have written rules for the lawyers to follow in their courtrooms. Although the lawyers in my court may tell you something different, I believe I have only one idiosyncrasy: *I want the exhibit.* I want you to let me see the exhibit at the same time the lawyer is questioning the witness about it.

I applaud attorneys who are trying to save our natural resources, but nothing frustrates me more than what I call the "one-exhibit trial." What usually happens is that the lawyer has only one exhibit and gives it to the witness. A direct examination is then conducted over the right shoulder of the witness while the other lawyer stands over the left shoulder to see what they are talking about. The following is an actual exchange that occurred in my court:

Lawyer 1: Would you read that line of the contract for the court? (*Witness reads*)

Lawyer 2: Objection, Your Honor, rule of completeness.

Me: May I see the exhibit?

Lawyer 1: No.

Me: Why?

Lawyer 1: I have not introduced it into evidence.

Me (*slightly exasperated*): Yes, but I'm the one who admits it into evidence.

Lawyer 1: Oh.

Did I mention that this was a *bench trial*?

I don't know how many times a lawyer has examined a witness concerning a multipart contract, a tax return, or a line-item budget without my having the benefit of a copy. Even if the judge had been a steno-

---

Mark A. Drummond is a judge in the Eighth Judicial Circuit of Illinois.

graphic court reporter in a former life, it simply is much easier to follow along with the exhibit in front of you. If you give the judge a courtesy copy, you are more likely to get the correct result for your client in the shortest period of time. Many of my fellow judges and I keep various colored highlighters and sticky notes on our benches to mark the courtesy copy of the exhibit. For example, I may highlight income in green and deductions in yellow on a tax return. I write the questions I want to ask next to the relevant part of the exhibit. Nothing is more frustrating for a judge than not being able to see what everybody else sees in the courtroom.

2. We Want the Law

What is the shortest distance between leaving the doors of your law school and winning the respect of judges? It's following Model Rule of Professional Conduct 3.3(a)(2), which reads, "A lawyer shall not knowingly fail to disclose to the tribunal authority in the controlling jurisdiction known to the lawyer to be directly adverse to the position of the client and not disclosed by opposing counsel."

In fact, I tell new attorneys to take the words "directly adverse" and change them to "arguably adverse." Why? There is nothing more impressive than the advocate who comes into court and says, for example, "Your Honor, this is our position. However, there are three cases that are arguably against us. We have cited those to you, but we believe two of those cases are distinguishable on their facts and one is just bad law. We also have two cases in our favor. . . ."

Judges learn very quickly on whom they can rely to tell them the current state of the law. Citing contrary authority builds your reputation as an ethical advocate. For judges who may be dealing with hundreds of files covering many legal issues, nothing is more powerful than being known as the advocate a judge can always count on for accurate statements as to the law.

There also is a persuasive power to citing contrary authority: It appears that you are less concerned about it when you admit its existence—and it is even more devastating for the other side when you cite cases that are against you that they have not found. No less an advocate than Cicero said that the perfect advocate is one who could argue both sides of any case.

3. We Want Objections that Matter

Judges become frustrated with what I will call "sport objections"—those made merely for the sport of it. Recently we were at the end of a trial that had to be continued. One of the parties had not shown up in court, and I asked the representative of an agency to explain the efforts that had been made to notify this party. The representative started to tell me that the party that was in court had told the representative that she had called the other party to advise him of the date. There was a hearsay objection. Now, the fact that this attorney's client had tried to notify the absent party of the hearing date didn't make a hill of beans' worth of difference to his client's case. Moreover, the fact that she took the time and effort to try to call the other party put her in a better light. The opportunity to object does not translate into actually objecting.

Every so often an objection actually hurts your case. In this case the lawyer who objected wanted the party to be making more money. The following exchange occurred:

> **Lawyer 1:** Now, do you have any chance to move up in the organization [from his vocal intonation, he assumes the answer will be no]?
>
> **Witness:** Yes, they told me—
>
> **Lawyer 2:** Objection—hearsay.
>
> **Me:** I would sustain that objection but the bigger question is why would you object since she started with yes.
>
> **Lawyer 2:** Objection withdrawn.
>
> **Witness:** Yes, they told me I would be in line for the manager's job, which ranges from $40,000 to $60,000 per year [a factor two to three times what she earned].

These are knee-jerk objections. Any time these lawyers hear the word "said," they make a hearsay objection without asking themselves, *Will this hurt me? Will this help me? Does this matter?*

4. We Want Good Jury Instructions

Lawyers work more hours than judges. Any judge who disagrees is either a rare exception or did not work many hours as an attorney. Therefore, I always try to accommodate the attorneys' schedules and try to save attorneys time. However, there is one group of people whose time I value more than the attorneys: jurors.

Nothing frustrates a judge more than having the jury twiddle their thumbs while we try to craft a usable set of jury instructions. Ninety percent of the jury instructions should be completed before trial and given to the judge. Alternate instructions based upon how the evidence may shake out should be typed and ready to go for the instruction conference. If you don't do many jury trials, ask someone who does, such as a state's attorney, how to do this. They'll know what I mean.

5. We Want You to Know Us

Most people know the Greek maxim "know thyself." Experienced trial attorneys will tell you to "know thy judge." As I said before, I would like to think that I have only the one-exhibit trial peeve, but I know many judges have more than one. (I know, you're shocked.) How do you ethically find out about the judge's preferences? Here are some suggestions:

- Call the judge. I have no problem with an out-of-town attorney calling me to ask about procedure in my courtroom.
- Call the judge's clerk. Some lawyers are uncomfortable contacting the judge directly or know that a particular judge does not want to talk to any attorney without the other attorney there, even on matters of procedure. Many judges' clerks or secretaries know the procedure.
- Ask for the written rules. Many judges have a list of the procedures they like in their courtrooms.
- Call another attorney who has tried a case in front of that judge. Start the conversation with, "Hey, I heard you got a good result in the Smith case." After the attorney talks for about 15 minutes, say, "Tell me about Judge Jones."

6. We Want to Be Affirmed on Appeal

For the most part, our biggest fear is having a jury trial overturned and having to do it all over again. In a perfect world, every judge would have a law professor's encyclopedic knowledge on the particular area of the law. Some judges do become specialists and have the luxury of knowing everything there is to know about a certain narrow area of the law. However, most of us rotate assignments, and, especially in rural counties, the jury trials may be few and far between. I remember when I was in practice, a judge thanked me for taking a civil case to jury trial. He had been a judge for eight years in that county and had never heard one civil jury trial.

If you are taking a jury case to trial, you probably have lived with that case for up to a year or longer. Probably the only person in the courtroom who knows as much about the case as you do is opposing counsel. We judges sometimes do not track why a particular piece of evidence is relevant, and we need time either to digest your argument or to have some law on the point.

What do you do? Make liberal use of offers of proof, and don't be afraid to ask the judge to reconsider a prior ruling during a break in the jury trial. An offer of proof made outside the presence of the jury preserves the issue for appeal. It also gives the judge more time to think about it without the pressure of 24 staring eyes expecting a split-second decision. I may need time to do some quick research on the law or a particular evidentiary point during the break. Don't assume that *Objection sustained* is the end of it. I don't want to have to do this again, and if I can trust you on issues of law or evidence, I will always give you a second chance.

7. We Want Civility

I once told a young attorney during a trial training course, "You can't treat witnesses as if they were born on this earth for the sole purpose of messing with your case." Some attorneys just can't help themselves and really emphasize the word "cross" in cross-examination. On a couple of occasions when I was practicing, I lost clients to attorneys who the clients thought were more "aggressive." I know that aggressive attorneys may give clients a certain dose of psychic gratification, especially in divorce cases, by the use of confrontational tactics. But as a judge and from juror feedback questionnaires, I can tell you that the people who decide the cases do not appreciate posturing, or put another way, "the show" put on for the client.

The question the attorney must ask is whether aggression is persuasive. To illustrate: The attorney wants to show that the witness (plaintiff) did not seek medical treatment after the accident. The aggressive attorney would do something like this:

Attorney (*in a loud voice dripping with sarcasm*): Ms. Smith, I didn't ask you how you felt, I asked whether you asked for an ambulance, yes or no? Now, can you answer that?

In contrast, another lawyer might simply repeat the question slowly and softly until getting the answer he or she wants:

Attorney: You didn't ask for an ambulance?

Witnesses: Well, I didn't feel hurt at that time.

Attorney (*softer*): You didn't ask for an ambulance?

Witness: Well, like I said, I didn't feel hurt at the time.

Attorney (*even softer and slower*): You didn't ask for an ambulance?

Witness: No.

By listening to the lawyer repeat the simple question and knowing that the lawyer is entitled to a yes or no answer, the jurors are soon siding with the attorney—looking at the witness and screaming in their minds, *Oh, just answer the question!* The longer it takes the witnesses to answer this simple question, the better it is for the attorney. The non-aggressive technique of repetition emphasizes to the jury how the witness is avoiding the question. Attorneys must realize that naked aggression, for the most part, is solely for their own gratification or that of their client. It rarely persuades the people who count.

8. We Want a Trial Notebook

I already have talked about having the exhibit in front of me. If you really want to impress a judge, make a trial notebook. In fact, make four of them: One for you and one for opposing counsel, the witness, and the judge. The original exhibits go in the witness's trial notebook.

Once the exhibit is admitted in a jury trial, it is shown to the jurors, either by their being instructed to turn to the exhibit in their own notebooks (in a document-heavy case) or by the exhibit's being projected on a screen. The jurors need to follow as the witness testifies. A judge's frustration at not seeing the exhibit does not even approach a juror's frustration at not being able to follow along. Believe me, they've told me.

For a bench trial, insert various items that will be useful to the judge. Many of my trial notebooks included the following: a chronology of the case; a list of witnesses, including their titles, if applicable; a request to admit facts and the response to that request; cites to the applicable statutory or case law; proposed judgement (on paper and disk).

My notebooks included my opponent's exhibits. Many times my opponents would tell me that we could just use my trial notebook, since it had all the exhibits. That allowed me to put the exhibits in the order that I wanted the judge to see them. I am not sure this is any great tactical advantage, but when you take a case to trial that, by definition, should be a close call, you should seek any advantage.

The trial notebook system eliminates the exhibit dance in the courtroom. It eliminates the attorney's having to ask permission to approach the witness, state for the record that she is now showing the exhibit to opposing counsel, and going back to her chair. The process becomes, simply, "Would you please turn to Exhibit 24," and everyone turns the page. It is so elegant. It is so surgical. It is so persuasive.

9. We Want the Judgment

You might want to ask the judge, with opposing counsel present, whether or not she would like the judgment you proposed on a computer disk so she can alter it as she sees fit. I heard of one judge who took this to the extreme. He would have both attorneys prepare a judgment, and he would sign whichever one he agreed with—no additions, no corrections, no deletions—or so legend has it.

There certainly is nothing improper in saying to the judge at the end of your closing argument, "Your Honor, this is our position in the case, and for your convenience I have drafted an order citing the underlying law that we believe is applicable, certain findings of fact, and a judgment based upon our argument. It is on this computer disk, and I also will give a copy to counsel." If a judge practices in a particular area for any length of time, she probably already has a skeleton form on her computer that she uses all the time. However, if you are in front of a judge who deals with many cases or is on special assignment, providing a copy of a proposed judgment on a disk that the judge can edit is a real help.

10. We Want to Talk About the Cases

The problem is, we can't. In some of the counties in our circuit, there is only one judge. It must be lonely. I have the benefit of being able to talk to six other judges in my courthouse. We would really love to be able to talk to the attorneys about the cases, but it becomes a slippery slope. We could possibly talk to the attorneys after appeals have been exhausted, yet we are still concerned about post-judgment matters. Most of us loved being trial attorneys, and not being able to talk to attorneys about particular cases, witnesses, or strategies is the biggest loss for us in taking the bench.

So, after we retire, regale us with stories. Until then, we former trial lawyers must live vicariously.

A Judge's Guide to Protecting Your Reputation
By James G. Carr

One of a lawyer's most important assets is his or her reputation. Each of us can create a good reputation by blending talent, intelligence, competence, and integrity. But we also risk destroying our reputation through deeds or words, whether deliberate or thoughtless, that undercut how others view us.

We are not always to blame for damage to our reputation. The spite, envy, and malice of others can result in negative, even noxious gossip. Vigilant and constant probity and competence remain the best—and perhaps the only—defenses against the corrosive consequences of innuendo.

My purpose here is not to suggest how to avoid the gossip that swirls around us all. I offer, rather, a list of steps that you can take to protect your reputation in the eyes of judges. Some may seem trivial. Others may help you avoid those missteps that occasionally cause even the best lawyers to stumble. Slip off the path, or stray too often, and you risk losing your good reputation forever.

First, be on time, or call.

Most lawyers are late once in a while for reasons beyond their control. They may be running late because another judge has detained them. They can hardly tell the first judge: "Sorry, but I have to leave you now. I've got another judge waiting for me." They may encounter unexpected traffic or have car problems. A family member may need attention. Whatever the reason for your tardiness, it is usually understandable and forgivable. But problems arise when a lawyer is routinely late and, what's worse, pins the blame on someone else.

Whenever you are late, you convey a message that your time is more important than the court's time. If the judge comes to believe that, it's likely that you are going to get less time and attention from the court than you would otherwise enjoy. Courts value their time. This is true even if the judge is chronically late. Few judges are late on purpose or make lawyers wait for no reason at all. Usually, judges are late because they are giving time and attention to other lawyers and litigants, who believe that their cases are at least as important as yours.

In this cell phone age, you no longer need to look for a pay phone and hunt for a quarter if you can't be on time. Give all who will be waiting

From the **Litigation Journal**/Spring 2010/ABA/Section of Litigation
James G. Carr is chief judge of the U.S. District Court for the Northern District of Ohio.

the courtesy of telling them where you are, why you will be late, and when you expect to be with them. Don't underestimate how long it will be before you arrive. A heads-up may not make the judge happy, but at least it will avoid giving the impression that you have a casual view toward the court's timetable.

Second, meet deadlines; don't wait to ask for more time.

Tardiness in filing or responding to a motion can have one of three consequences, none of them desirable. The court will have less time before the trial date to read the briefs and decide the motion. So it may overrule the motion if you are the tardy movant, or it may grant the motion if you are late with your response. Or it may become necessary to postpone the trial, which disrupts the court's calendar and causes inconvenience to other lawyers and litigants.

Courts set calendars with an eye on the volume of work they need to do within the time available. Most judges don't want a reputation for not being able to handle their dockets promptly and efficiently. From time to time, you may be unable to meet a court deadline because other clients have emergencies, other courts make demands, or life intrudes, interrupts, and interferes.

For many lawyers, predicting what they will be doing next week or month is difficult. Their time is at the mercy of the needs and schedules of others, including judges. Judges, in contrast, depend on predictability to make best use of their time. Without control over the course of the cases on their docket, judges cannot well serve the litigants and lawyers before them. Therefore, judges want the time they have set aside for something to be used for that purpose.

Judges also are cognizant of the inconvenience to others, especially litigants, that postponement causes. Requests for continuance seem rarely to consider the needs and commitments of litigants and witnesses.

Because you sometimes have no choice but to ask for additional time, let the court know as soon as possible of your inability to meet a deadline. Explain the reason candidly. Admit that you simply weren't able to get something done within the set time. That's better than inventing an excuse that the court might view as implausible.

Don't make a habit of asking for more time. When discussing a trial date with the court, estimate realistically the time needed for discovery and motion practice. Anticipate the delays involved in getting medical and expert reports and depositions. Build in time for mediation or other settlement efforts. Know what else you have to do in the meantime. Ask for deadlines and a trial date that you reasonably expect to meet.

Once a schedule is in place, keep to it if at all possible. Avoid procrastination. It takes only a couple of requests for postponement of trial, especially requests made shortly before trial dates, for your standing in the court's eyes to dwindle.

You never want to provoke a court into saying no when you and your client really need a yes. When you deal with judges, your reputation for diligence may be second only in importance to your reputation for integrity.

Third, be prepared.

Tardiness and requests for extensions of time are, at worst, venial sins. Being unprepared is a much more serious professional failing. Lack of preparation, especially if manifested during trial, can injure a lawyer's reputation irremediably.

Coming to an initial pre-trial conference without having done what a judge expects or orders—going over the agenda with all counsel or providing an initial status report and proposed schedule—gets things off to a bad start. At best, it causes the conference to take more time, and perhaps accomplishes less, than it otherwise might.

Lack of preparation for settlement conferences and, concurrently, lack of consideration for the court, opposing counsel, and your own clients are even more dismaying. Many courts have a timetable for offers and responses and for submissions of ex parte or similar statements. Where counsel fails to meet those deadlines, the settlement conference is not likely to be successful.

The court's annoyance may not be the worst consequence. Failure to prepare for a settlement conference, especially where the judge takes an active role, can seriously disadvantage your client. If the court has received settlement statements from everyone but you, its view of the case, its merits, and its potential value will be unavoidably distorted. Not knowing your view of the case, the court may encourage an outcome that, if ultimately accepted, might be less favorable than if you had been a fully prepared participant.

Lack of preparation for trial is, of course, most unpardonable and most dangerous—not just to your reputation, but to your client's well-being as well. Direct examination is no time for discovery of what a witness has to say; doing so on cross-examination is even more risky.

Even if a lawyer has conducted all necessary discovery and mastered what it discloses, failure to prepare carefully for direct and cross-examination will put off both the court and the jurors.

There rarely is too short an examination. Jurors dislike an aimless, rambling, and seemingly unending examination—especially a cross-examination. The longer an examination goes, the less productive or, at least, the less persuasive it may be. More cases probably have been lost by cross-examination that lasted too long than by cross that ended too soon.

Failure to prepare carefully for cross-examination is like setting sail in a rudderless boat without a chart. There will be a lot of movement but not much progress. Sinking on the shoals of unanticipated and unwelcome answers will be a constant danger.

Less dangerous manifestations of lack of preparation may also hurt your case and your reputation with the court. Your fumbling through a file or box of documents for the next exhibit may be recalled when the exhibit is not. The equivalent in today's electronic world—not knowing how some technological marvel works—will leave jurors, especially those under 30, distracted and unimpressed in equal measure.

Fourth, be meticulous when you write.

Most lawyers pride themselves on their oral skills and assume that they are just as persuasive when they put pen to paper. Sadly, that is often not the case. Turgid prose makes for unpersuasive arguments. Native talent alone rarely results in good writing. Effective legal writing doesn't just happen. It comes from careful thought, deliberate effort, and thorough editing, all of which take time.

Good writing pays handsomely. A well-written brief is always more persuasive, even where the facts and the law would favor the author of a poorly written brief. More than ever, your stature as an advocate depends not on how well you can present your case orally but on how well you do so in writing. Trials are few and far between. The outcome of cases increasingly depends on motions and briefs.

You want your name on a brief to be a sign that it will be comprehensive and concise. You want the judge to expect that you will state the facts and the law accurately and clearly. You want the judge to look forward to arguments that will be instructive, illuminating, and persuasive. The last thing you want is for a judge, on seeing your name on a brief, to open it with a heavy heart, mentally exhausted from the anticipated travail of working through dense and dull legal prose.

Content alone does not suffice. Proofread. Otherwise, typos and other errors will be distracting and may even cause the judge to lose sight of your argument.

Bad writing can be remedied, and the writing of even chronically poor writers can become—with enough attention and work—robust and vigorous. Good writing is an excellent way to create a good reputation in the mind of a judge.

Fifth, state the facts and cite the law accurately.

Nothing devalues an argument more thoroughly than misstated facts. A misstatement of facts, even if unintended, stains your reputation for care and candor.

Recite not just the facts that make your case. It is just as important for your credibility and the forcefulness of your assertions to acknowledge the unhelpful facts.

Be equally accurate and complete with your exposition of the law. Misrepresentation of the law will indelibly tarnish your reputation for competence and probity.

Good research uncovers cases in support of your claim. Better research discovers those that challenge your contentions. The best research finds them all, good and bad, recites their holdings accurately, and shows the court why it should follow one line of cases and ignore the other.

Bad research either fails to find the unhelpful cases, or, if they are found, acts as though they do not exist. Worse research claims that such cases are distinguishable without telling the court why that is so. The worst research misquotes cases, pretending that they stand for something other than what the court will learn when it reads them.

Don't assume that the court won't bother to read the cases. It will. If a court believes you led it astray, whether intentionally or not, all your assertions will be suspect. Once the court thinks that you failed to read even just one case carefully, it will doubt the accuracy of your recitation of all the cited cases. Few briefs, no matter how well written or otherwise persuasive, can recover from such doubt on the part of the court.

The effects of poor research last well beyond the ruling in a particular case. Once a judge (or a law clerk) views a lawyer's research as unreliable, that lawyer's future handiwork will be discounted, if not disregarded, before the first page is turned.

Moreover, a judicial declaration in an opinion that a brief inaccurately stated the facts or law can never, in the age of Westlaw and LexisNexis, be stricken from your professional record.

Sixth, emphasize the essential and ignore the trivial.

Some cases are simple, and all can agree on the significant facts, even when the parties dispute those facts and controlling law. Other cases have lots of facts and many issues, some significant, others far less so.

If you can't prevail on your strongest contentions, you're unlikely to win with ones that are trivial. Be selective. Focus on what matters and will make a difference. Don't squabble over every bagatelle and bauble in the case. Pick the fights you need to win.

If you can't discern the major issues in your case, or if you obscure them in a mass of pages about things that don't matter, don't expect the court to see and rule on what counts. This is especially true with discovery disputes, which most judges heartily dislike. They expect and want counsel on their own to resolve nearly all discovery issues. The heavy heart with which most judges turn to motions to compel is not lightened where the response to every interrogatory is "overbroad, unduly burdensome, and not calculated to lead to discoverable information."

If you don't pick discovery disputes with care, and habitually run to the court needlessly, you'll come to be known for crying "Wolf, wolf." Don't wear down a court's patience; if you do, you may not get the attention you need and your client deserves when you want it most.

Seventh, don't sandbag your opponent in your reply brief.

Some lawyers withhold their strongest arguments and cases until their reply briefs. This may seem to be an effective way to disarm the opposition and beat back its arguments.

It is not. All it does is annoy the court. As a result, the court may sua sponte strike your reply brief for failing to be limited to arguments in the response brief. Or it may give your opponent leave to file a surreply brief. This will shorten the time available to the judge to read and decide the motion. The judge will view you as acting both unfairly and unprofessionally. The court will give less credence to whatever you have to say. Sandbagging is no way to gain a good reputation as a fair and competent advocate.

Eighth, avoid ad hominem arguments, sarcasm, and similar rhetorical techniques.

No judge likes to watch grown-ups being nasty to each other and calling each other names. Even if you genuinely believe that opposing counsel is being deliberately dishonest with the court, don't call him or her a liar. Don't say your opponent is being purposefully inaccurate. Don't say "tain't so."

Simply tell the judge what you believe the facts are and then prove them to be so. Keep in mind the old saying: "You draw more flies with honey than vinegar."

Aside from not liking the spectacle of a verbal food fight, judges are likely to conclude that if all you have to offer are insults, sarcasm, and snide comments, there's nothing of substance in what you have to say or write. The mud you throw is as, if not more, likely to stick to you as to the other guy.

165

Even if you prevail in the exchange, the judge will infer that in the future you'll be a troublemaker in need of close monitoring.

Ninth, let opposing counsel speak without interruption.

Sure, you have a right to be heard, but then so does the other lawyer. You are less likely to get a fully attentive and sympathetic hearing if you interrupt while your opponent is in the midst of speaking.

Let the other lawyer speak at will for whatever time the court is willing to listen. Be patient and attentive. When it's your turn to speak, make good use of your time, anticipating that you'll be able to do so without interruption (except from the court).

Interruption never makes a weak argument stronger. Rudeness, whenever it occurs and whatever form it takes, simply marks you as unprofessional.

So wait your turn. Patience is not just a virtue—it is always a desirable and worthy professional attribute. Your reputation for patience will stand you in good stead. The lawyer who listens attentively and quietly while others speak is often the lawyer whom the court hears best.

Tenth, let the judge speak without interruption.

Judges generally believe that what they have to say is worth listening to. They even believe that what they have to say, if not necessarily incisive, is nonetheless decisive. You will hardly help your case by trying to keep the court from coming to the end on its own.

Interrupting the judge is unlikely to lead the court in the direction you wish it to go. At best, it shows that you believe that what you have to say is more important than what is on the judge's mind.

Eleventh, answer the judge's questions.

Good lawyers do not see questions from the bench as getting in the way of their eloquence and the elegance of their arguments. On the contrary, even when the judicial question disrupts a train of thought or argument, the seasoned advocate welcomes the interruption. Judicial questions allow the lawyer to understand and respond to issues troubling the court.

Sometimes judges miss something important, either factual or legal. A judge's questions can alert you to that possibility and allow you to clear away the fog of judicial confusion.

If you don't understand a judge's question, say so. Ask that it be repeated or rephrased. Under no circumstance should you ignore any question. Every ignored question is a hole drilled in the bottom of your legal boat. If you don't know the answer, ask to leave to supplement your brief. You may not help your case by telling the court you don't know the answer, but you'll hurt it less than by making up some off-mark response or imagining that no response is necessary.

Don't be upset if the judge seems to ask hard questions of you but not your opponent. The judge is doing you a favor by letting you know what you have to do to prevail. Welcome that opportunity. Keep in mind that an unexpected question, if you pay attention and think about it, may not be off base; indeed, it may be on point—perhaps even on a point helpful to you.

Never tell the court that you'll get to a question "in a minute," or "I'm coming to that." Such reactions are not just unresponsive, they are rude and counterproductive.

Unanswered questions obstruct the force and flow of the arguments that follow. To be most persuasive, focus primarily on the issues the court raises and then turn to the ones you wish to present.

Every unanswered question leaves an impression of evasiveness and lack of confidence in your argument and case. That impression can never help. At worst, the unanswered question will be on the judge's mind when deciding the case. The answer the judge then comes to is not likely to be as favorable to your case as the one you had a chance to give.

Twelfth, know the rules of evidence.

At some point, judges will form impressions of how well you know and follow the evidentiary rules. If, for example, you constantly place a gag on your witnesses by asking them leading questions on direct, judges will be frustrated at not being able to hear what the witnesses have to say. You also risk the disruption of objections and a disjointed presentation. Frequently sustained objections will lessen your credibility with the jurors as well.

Even if leading questions don't evoke an objection, the jury will be far less convinced if the lawyer is the source of information, rather than the witness. Jurors want to hear the story from the witness: If leading questions keep them from doing so, they may conclude that the witness or the lawyer, or both, have something to hide.

If you give the judge the impression that you either don't know or care to follow the rules of evidence, you will be less likely to prevail when the outcome of an objection is a close call.

Few attributes enhance a trial lawyer's standing in the courtroom more than a reputation for knowing and following the rules of evidence. Lawyers who have that reputation often receive from judges the deference that attentive students give to a learned teacher.

The courts of appeal know that trial judges, when confronted with an evidentiary issue, usually have little time for reflection and none for research. Appellate judges understand that the exigencies of trial compel judges to rule in haste. The standard of review is highly deferential, and erroneous evidentiary rulings almost never result in reversal.

That being so, favorable rulings on close evidentiary calls can prove decisive. Develop and deserve a courthouse reputation as a master of evidence. If you do, judges, especially newer and less confident or knowledgeable judges, will respond favorably when you assert that the rules of evidence require the result you want. The strike zone will be wider for you and narrower for your opponents.

Thirteenth, accept adverse rulings.

Some lawyers continue to argue even after they have won a ruling. Many more continue to argue after they have lost one. The message to the judge is that what the court has said either remains open to debate or doesn't matter. Either way, the message is highly annoying. Once a judge has ruled, stop arguing and don't ignore the ruling. Make your record and move on.

Even if you are firmly persuaded that the judge has made a prejudicial error, let the adverse ruling lie until you have a chance to present controlling authority to the court. Even then, proceed with caution, and be certain that the point is worth renewed pursuit.

No judge welcomes or likes motions for reconsideration. Rightly or wrongly, courts believe they decide matters correctly. The last thing any judge wants to do is revisit something that has already been decided. If you make a habit of filing motions for reconsideration each time you lose a motion, you will make judges very unhappy to see you again. And you are unlikely to prevail.

Fourteenth, don't tell the court it has committed reversible error.

No judge likes to be reversed. But it is a fact of judicial life that goes with the territory. For an advocate to tell a court that it has just committed reversible error is usually seen as an insulting threat. "Change your mind or else" is, however, hardly likely to cause the court to change its mind. It is more likely to brand you as an impertinent would-be bully who has probably—and to the misfortune of his reputation, case, and client—forgotten who is in charge.

What should you do if you believe that a ruling or decision is, in fact, erroneous and irredeemably harmful to your case? First, make sure the error is preserved for review. Next, if you have not done so before, call the judge's attention to controlling authority. If you have not given the court that authority sooner, tell the judge why you did not do so. Then wait until you are in the court of appeals to contend that the error is reversible.

Fifteenth, don't view every negative event as a manifestation of judicial hostility.

Some, but far from all, adverse rulings are an indication of judicial unfriendliness. If that seems so, ask yourself, as objectively as possible, whether you might be the cause of the judge's apparent petulance.

Usually, the judge is truly calling them as they appear to be. Give the judge credit at least for trying to do so. By all means, never display annoyance or incredulity when a ruling goes against you.

Don't be discouraged if you seem to be losing a lot more evidentiary rulings than your opponent. Seasoned lawyers understand that the time to start worrying is not when they are losing objections but when they are winning them all. Courts like to protect the record once they view the outcome as clear. Nothing more quickly and properly dissuades a potential appellant than a record replete with rulings in his or her favor.

Communicating, no matter how subtly or obliquely, a belief that the judge is wrong-headed will only lead the judge to think the same of you.

Sixteenth, don't get angry when the judge does.

Judges get paid to keep their tempers. Some judges habitually don't deserve a paycheck. Others, even those whose judicial temperament normally is exemplary, occasionally erupt.

You'll not help an already volatile situation by losing control as well. The best response after a judge has unfairly pinned your ears to the far wall is to ask for a recess. It will give the judge time to cool off and calm down and for you to figure out how to extricate yourself from a painful impasse.

Someday you may find a lawyer who won a shouting match with a judge. When you do, ask how it was done. It probably won't be an example or experience worth replicating. Until then, the hotter the judge becomes, the cooler you must be.

Seventeenth, be forthright.

A well-founded reputation for integrity is the lawyer's most important attribute.

Whenever you do something as a lawyer that causes someone to doubt your candor and honesty, your professional standing slips. Let it slip often enough, and whatever good reputation you once had will be lost forever.

Whence comes a reputation for integrity? From dedication to making the judicial system function as it ought. This means telling the full story—what Mark Twain called "the plain unvarnished" truth—in your briefs and statements to the court. Nothing is gained from not doing so:

Your opponent will fill in what you've left out, and, what's worse, correct any misstatements of fact or law.

Don't make up excuses—whether for being late or unprepared or for honest mistakes. Don't attribute your mistakes to the judge's staff or anyone else. Don't claim that something was not on your calendar—especially not, as once happened to me, after your secretary has told the judge's office that it was.

It's not a sign that you stand high in a judge's regard if, whenever you speak with the judge, even on the most insignificant of occasions, a court reporter is at the judge's side.

Judges may forget much and forgive more, but they never forget or forgive a lawyer's dishonesty. Just as there is no such thing as being a little bit pregnant, there is no such thing as being a little bit dishonest.

A good reputation is invaluable. Honesty really is the best policy. Make that your guiding star and you will earn, deserve, and keep the best of all possible reputations.

The Road to Lead Plaintiff: The Basics

By Aimee Williams

Becoming lead plaintiff in a private securities class action can be a contentious process, complicated by inconsistent opinions regarding what constitutes sufficient notice, who has the largest financial stake and is the most adequate plaintiff to represent the class, who has standing to challenge the notice and lead plaintiff motions, and other related issues. Rather than exploring the intricacies of such case law, the purpose of this article is to provide the new practitioner with a basic road map of the process, which is guided by the Private Securities Litigation Reform Act of 1995 (PSLRA), in keeping with its intent to prevent lawyer-driven litigation.

CERTIFICATION MUST BE FILED WITH THE COMPLAINT

The road to becoming lead plaintiff begins with the filing of the complaint on behalf of a purported class. In addition to filing the complaint, a plaintiff seeking to serve as the class representative must file a sworn certification, personally signed by the plaintiff, that meets each of the requirements enumerated in the PSLRA.[1]

ADEQUATE NOTICE MUST BE PROVIDED

Once the complaint and certification are filed, a plaintiff must satisfy the PSLRA's notice requirement. No later than 20 days after filing the complaint, the plaintiff must publish a notice advising members of the purported class of the pendency of the action, the claims asserted in the action, and the purported class period.[2] The notice also must advise that, no later than 60 days after the date on which the notice is published, any member of the purported class may move the court to serve as lead plaintiff.[3] If the notice lacks sufficient detail to inform the reader of the general nature of the claims and fails to provide an avenue for further inquiry, the court may deem it insufficient and require the plaintiff to republish the notice.[4]

From the **Securities Litigation Journal**/Spring 2006/ABA/Section of Litigation
[1] *See* 15 U.S.C. § 78u-4(a)(2)(A) (2005).
[2] *See* § 78u-4(a)(3)(A)(i).
[3] *See id.*
[4] *See, e.g.*, Haung v. Acterna Corp., 220 F.R.D. 255, 258 (D. Md. 2004) (PSLRA requirements not met where notice failed to inform reader of legal basis for claim and lacked the case name, docket number, judge's name, and court's address).

Publication of the notice must be in a "widely circulated national business-oriented publication or wire service."[5] Although this phrase is not clearly defined by the PSLRA, the publication is intended to be "reasonably calculated to reach, at the least, sophisticated and institutional investors."[6] Courts' interpretations of this requirement have varied. For example, one district court concluded the *New York Times* was not sufficient, while another court determined that publication on *Business Wire* satisfied the notice requirements.[7]

Frequently, multiple actions are filed on behalf of a purported class. If the actions assert substantially the same securities claim or claims, only the plaintiff in the first-filed action is required to publish a notice.[8] It is not uncommon, however, for other plaintiffs' firms to publish notices similar to the initial notice in hopes of attracting a potential lead plaintiff as a client. This practice is starting to draw reactions from the plaintiffs' firms that filed the first action and published the initial notice.

THE COURT APPOINTS LEAD PLAINTIFF

As previously noted, any member of the purported class may file, no later than 60 days after publication of the notice, a motion seeking to serve as lead plaintiff. Within 90 days of publication of the notice, the court must consider any motion made by a purported class member in response to the notice and appoint as lead plaintiff the member or members of the purported plaintiff class determined by the court to be the most adequate plaintiff.[9] If consolidation of multiple class actions asserting substantially the same securities claims is sought, the decision on the motion to consolidate must be rendered before the court may appoint the lead plaintiff.[10] Under these circumstances, the court must appoint the lead plaintiff "[a]s soon as practicable" after the consolidation decision is rendered.[11]

The most adequate plaintiff is the purported class member most capable of adequately representing the interests of class members. The PSLRA imposes a rebuttable presumption that the most adequate plain-

---

[5] § 78u-4(a)(3)(A)(i).
[6] Greebel v. FTP Software, Inc., 939 F. Supp. 57, 64 (D. Mass. 1996).
[7] *See Haung,* 220 at 258; *Greebel,* 939 F. Supp. at 64.
[8] *See* § 78u-4(a)(3)(A)(ii).
[9] *See* § 78u-4(a)(3)(B)(i).
[10] *See* § 78u-4(a)(3)(B)(ii).
[11] *See id.*

tiff in a private securities action is the person or group of persons that, in the determination of the court, has the largest financial interest in the relief sought by the class and otherwise satisfies the requirements of Federal Rule of Civil Procedure 23.[12] This presumption may be rebutted only upon proof by a member of the purported class that the presumptively most adequate plaintiff will not fairly and adequately protect the interests of the class or is subject to unique defenses that render such plaintiff incapable of adequately representing the class.[13] A plaintiff may conduct discovery to rebut the most adequate plaintiff presumption if the plaintiff first demonstrates a reasonable basis for finding that the presumptively most adequate plaintiff is incapable of adequately representing the class.[14] Although beyond the scope of this article, it is important to note that courts differ as to whether a group of otherwise unrelated investors may satisfy the most adequate plaintiff presumption by aggregating their individual losses to give the group the largest financial stake in the litigation.

To further discourage lawyer-driven actions, the PSLRA imposes limitations on "professional plaintiffs." Except as otherwise permitted by the court, a person may not be a lead plaintiff, an officer, director, or fiduciary of a lead plaintiff, in more than five securities class actions brought as plaintiff class actions pursuant to the Federal Rules of Civil Procedure during any three-year period.[15] Courts have discretion in enforcing this provision and have made exceptions, particularly where institutional investors are involved.[16]

CAN DEFENDANTS CHALLENGE THE LEAD PLAINTIFF PRESUMPTION?

The PSLRA is silent as to whether a defendant may rebut the presumption regarding the most adequate plaintiff, and courts are divided on the issue. Many courts have concluded that, based on the plain language of the statute, formal challenges to the appointment of the most adequate plaintiff are limited to those of other purported class members. For example, in *Greebel*, the court determined that defendants could not oppose a lead plaintiff motion on grounds related to movants'

---

[12] *See* § 78u-4(a)(3)(B)(iii)(I).

[13] *See* § 78u-4(a)(3)(B)(iii)(II).

[14] *See* § 78u-4(a)(3)(B)(iv).

[15] *See* § 78u-4(a)(3)(B)(vi).

[16] *See, e.g., In re* Fannie Mae Sec. Litig., 355 F. Supp. 2d 261, 264 (D.D.C. 2005).

satisfaction of criteria for lead plaintiff prior to the class certification stage.[17] On the other hand, defendants could raise procedural objections to the adequacy of plaintiffs' certification and notice.[18]

Other courts disagree with the *Greebel* court's interpretation of the PSLRA provisions governing appointment of lead plaintiff, concluding that nothing precludes or limits defendants' right to oppose a lead plaintiff motion.[19] And a few courts that have declined to acknowledge defendants' formal standing to challenge the appointment of the most adequate plaintiff have nonetheless considered, sua sponte, defendants' arguments and authorities in making their appointment.[20]

---

[17] *See Greebel*, 939 F. Supp. at 60–61.

[18] *See id.*

[19] *See, e.g.*, King v. Livent, Inc., 36 F. Supp. 2d 187, 190 (S.D.N.Y. 1999).

[20] *See, e.g., In re* First Union Corp. Sec. Litig., 157 F. Supp. 2d 638, 641–42 (W.D.N.C. 2000).

Oral Argument— Comportment in the Courtroom

A Few Do's and Don'ts of Oral Argument
By Thomas J. Donlan

One of those old sayings—that happens to be true—is that "experience is the best teacher." Unfortunately, at today's billing rates, most clients do not want to pay for you to get that experience at the appellate level. Nor can you afford to lose an appeal for a client because of a lesson you had not learned yet. Fortunately, in the words of another old saying, an inexperienced attorney can "learn from the mistakes of others." A good way to do that is to go to an appellate court and just watch. You will be surprised at how many lawyers, even some experienced ones, make obvious mistakes during oral argument. If geography or finances makes going to the appellate court yourself unrealistic, you can talk to other attorneys who have been there. Old "war stories" have been a favored teaching tool, probably since Neanderthals were hunting mastodon. The following are some practical do's and don'ts based on anecdotes (which are just "war stories" told somewhere other than a veterans' bar) from appellate courts across the country.

1. DO KNOW THE RECORD

You may think that of course the lawyer knows the record; she tried the case. However, often that is not true. There are good reasons why the lawyer who argues the appeal may not be the lawyer who tried the case. Trial advocacy and appellate advocacy often require different skills. An attorney may be dynamic at trial, able to connect with a jury, but not as comfortable or effective in the intellectual interplay with a panel of judges about pure legal issues. Some trial attorneys do not like appellate work. It doesn't provide the rush of slugging it out with the other side, setting up the witness for the one critical question, or delivering that stirring summation. Other attorneys simply do not get enough opportunities to feel comfortable arguing an appeal.

In addition, a fresh point of view at the appellate level often benefits the client. An attorney who has lived with the case all the way up through trial develops a certain set view of the issues and evidence. This may be hard to change on appeal, particularly when the decision went against her at trial. The new appellate attorney comes to the case without those fixed perceptions. Finally, some clients simply want a new attorney to handle the appeal because the previous one lost at trial.

Whether you tried the case below or not, however, you must master the record. Your credibility with the appellate court can be severely damaged if you do not know what the record says on a critical point. Yet this happens far more frequently than you would think.

The attorney is arguing an issue of liability. His legal arguments are well constructed and appear persuasive. Then one of the judges interrupts and asks, "Counsel, didn't one of the witnesses say that the instrument was broken?" The attorney pauses, perhaps flips through notes furiously and then looks up at the judge, says that he is not sure and continues, "Well, you know, your honor, I did not try the case."

Whatever the point was, odds are that the attorney just lost the judge. Remember, the appellate judge did not try the case either. However, she has prepared, read the briefs and record excerpts, and is ready to discuss how the facts influence the legal argument being made. At the very least, it shows a lack of respect not to have worked as hard as the judge. Further, such lack of knowledge certainly is a failure of the duty owed to the client. The lawyer who makes such a statement had better hope that his client is out of town, not sitting in the courtroom listening to such a telling admission.

The requirement to know the record applies equally to the attorney who did try the case below. It is frequently a long time between the end of trial and the argument on appeal. Do not think that just because you were there at trial, you will remember everything that happened—or the way it happened. (Attorneys are often surprised after trial by what actually appears in the transcript—"Did I really say that?") Review of the record is vital even if you were there when the trial took place.

One subset of this rule concerns the situation where the person arguing not only did not try the case, but also did not write the brief. Although this more likely involves an experienced advocate in a large firm, it can happen anywhere, depending on the division of labor. The appellate advocate has two demands now: to know the record and to know the brief. In truth, the most devastating question is not "Didn't the record say . . . ," but rather, "Didn't you state in your brief . . ." (something different from what you just argued to the panel). That actually happens, too.

Every rule has exceptions, of course. The appellate court usually will understand if you cannot remember some less significant point. Depending on the court, you may be able to offer to review the record after the argument and clarify the issue with the court by letter. For the most part, if the point has any importance at all, the judge rightly expects you to be prepared to discuss it at the argument. For the attorney trying to hide behind not having tried the case below, there is simply no reprieve.

2. DO PREPARE TO ANSWER QUESTIONS

Another old saying is: "How do you get to Carnegie Hall? Practice, practice, practice." It is the same for oral argument. You must be prepared not only for questions about the record but also for questions about your argument. The best way to prepare for questions is to practice answering them. Do not write a speech. This is not a trial where you get to present an eloquent closing and the jury has to sit there. Unless you have an ice cold bench, you will get questions—and be expected to answer them. The judges already have your brief (and in most cases have read it). Oral argument, as the experts constantly remind us, is intended to be a dialogue. Whether or not you think a judge has already made up her mind, this is your last chance to convince her. So you need to be ready with the answer that persuades her (or at least tries to disguise the hole in your argument).

The best form of preparation involves others. You have lived with this case, perhaps since trial. You have developed your arguments, refined them, and now, as the date for oral argument approaches, you feel pretty good about them (except for those cases where the client demands to take an appeal after you tell him that he has no chance). The problem is that you may be wearing blinders as to problems with your argument.

Involving other attorneys, especially ones who have not been working on the case, allows you to get ready for the unexpected. What is it that even your opponent might not have focused on, which can threaten or even derail your argument? Once again, a fresh set of eyes is a benefit.

How you involve others is a matter of individual preference. Many attorneys like to do a moot court. Go to a conference room with two or three attorneys and the clock running, and have the attorneys fire questions at you. Afterward you can get feedback on your answers and refine and improve them. Repetition is important, so depending on the importance of the case, doing more than one moot court can be a great tool. One prominent attorney in a CLE program explained that he was unable to craft a satisfactory answer to a question until his third moot court. But when he appeared before the U.S. Supreme Court and got the same question he was prepared—and won.

Other appellate advocates prefer brainstorming sessions to moot courts. A group of attorneys joins with the advocate and tosses out ideas, issues, and potential questions. Charles Fried, a former U.S. Solicitor General used this approach. Before a Supreme Court argument on an important issue of military law, he gathered together both civilian attorneys from the Department of Justice as well as active duty military lawyers. For a couple of hours, Fried led a spirited discussion sitting on the couch in his office overlooking the Mall in Washington, D.C. Fried's subsequent impressive—and successful—argument was a tribute not only to his skill as an advocate but also to the depth of his preparation. The method you choose is up to you. Perhaps it could even be a combination, moot court followed by brainstorming. However, take the time and prepare for the court's questions.

3. DO ANSWER THE JUDGE'S QUESTIONS

Oral argument is not a presidential debate. The judge has not asked a question merely so that the lawyer can go off on a tangent to make a scripted statement. A good, experienced advocate can use an answer to a question as a springboard to make a point she wishes to get in. However, first you need to answer the judge's question.

Every attorney has a question she dreads and hopes to avoid. But when the question comes, it is far better to give the best answer that you came up with during all of that preparation—and then take the heat, if necessary. If you try to avoid answering, you could end up like an unfortunate lawyer appearing before Judge Posner of the Seventh Circuit. Judge Posner asked a question, and the lawyer danced around the answer. Undeterred, Judge Posner asked the question again. The lawyer once more sidestepped the question, perceiving, quite correctly, that there was no good answer for the argument he was making. Judge Posner then told the attorney to stop and answer the question, "yes" or "no." The lawyer tried again to avoid answering, claiming that the question could not be answered "yes" or "no." Finally, a visibly exasperated Judge Posner said: "Counsel, just answer yes or no." The result? The lawyer ended up aggravating the judge and still had to give an answer that was damaging to his argument.

At an oral argument, the judges are in charge. They get to ask the questions. Whether you like the question or not, whether there is an answer that helps your case or not, you need to answer the question. Every case has weaknesses or issues you wish were not there. The skill of an advocate is addressing them in such a way that the rest of your argument remains standing. Trying to dodge and weave occasionally may look like it's working, but the judge knows whether her question received an answer. At best, dodging a question hurts your effort to be persuasive. At worst, you can be publicly embarrassed, like the attorney before Judge Posner.

You should never be afraid to answer a question. This is your opportunity to persuade. No appellate case is perfect. Every one has some weakness, large or small. Your job as an appellate advocate is to convince the members of the panel that, on the whole, your arguments are the better ones. If you have prepared, the question should not be a surprise, and you can give your best answer. Your candor with the court will help your presentation, even if you do not succeed on that particular point.

Answering a question is not the same as conceding an issue. You may perceive that a line of questioning is focused on forcing you to surrender part, or all, of your argument. The way out of this trap is not avoiding the question but, instead, standing up for your position by saying no to the requested concession. Again, you may not win the point, but you will not antagonize the court or appear evasive, which is detrimental to your credibility on other points.

4. DO NOT MAKE SWEEPING STATEMENTS THAT MAKE YOUR JOB HARDER

Most lawyers long for the chance to strike a blow for justice, to stand up for the little guy, to make a real contribution to the law. In practice, few cases offer that opportunity and even fewer often a chance to make an impassioned argument to an appellate court. Most appeals turn on rather narrow issues of law (or less frequently, of fact). Yet you will see lawyers include in their argument grand proclamations, which are far broader than necessary to win an appeal. The problem with such statements is that they are often more difficult to defend than the essential point. Moreover, sweeping generalizations invite tougher questions from the bench.

In a case before the U.S. Supreme Court, an advocate began his argument with such an expansive statement concerning jurisdiction. He barely finished the sentence when Chief Justice Rehnquist demanded,

"Where in our case law do you find support for that, counsel?" The problem was that none of the prior cases had ever gone as far as the lawyer was stretching the law. The attorney was on the defensive and stayed there throughout his argument. The sad point was that there was good case law supporting the attorney's central argument. Clearly Chief Justice Rehnquist was hostile to the attorney's position and unlikely to vote in his favor. However, by reaching too far, the lawyer opened himself up to the Chief Justice's attack and an entire range of questions, with no good answers, on ground he did not have to defend.

It is important before the argument to decide just what you need to win. While it may be exhilarating to deal with big issues, it may not be necessary. Focusing in on the central elements of your case also helps define the other limit to your argument—what you cannot concede. When pressed by a judge to abandon certain arguments, you will know what you must preserve and not be trapped into giving away your crucial points. Careful selection will ensure that your argument is aimed at what is really important for your client to succeed rather than what makes you feel important.

Obviously, there are cases that you cannot win without expanding the scope of prior decisions. That is better done openly, rather than by appearing to claim that the prior case law has gone farther than it has. Attorneys too frequently mischaracterize the scope of existing decisions to make it appear that their point is included. While occasionally an overworked trial judge may accept such a misrepresentation, a panel of appellate judges is all too likely to see through it.

There are those cases where great principles are at issue, where the advocate is indeed striving for a tectonic shift in the law. If you are privileged to argue one of those rare cases, cherish the opportunity. Yet even there, the rule applies—do not reach or claim more than you must to win for your client.

5. DO KNOW WHEN TO SIT DOWN

One of the hardest things, once the argument begins, is knowing when to stop. You have prepared for a long time, you have waited during the arguments before yours, you have waited for your opponent—finally it is your turn. So far, things have gone well; the panel really hammered opposing counsel. In fact, the judges have made most of your points. You launch into your argument and notice that you are not getting any questions. What a great opportunity to make your highly polished points without interruption—or is it?

Perhaps, instead, it is time to ask the panel if they have any other questions and, if not—sit down. This is a difficult decision and only the most experienced and accomplished advocates are comfortable when the situation arises. Solicitor General Fried, in arguing the military law case to the U.S. Supreme Court, gave a stunning demonstration of how less can be more. The Solicitor General was arguing that the Supreme Court should overrule a precedent. After a little more than twenty minutes of dialogue with the Court, the justices appeared to run out of questions. So Fried politely said "If the Court has no further questions, I will relinquish my remaining time"—and he sat down, with almost ten minutes of time remaining.

Most advocates before the U.S. Supreme Court would not even consider giving up some of their precious time, but that may be the best choice. If the panel gives a clear signal that you are winning, do not risk changing their mind by saying anything more. It is not about your moment in the sun, but the best result for your client. You need not fear that the court has secret questions you will fail to address by stopping before your full time has expired. If the court has additional questions, they will inevitably tell you, if you politely ask them, before sitting down. You only have to see one lawyer snatch defeat from the jaws of victory by talking long after she should have sat down to realize that silence can be golden.

6. DO LOOK IN THE MIRROR

Personal appearance is a delicate issue in today's American society. It is tied up in issues of self-expression, popular culture, conformity, and tradition. Few attorneys would show up to argue an appeal in jeans and a flannel shirt, regardless of what is acceptable at Microsoft. However, you occasionally see strange sights in the courtroom. You need to keep in mind who you are representing and what you are trying to say.

Once an attorney appeared in the U.S. Supreme Court to argue a search and seizure issue. His client, whom the lawyer had represented at trial and before the Ninth Circuit, had been convicted on a drug charge involving a substantial amount of money. The attorney appeared in a striking silver grey suit and photogray glasses. Being from a warm climate, the attorney's glasses were designed to deal with very sunny days. As the attorney approached the lectern, he looked up at the lights above the bench—and his glasses immediately darkened. There he stood, arguing for his drug-dealing client wearing the equivalent of Hollywood shades.

A set of do's and don'ts is not intended to double as fashion advice, merely to pass on experiences. Perhaps in thinking about your appearance, you might consider that the judges you will argue before are dressed in black robes that go back centuries and have not been seen elsewhere in modern society, outside of choirs and graduations, in almost that long.

Whatever you decide to wear, it is best to keep it on. In another courtroom, on a warm sunny day, a lawyer was sitting at counsel table while his opponent argued. Apparently affected by the heat, the lawyer rose and—while the panel looked on in amazement—removed his coat, hung it on the back of his chair, loosened his shirt and sat down again. Nothing was said by the judges at the time or when the attorney arose to present his argument. However, one of the judges was heard to remark, at a subsequent social event, that he had never seen such a disrespectful display in his entire time on the bench. While the judge never said the attorney's actions affected the decision, when the opinion came out, the undressed attorney lost.

Looking in the mirror involves more than what you are wearing. It includes what you are saying and how you are saying it. Appellate advocacy requires heightened self-awareness and a willingness to change. No one style of dress or presentation is appropriate to all cases. While you must ultimately be comfortable with the approach in a given case, you should always be checking the mirror to see how that approach looks from the outside.

Appellate advocacy is challenging, rewarding, and on occasion nervewracking. There is much to be learned by watching the masters, lawyers who regularly appear before the appellate courts. They provide a model to which to aspire. However, for many attorneys, better lessons can be learned by watching or hearing about the lawyers who really foul up. You may not be blessed with the special ability to argue with the very best, but by paying attention to the basic do's and don'ts, you can easily avoid being thought of as among the worst.

Young Lawyer Focus: "A list of the things, in no particular order, that I wished I was told and was not . . . and the things I was told but only really understood during or after the argument"

By J.D. Barnea, Gabrielle Bina, Elisabeth Brown, Ethan Glass, Adam Gromfin, Doug Keller

1. **Conduct mock oral arguments with "judges" unfamiliar with your case.** While the attorneys you've worked with on your appeal can, and will, hit you with hard questions during your mock oral arguments, they are likely to be questions that you have previously discussed, researched, and perhaps even briefed. Involving attorneys in your mock oral arguments who are unfamiliar with your case—and even unfamiliar with the area of law at issue in your appeal—will force you to respond to questions that you had not anticipated. For example, your mock judge may come up with a sticky procedural question or an issue related to the standard of review that is potentially dispositive of the case, but was never identified by opposing counsel. Even if such questions never come up during your real argument, it is beneficial to prepare yourself for the feeling of having to respond to unanticipated issues on-the-fly.

2. **Don't assume your entire oral argument will be consumed by answering judges' questions.** Rather, prepare an entire presentation of the case, just as if you were not going to be asked questions by the judges. This way, in the unlikely (but still possible) scenario in which you are the recipient of a panel of blank stares—as I was during my first argument—you'll have something prepared to say. Also, if at any point the lively discussion dies down, you'll have somewhere to return to.

3. **The judges are unlikely to be convinced that your criminal client is in fact innocent.** By the time one finishes writing a criminal appeal, it is quite easy to be convinced that your client has been wrongly accused and convicted. One can even convince oneself that it has to be obvious to anyone upon the reading of the introduction of your brief.

4. **Don't assume that the judges will care about the gross injustices involved in your client's case.** After spending many hours

thinking about your client's plight, you're likely concerned about the gross injustices involved in your client's treatment—this is particularly so in immigration and criminal cases. But don't assume that the judges will see the same injustice as you or that they'll have a similar reaction to the injustice. The judges will have a much wider range of experiences than you and they've likely seen much worse.

5. **Even though it's easy to be intimidated by the panel, treat the argument more like a conversation and less like a debate.** It's easy to view the argument as, well, an argument. And it obviously is insofar as you'll hopefully convince the panel that you're right and your opponent is wrong. But the discussion is much more likely to be fruitful (and convincing) when you aren't trying to score points or be overly defensive. Instead, the tone of the debate should be one of equals exchanging ideas on the issue before the Court. It's easy to be overly deferential to the panel, which does your client a disservice. Speaking to the panel respectfully, yet as an equal, lends your arguments a lot more credibility than they otherwise might have.

6. **Learn every page of your excerpted record/joint appendix—not just the pages you quote from directly.** Having been told repeatedly, "learn the record," when it came time to prepare for argument, I diligently read both parties' briefs, being sure to look at corresponding record cites as I proceeded. I thought surely I was learning the record that way. At oral argument, however, one of the panelists asked a fact question about my client's verification of his complaint. Because neither side had briefed the (in)adequacy of the verification, I had not focused any attention on it during preparation. This left me in the uncomfortable position of having to find the verification, read it, think about it, and advocate around it, all while the clock was ticking and the judge grew impatient. Had I approached the record differently—by reading it not only in conjunction with the briefs, but also independently—I would have been more familiar with the issue. I may not have been able to predict the judge's question (neither side having raised it), but I would have at least had a more solid foundation on which to build.

7. **If you don't have a direct answer to a direct question, say so and offer to submit supplemental briefing.** It's easy to feel like you have to answer every question the judges ask you. And you should prepare in such a fashion that you'll be able to answer

every question. But if you get a question that you simply don't know the answer to—a question about where in the record something is located, perhaps—be honest with the panel: you don't know, but you're happy to submit supplemental briefing on the point. Don't waste the court's time with an attempt to come up with an answer that will only mislead the court.

8. **Directly answer judges' questions.** We all have been confronted with a question that seems to misunderstand an argument, and our natural response is to say something like, "well, that's not really the right question" or "that is actually irrelevant to my argument." At least that was my approach during my first argument. While preparing for my next argument, another lawyer suggested that I directly answer such questions before qualifying the answer or quibbling with the question, not just as a matter of respect (which is important!), but also to improve the flow of the argument. At that next argument, I fielded a question that I thought was misdirected and answered it, "I think the answer is no, your Honor. But let me explain why I think that question does not really get to the heart of the matter. The real question is ____, and the answer to *that* question is yes." The judge responded, "Oh, I understand. Thank you."

9. **Get your outline/notes down to one page.** While it is common (and even suggested) to prepare an outline of your argument, anything more than a page is likely to be a crutch rather than an aid. When notes/outlines are too detailed, we have a tendency to get wedded to them, often losing the flexibility that is necessary to field unpredictable questions and to adjust as necessary. In my experience, my detailed 8-page topical outline proved far less useful (I never referred to it once argument began) than the very skeletal 1-page outline I brought to the next argument. I included a couple introductory sentences just to get the argument flowing, and then a very simple sketch of the points I thought I had to make before argument ended. That simpler outline acted as a good roadmap and checklist, especially when the argument tended to stray a bit.

10. **Be willing to adjust the angle/theme of your arguments; you do not need simply to repeat your written arguments.** We have a tendency to think that oral argument is simply about defending our briefing. This is true to an extent, of course, but only to an extent. Oral argument is a chance to *supplement* arguments you made in your briefs—to highlight a particular angle that seems to

make more sense once you have had a chance to take a step back from briefing, to fill holes that moot argument revealed, etc. Trust that your briefs speak for themselves, and use oral argument as a chance to be more fluid and less rigid. As a panelist told me at oral argument, "Yes, I've read your brief on that matter. I'm interested if you have anything else you'd like to add." That welcomed invitation gave me an opportunity to focus on a point that I thought needed some bolstering. The court appreciated it, and actually relied on the point I made at oral argument when writing its opinion. Next time I will not wait for such an invitation to veer a bit from my briefing.

11. **There are ways to get extra-record evidence before the panel.** We all know that an appeal is generally limited to the documents on the district court's docket. But don't fall prey to ignoring important evidence that is not on the docket. For example, the most common tool is to ask the court of appeals to take judicial notice of the facts. Additionally, you can move the court of appeals to correct omissions or misstatements (rare), consider matters before the district court but not entered on the civil docket, supplement the record to avoid dismissal for lack of subject matter jurisdiction or in other "extraordinary cases." While you should be aware of, and use, these tools, you should also be aware that they all have strict limitations is generally limited to the documents on the district court's docket. But don't fall prey to ignoring important evidence that is not on the docket. For example, the most common tool is to ask the court of appeals to take judicial notice of the facts. Additionally, you can move the court of appeals to correct omissions or misstatements (rare), consider matters before the district court but not entered on the civil docket, supplement the record to avoid dismissal for lack of subject matter jurisdiction or in other "extraordinary cases." While you should be aware of, and use, these tools, you should also be aware that they all have strict limitations that should not be breached.

12. **Oral argument may not be the end of the case.** Oral argument may not be the end of your case. If the other side thinks they are going to lose, you may end up dealing with mediation or settlement. Despite your own inclination to get a ruling from the panel, you have to make sure it is what your client wants.

Method Acting for Lawyers
By Kathleen B. Havener

The legal affairs commentator on TV described the defense lawyer's closing argument in the celebrity case du jour: "Spellbinding!" he gushed to the newscaster. "The jury was enthralled." Surely every trial lawyer wants to captivate the jurors with such courtroom delivery, but how?

Consider, as you contemplate how to go about enchanting your courtroom listeners, who your competition is. Real-life jurors don't know about the hours of waiting, the insufferable boredom, the endless delays. All they see is what the actors do on *Law & Order, The Practice, Boston Legal, Presumed Innocent, A Civil Action,* and *A Time to Kill.*

Actors use techniques to help them weave believable tales. What can we learn from them? When you talk to the jury, look at the jurors. Watch each one just as you would look at a friend. Like an actor in live theater, pay attention to how the audience is receiving you and adjust your delivery accordingly. The subtle signals you pick up from the jurors will tell you what you might need to repeat, emphasize, or downplay. Pay attention to your own body language, and not just when you speak. You don't have to stand at attention like a guard at Buckingham Palace, but pay attention to your posture. Show respect for where you are and what you are doing. Actors pay attention to their posture because good posture helps the whole body move more fluidly, and they feel more confident. In addition, good posture helps you to project your voice without strain because your diaphragm has more room to do its work. Because your breath supports your voice, everything that impacts your breathing is important. And, as every actor knows, a person with good posture is more pleasing to watch. Slouching is distracting.

When you're not speaking, you're not invisible. Just as actors must remain in character whether or not the scene revolves around their role, you must be conscious of how you look to your audience at all times. Jurors will certainly notice how you conduct yourself, in the spotlight or not. Leaning back in your chair looks sloppy and inattentive. Remember the "bad boys" in junior high who slouched in their desks at the back of the classroom? Somehow, they made their languorous physical

From the **Woman Advocate**/Summer 2007/ABA/Section of Litigation
Reprinted with permission from Litigation, 31:4, *Summer 2005. Copyright 2005 by the American Bar Association.*

posture convey haughtiness and superiority. Hunching makes you appear as if you don't care what's going on, so sit up straight. Letting your eyes wander doesn't make you look thoughtful; it makes you look bored. As the day wears on and your level of fatigue increases, you might have to force yourself to pay attention to your demeanor; but if you're bored and fed up with being in court, think how the jurors may feel about being there.

Sometimes the smallest things about your clothing, as with theater costumes, can make an enormous difference. If you will have to reach up to write at the top of an easel, for example, don't wear clothing that constricts your movement or, worse, rides up when you lift your arms. Make sure your suit fits—no frayed cuffs or torn pockets allowed. The jury will almost certainly note anything that doesn't feel or look right.

If you have not dressed warmly enough, folding your arms across your chest to stay warm can make you look defensive or even frightened, especially if you're a woman. It can also make you appear overly confident and unwilling to listen to another point of view. It definitely puts a barrier between you and everyone else. You're inaccessible and closed off. So don't cross your arms. Another thing to question is the general belief that a room that is slightly too cool helps people to stay alert. For me, it has the opposite effect; I become drowsy and find it difficult to pay attention. Visiting the courtroom in advance will help you dress appropriately and feel more comfortable.

Know how to be still. Shifting your weight from one leg to the other, tapping your foot, tapping a pencil, and even shuffling papers can make you look nervous or, worse, bored. In the courtroom as onstage, every movement is magnified. Hence, one of the cardinal rules of acting: Every movement must have a point. Don't make a single move without a purpose. If you don't have somewhere to go, stay where you are and be still.

Even the most experienced actors have to deal with stage fright. It can make your voice tremble and your hands shake and make you feel and look incompetent even though you aren't. Here are a few simple ways to deal with stage fright.

Remember that the jury is more important than you are. Your purpose is to make them feel comfortable and to help them understand the case in the right way.

Know that fear is contrary to your purpose. In fact, it can project such a negative feeling that it makes you seem hostile. Pretend instead that the jurors are your guests; you'll forget your own fear if you're trying to make sure the jurors feel welcome and important.

Breathe as deeply as you can, concentrating on inhaling to a count of four and exhaling to a count of eight, for a series of ten breaths. Consciously relax your shoulders while you breathe. Just the exercise of concentrating and controlling your breathing really will go a long way toward calming your fear. Deep breathing can even lower your blood pressure.

Consciously relax your jaw. This will help you to sound normal—especially to yourself—when you begin speaking, which will make you feel more comfortable right away.

Never act or feel rushed. Your presentation isn't a race. Express every important word and speak so that the whole room can hear you. If you feel pressured to hurry, deliberately slow yourself down, at least until you feel calmer.

Pretend that the people who are listening couldn't intimidate you if they tried: Imagine your daughter's Brownie troop, your kid brother, the guys you play poker with once a month, a gang of cartoon characters.

Think of yourself as a member of the trial team. It will draw your focus away from yourself and remind you that others matter as much as or more than you do.

Believe in your position, and believe the story you are telling. When you believe with all your heart that you know the truth and are the medium that can convey the truth to the jury, your fear will almost certainly abate. Enthusiasm and conviction are good qualities, not negative ones.

If your true fear is that you will fail in front of your colleagues, remind yourself that your feelings about the case are for the jury and that no one else matters. Forget about what your colleagues think. They don't deliberate, and they can't deliver a verdict. In the courtroom, they are irrelevant.

Pay attention to your voice. Controlling your vocal inflection helps communicate your ideas, and it automatically helps you control your breathing. When you need real power in your speech, forget volume, and use rising, falling, and sustained inflections instead.

Another powerful tool is silence. All actors know that sometimes a pause between lines is not just appropriate but crucial to the scene. Use silence before you begin to speak, to get everyone's attention. Use silence instead of filler, like "Um . . ." Before you make a critical point that you want to drive home, pause for a long moment. Take a sip of water. If the other side or the gallery is making noise and distracting you or the jury, stop talking until the room is quiet again. The room is yours, after all. When jurors are surprised by something, they need a moment to absorb what they've heard. That calls for a strategic pause. If you make the jury laugh, stop and enjoy the joke along with them. Remarkably, the more you use silence effectively, the less anxiety you will feel.

With a little practice, just like an actor, you can use the power in words to persuade juries of the rightness and justice of your cause. All you have to do is play your part.

Using the Lessons of Aristotle to Present Outstanding Oral Arguments, Part I

By Lawrence D. Rosenberg

He would like to thank his college debate partner, Peter Smiley, his former colleagues at the U.S. Department of Justice, and his present colleagues at Jones Day, most notably, Donald B. Ayer, Glen D. Nager, Robert H. Klonoff, and Gregory A. Castanias, for having discussed with him their views on and for shaping his approaches to these subjects.

Delivering oral argument can sometimes appear to be a daunting task. An advocate may experience pangs of self-doubt. He or she may wonder: What if the Judge doesn't like me? What if the Judge thinks my case is terrible? What if the Judge is bored by what I say, or worse, falls asleep? Such concerns are natural. Oral arguments are often difficult. They are sometimes down right unpleasant. But, if you understand what is entailed in presenting an effective oral argument and with some practice, delivering an oral argument to a judge, arbitrator, or mediator can be highly effective in advancing an advocate's position, while being very rewarding for the advocate.

This article sets forth a number of approaches, strategies and tips for presenting outstanding and compelling oral arguments to trial judges, arbitrators and mediators. It begins by turning to an old friend of oral advocates—Aristotle—for some fundamental principles for delivering effective oral arguments. It next examines the critical steps in preparing for an oral argument. Finally, it discusses a number of techniques for presenting outstanding oral arguments in today's courts and ADR settings.

THE BASICS OF EFFECTIVE ADVOCACY AS DEFINED IN ARISTOTLE'S *RHETORIC*

As college debaters and students of "rhetoric" will tell you, the original master of rhetoric was the ancient Greek philosopher Aristotle. Many of his works addressed effective methods for presenting arguments. Perhaps his most important work in this regard is his tome dedicated entirely to the subject, *Rhetoric*. That work goes into great detail about how a public or legal speaker can most effectively convey arguments and represent a client.

From the **Trial Practice Journal**/Summer 2007/ABA/Section of Litigation

Three basic principles guide Aristotle's advice for effective advocacy: *ethos, pathos* and *logos*. *Ethos* is defined as "the speaker's power of evincing a personal character that will make his speech credible." *Pathos* is defined as the speaker's "power of stirring the emotions of his [audience]." *Logos* is defined as the speaker's "power of proving a truth, or an apparent truth, by means of persuasive arguments." *Aristotle's Rhetoric* (W. Rhys Roberts Tr. 1954), *available at* www.iastate. edu. Each is important for an effective oral argument. And each can be cultivated by the careful actions of an oral advocate.

Ethos. Looking at *ethos* more closely, there are a number of things that a speaker can do to enhance his or her "personal character" and "credibility":

- **Likeability.** First, and most obviously, it helps the advocate to be likeable. That means that the speaker should be polite to both the court or tribunal and his or her opponent, even-tempered, responsive to questions, mindful of time limits, and respectful of the concerns of all present in a courtroom or other forum. One of the quickest ways to lose the quality of likeability is to be rude or abrupt to the court or one's opponent. Failure to answer questions or to answer them in an evasive manner can also get the advocate off on the wrong foot.

- **Preparedness.** It is critical for an effective advocate to be prepared for an oral argument. That means knowing the case, the key authorities, the record, and all of the salient facts extremely well. While a court may have never encountered a particular advocate in the past, the court will very quickly determine if an advocate knows the case factually and legally. Just as a rude or obnoxious advocate can be off-putting to a tribunal, an unprepared advocate will not be taken seriously, and thus will jeopardize any chance of communicating effectively.

- **Honesty and forthrightness.** It is also very important for an advocate to be honest and direct with a tribunal. An advocate must acknowledge the weaknesses in the record or the relevant authorities when identified by the court. And the advocate must directly answer questions, rather than evade them. This is not to say that an advocate should simply give up when confronted with troublesome cases or deficiencies in the record. Rather, the advocate should acknowledge those issues and provide the best and most persuasive responses to questions identifying case problems. Credibility is paramount, and one of the worst ways to harm your credibility is to give the impression that you are being dishonest with the court or that you are playing fast and loose with the record or facts.

- **Organization.** Another key to an effective argument is to appear organized as well as to deliver an organized argument. When delivering an argument, the advocate should have all necessary materials close at hand and neatly arranged. When notes are flying off the table toward the judge or when an overlarge stack of legal briefs collapses in the middle of your argument, you are likely to take a major hit to your credibility. Moreover, an advocate who presents a disjointed argument without a clear theme and progression will lose the attention of the audience, regardless of how compelling the substance of the argument actually may be.

- **Clear and understandable delivery.** It is very difficult to accept the resounding persuasive appeal of an argument when one can't understand it. Therefore, it is essential that an advocate deliver the argument in a clear and understandable manner. The advocate must enunciate words clearly, speak with a moderate, easily understood pace, avoid using unfamiliar jargon or idiomatic expressions, and should use pauses and vocal inflection appropriately to emphasize the key points of the presentation.

- **Professional appearance.** While probably not as important as some of the other key qualities noted here, it is always helpful for an advocate to have an appropriate appearance and sense of decorum. It is rarely helpful, for example, to wear ripped or heavily wrinkled clothing when delivering an oral argument. It could be quite harmful to wear attire that is simply not appropriate. While very few prospective advocates would wear a tee shirt and jeans for such an occasion, articles of clothing such as cowboy boots, extremely loud jackets, ties or scarves may be distracting to the court and focus the judge's attention on the advocate's attire rather than upon the case. Such distractions are not helpful.

Pathos. Turning now to *pathos*, There are also a number of things an advocate can do to elicit a favorable emotional response from the court or ADR audience:

- **Highlight the crucial equities favoring your client's position.** While it is always important to present the logical reasons why your client's position is correct, it also helps to highlight why ruling in your client's favor is the fair and just outcome in a particular case. To be sure, harping upon fairness and justice to the exclusion of a persuasive legal argument will not get you very far, but the best oral arguments convey to the audience the sense that your client's position is not only the legally correct one, but is also fundamentally fair, reasonable and just.

- **Highlight the best and most sympathetic facts favoring your client's position.** All legal cases are rooted in their key facts. In most cases, however unsympathetic, there are at least some facts that favor your client's position or side of the story. And persuasive arguments apply the relevant authorities to the facts of your case. Thus, it is natural to highlight the most helpful facts and those suggesting that your client's position is the most sympathetic.
- **Highlight the worst and least sympathetic facts relevant to your opponent's position.** Aristotle has explained that the concept of *pathos* also may require stirring the passions of your audience against your opponent's case. While you must be very careful about pushing this too far, it is certainly reasonable and advantageous to highlight the worst facts for your opponent. The idea is not to make ad hominem attacks on your opponent or to blatantly state that your opponent did awful things. Rather, the skillful advocate can mention certain pejorative facts that will lead the audience to conclude that your opponent has acted improperly.
- **Tell a coherent, compelling, and consistent story.** Oral arguments rarely permit time for lengthy factual recitations. Nonetheless, it is important to highlight the important factual aspects that underlie the case. They provide the essential context. It is critical that those details are packaged to present a compelling, consistent, and reasonable explanation for the actions taken by your client. The facts you highlight and the language chosen to describe those facts can significantly help convey the message you wish to communicate to your audience.

Logos. Arguments to juries may rely primarily on *pathos*. But *logos* is usually the key to persuade adjudicatory tribunals. Indeed, attempts to rely primarily on either *ethos* or *pathos* may backfire badly. That is not to say that professional tribunals are indifferent to either *ethos* or *pathos*, but *logos* is usually most important. It is critical to present your argument in a logical and persuasive fashion. There are a number of things an advocate can do to accomplish this:

- **Select your key issues.** One of the most important steps in preparing for an oral argument is to select the key issues you will focus on during your argument. While there is no "magic number" of exactly how many issues you can present, in most cases you can expect to focus on no more than two to three issues at oral argument. On rare occasions four or more issues can be coherently and persuasively presented, but usually only when arguments in excess of thirty minutes per side are permitted. If you are presenting an oral argument of about twenty minutes per side or less, it will be virtually impossible to present more than three key issues to the court. Select your best issue for oral argument and present that issue first. If your first issue is complex or particularly interesting to the court, it may be the only issue you have time to address in any detail. The process of issue selection is critical. It is the very rare circumstance where an advocate will win a case on the third or fourth argument presented orally to the court. However, it is very common that an advocate's best argument gets muddled and lost among a sea of less persuasive arguments.
- **Carefully structure your argument.** It is critical that an advocate has an organized and logical argument that flows naturally. It is very important to have a coherent structure to your argument. Begin with a preview that quickly mentions the theme or main thrust of your argument and lists your two or three main points. It is then necessary to proceed quickly to your first main point, make a brief affirmative argument on that point and respond to the tribunal's questions as they arise, and move on to your next point or points, if possible. It is also helpful, although not as important, to quickly sum up your argument before you conclude.
- **Develop a coherent and compelling theme.** Each oral argument is designed to persuade the audience to do something. It is critical that the action you wish your audience to take (whether it be to rule in your client's favor on a dispositive motion or to grant some specific form of relief) be clearly stated at the outset. Justification for the tribunal taking the requested action should be provided. For example, you may wish to urge as your theme in an appellate argument that the judgment below should be reversed because the trial court misconstrued the plain language of the contract at issue. Since *logos* is the primary factor when arguing to an adjudicatory tribunal, a theme such as "this stale, twenty-year old case should

be dismissed under the statute of limitations," will generally be more effective than a theme such as "this is a case about refusal to take responsibility for one's actions."

- **Rely on your best and most persuasive authorities.** Obviously, in an argument before a court or ADR panel, you will likely rely on key precedent and other authorities. It is critical that you select the most important and most persuasive authorities that support your position. In a typical oral argument of twenty minutes or less per side, you will only have time to discuss a few key authorities in detail. Before your argument, you should carefully select the cases you want to discuss and mention them where appropriate in your argument. While you must be prepared to address every case cited in the briefs or other materials, you should stay away from any lengthy discussion of authorities that you don't believe are particularly pertinent to your argument. However, that does not mean that you should ignore or sidestep adverse authority. Rather, you must directly address such authority when raised by the court or your opponent.
- **Carefully apply the key authority to your case.** It is not enough to cite and discuss key authority. Moreover, it can be quite dull. To make a compelling legal argument, the advocate must carefully apply that authority to the case at hand to show why and how that the authority prescribes a decision in your client's favor.

"Lame-o"s. My college debate partner added a basic principle to Aristotle's three, which he dubbed as *"lame-o"s*—the speaker's power to make himself or herself look like an idiot. Obviously *lame-os* is something to be avoided. *Lame-os* can take many guises in presenting an oral argument. Obviously, a complete breakdown in front of the court or an inability to answer even fundamental questions about the case demonstrate a severe episode of *"lame-o"s*. However, there are many more subtle ways to practice *lame-os*. Interrupting a judge's question is not a way to endear yourself to the court. Moreover, failing to answer a question or series of questions or doing so evasively or with answers that simply don't make any sense will also dramatically undermine the persuasive value of your argument. If you don't understand the court's question, say so up front. The court will likely respect your honesty instead of believing you to be either dense or deceitful.

I recently attended an oral argument where both advocates managed to come up with bizarre answers to the court's questions. The case involved a criminal defendant, whose lawyer argued that the police had not waited a sufficient period of time between "knocking and announcing" and breaking down the defendant's front door—a period of about four seconds. A particularly interesting colloquy between the court and the defense attorney went as follows:

Q. Is it typical for over thirty police officers to arrive in an attempt to arrest a criminal suspect?
A. Yes, that happens frequently.

Q. Are you serious?
A. Sure.

Q. All right, let's talk about the rocket launcher. You concede that the police had credible information that your client possessed a rocket launcher capable of taking down large aircraft?
A. Yes. But the informant didn't mention the presence of any ammunition.

Q. No ammunition? What, are we supposed to believe your client was doing with the rocket launcher: using it as a coffee table?
A. Possibly. He might have been a collector.

Q. Or maybe he was using it as an umbrella stand?
A. Sure. That's possible too.

Not surprisingly, the court was having difficulty accepting these answers. However, the prosecutor also decided to liven up the proceedings. A colloquy with him proceeded as follows:

Q. So, are you saying that when the police have credible information that an individual possesses more weapons of mass destruction than we have found in Iraq, the police are justified in breaking a door down four seconds after "knocking and announcing?"
A. No. I'm not saying that at all. In this case we had other important facts.

Q. Really, the weapons of mass destruction aren't enough? What other facts should we be considering?
A. The dog.

Q. What are you talking about?
A. The police had been informed that the defendant had a dog. But when they arrived, the dog was nowhere to be seen. Thus, the police reasonably concluded that the dog may have been warning the defendant that the police had arrived.

197

Q. Really. Perhaps the dog was inside arming the rocket launcher.

Needless to say, these colloquies demonstrate both that giving incredible answers to questions posed by the court are not likely to advance your client's case and also that giving defensive answers to helpful "softball" questions is also not likely to help your client's case.

The concept of "lame-o"s highlights that while an advocate is striving affirmatively to advance the *ethos*, *pathos* and *logos* of his or her presentation, saying things that just don't make sense or aren't credible are best avoided.

THE KEY STEPS TO PREPARING FOR AN ORAL ARGUMENT

How do we implement Aristotle's fundamental concepts of *ethos*, *pathos* and *logos* (and avoid the associated concept of *lame-os*) in preparing for an oral argument? Preparation is in many respects the most important process necessary for delivering a compelling oral argument. An advocate must be intimately familiar with the important issues in the case, the primary authorities relevant to the case, the record and facts of the case, and the audience before whom the case is to be argued. The advocate must also anticipate what the opponent is likely to emphasize and what questions the court or ADR panel will likely have. Moreover, most excellent oral advocates practice their argument and the answers they likely will give to the court's or ADR panel's questions many times before they actually deliver their argument. I suggest the following steps to preparing for oral argument; these steps already assume a very good working knowledge of the case, which is a prerequisite to serious oral argument preparation:

1. **Select the key issues for oral argument.** Once an oral advocate has a good working familiarity with a case, the first step is to isolate the key issues to be emphasized at oral argument. I have said that in most circumstances there should only be one, two or three key issues for oral argument. Nonetheless, at the beginning of the preparation process there can, and in some cases should, be more than this. After all, part of the purpose of preparing for an oral argument is to winnow down the issues that you will want to emphasize. With this said, there should be some initial paring down of the issues. There is no magic number, but in most cases there shouldn't be more than five or six issues that you seriously will consider emphasizing at oral argument. Paring down the issues at

this initial stage will improve the *logos* of your argument and will make it much easier to focus the remainder of your preparations.

2. **Become intimately familiar with the record and the facts of your case.** Once you have pared down the issues that you may emphasize at oral argument, it is critical that you carefully evaluate the record and the facts of your case, particularly with respect to those issues that you have chosen to focus upon. You should know every detail relevant to those issues and where that detail can be found in the record. Obviously, the extent of this task will depend upon the stage of the case at which your argument has arisen. If your argument relates to a motion to dismiss in a trial court, the "record" may consist of the complaint and the briefing on the motion to dismiss and little else. If your argument relates to a summary judgment motion or mediation, there may be a voluminous record containing briefs, discovery responses, deposition transcripts, and other materials.

   In all events, the tribunal will likely have questions about the facts of your case and how the key authorities should be applied to those facts. As Judge Alex Kozinski of the U.S. Court of Appeals for the Ninth Circuit has put it, "The law doesn't matter a bit, except as it applies to a particular set of facts. So you will find that judges at oral argument often have a lot of questions about the record." Hon. Alex Kozinski, *How You Too Can . . . Lose Your Appeal*, 23-OCT Mont. Law. 5, at *23-*24 (Oct. 1997).

3. **Become intimately familiar with the primary authorities relevant to your case.** It goes without saying that an oral advocate is expected to know every primary authority very well and to be able to discuss those authorities at oral argument. Accordingly, an oral advocate should very carefully read those key authorities and note the important points from each that may be emphasized at oral argument. This is not to say that an advocate must be intimately familiar with every case cited in every pleading filed during the course of litigation. Rather, the advocate should become intimately familiar with all of the important cases pertaining to the issues that the advocate will emphasize or that may become the subject of discussion at oral argument. It is better to be overinclusive rather than underinclusive. Thus, if you are not sure what cases might become important at oral argument, you should become familiar with all of the cases that might be raised.

4. **Carefully analyze how the primary authorities apply to the facts of your case.** The real "trick" to the *logos* of your legal ar-

gument is to convey effectively how the primary authorities, when applied to the facts of your case, compel the result your client seeks. As Judge Kozinski has noted, "[e]ach case is different insofar as the facts are concerned. Where the lawyer can really help the judges—and his client—is by knowing the record and explaining how it dovetails with the various precedents." Kozinski, 23-OCT Mont. Law. 5, at *24.

5. **Anticipate the main arguments that your opponent will make.** In most circumstances, oral argument in the United States involves both sides presenting their arguments about a particular issue. It is important to anticipate what arguments your opponent will emphasize, what authorities will be used to support those arguments, and what facts in the case your opponent is likely to highlight. By carefully thinking through what your opponent is likely to do at oral argument, you can determine how best to respond to those arguments or how to preempt them with your affirmative arguments. One way to approach this part of the preparation process is to pretend that you are delivering your opponent's argument. By doing so, you can focus on the best authorities and facts for his or her side of the case. Some advocates even go so far as to deliver what they see as their opponent's best arguments to colleagues who have familiarity with the case, so that those colleagues can help determine the best ways to counter those arguments.

6. **Anticipate the questions your judge or panel is likely to ask.** A critical component of the preparation process and to bolstering your *ethos* and *logos* is to determine what questions the tribunal will likely want answered. In one sense, this may be the most important part of the preparation process. After all, your main objective during oral argument is to satisfy the concerns of the tribunal. One way to anticipate such questions is carefully to examine the weaknesses on both sides of the case. Quite often a tribunal will seize upon such weaknesses to determine whether they are fatal to your case or to one of your arguments. Another useful tactic is to have colleagues who are familiar with your case draft a set of possible questions that they think the trubunal may ask. It also is helpful to examine any confusing or controversial aspects of your case and of the primary authorities to determine questions that such aspects may suggest.

Once you have determined what questions that the tribunal may ask, you should then attempt to craft your best answers to each of those questions. By doing so, you can focus on the best authorities and facts for his or her side of the case. Some advocates even go so far as to deliver what they see as their opponent's best arguments to colleagues who have familiarity with the case, so that those colleagues can help determine the best ways to counter those arguments.

7. **Find out as much information as possible about your judge or panel.** As early as possible in the preparation process, you will want to learn the composition of and proclivities of the judge or panel before whom you will be arguing. You will also want to know how the argument will be conducted, the applicable time limits, where you will stand to present argument, and the order of presentation at argument. You will also want to know whether your judge has written any decisions relevant to your case, whether the judge is likely to ask many questions or just a few, whether the judge or tribunal members have any particular academic or ideological philosophy. And you should also try to find out if the judge is personally familiar with any of the lawyers who will attend the argument. If you are able, it is generally a good idea to observe your judge or tribunal before the day of your argument to get a feel for how the proceedings are managed. Once you have acquired all the information possible about your judge or panelists, you will want to reexamine the questions that you determine are likely to arise at oral argument to see whether you have overlooked something that is likely to be of concern to the tribunal.

8. **Prepare an oral argument outline or "cheat sheet."** Once you have completed the prior steps, it is useful to prepare a concise oral argument outline or "cheat sheet" that includes the key points you want to address at oral argument along with the key authorities and citations to the record that you believe will likely arise at argument. As part of this process, you likely will pare down your list of key issues even further. For each issue, list your primary authorities and record citations with a one sentence description of the key points from each. From this, you can create either an outline of approximately one page for each issue, or a "cheat sheet" that is written on or fastened to a folder for which each surface corresponds to one of your main issues for argument (*e.g.*, the front for issue 1, the inside for issue 2, and the back for issue 3). While advocates differ on the kind of outline they may prepare, it is very useful to synthesize the knowledge of your case that you have gained during the preparation process by creating such a tool.

9. **Craft your introduction, conclusion and argument structure.** Once you have completed your oral argument outline (or as part of that process), it is helpful to craft your introduction and the structure of your argument. Your introduction should include a statement of the main theme of your oral argument as well as a short preview of the points you wish to emphasize at oral argument. Typically it should be 30-90 seconds in length, depending on your judge or panel and how likely you are to be able to speak uninterrupted for a given period of time. Your theme can be something very simple such as "under the controlling law, plaintiffs have failed to state a claim for relief, and thus their complaint should be dismissed," or "my client is entitled to summary judgment because the defendant has, as a matter of law, violated the federal antitrust laws in two independent ways." Your introduction should include a very brief statement of the main two or three points you want to emphasize in the order that you intend to present them. Your best and most persuasive point should go first. Your introduction should also include a very brief statement of the relief you seek. You should also craft a very short conclusion—of perhaps ten to fifteen seconds in length—that summarizes your argument and restates the relief you seek. It could be something such as "accordingly, defendant's expert is unqualified and has not used an appropriate methodology in his analysis; his testimony should be excluded at trial."

10. **Determine whether you wish to use any demonstratives or visual aids.** The topic of using demonstratives or visual aids during oral arguments is one that could merit pages of discussion. It engenders severe disagreement among experienced advocates. Certain advocates (in my experience, a minority) believe that visual aids are critical whenever an advocate is communicating orally and attempt to use visual aids in arguments before trial and even appellate courts. They may use boards with documents, charts, graphs or argument points, more complicated computer presentations, or even play video clips when a tribunal will permit such visual aids. Other advocates believe that oral argument (especially on legal motions before trial courts and on appeals) primarily represents an opportunity to answer the questions troubling the judge or panel. Such advocates usually avoid visual aids except in compelling circumstances such as very technical cases were one or two visual aids can demonstrate a complex machine, computer algorithm, chemical compound, or the like. My

advice is to consider carefully your audience, the complexity of the case, and the focus of your argument when determining whether to use visual aids. I have used them and seen them effectively used in trial court arguments and presentations to ADR panels when the case involved complicated facts that had to be understood by the judge or tribunal. On the other hand, I have also talked with and argued before a number of appellate judges who very much dislike such visual aids, particularly in cases that primarily involve a legal issue. Similarly, I have seen trial court judges refuse to permit such visual aids, even after they have been set up in the courtroom. While visual aids are often essential for presentations to juries and may be very useful in certain oral arguments before judges or ADR panels, an advocate must make a careful decision whether to use them at all and must carefully choose any visual aids to use at oral argument.

11. **Perform a moot court or practice argument.** After you have put together your oral argument outline and determined whether to use any visual aids, it is usually very helpful to perform a moot court or practice argument. You could convene a formal moot court with a number of "judges," or simply perform a practice argument before one or two colleagues, who are familiar with your case and who will be able to ask pertinent questions. While excellent oral advocates differ with respect to how they perform such practice arguments (some prefer to treat them much like an actual argument in court, others may prefer simply to have colleagues ask them questions), most generally perform moot courts or practice arguments at least before important or difficult oral arguments. This process can be very important in further paring down your issues for oral argument, examining the weaknesses of your case, and building your confidence as you approach your oral argument. It can also help you to tailor your arguments and your delivery in a manner that will likely achieve the most favorable response from the tribunal. Therefore, this process can strengthen the *ethos, pathos* and *logos* of your advocacy. It also can uncover any tendencies you have that are likely to annoy or offend your audience (such as raising your voice when answering a question that you think is stupid), and therefore can help eliminate *lame-os*.

12. **Revisit your issues for argument and make your final selection of the one, two or three that you wish to emphasize.** Once you have completed the prior steps, you are ready to choose the issues to emphasize at argument that are most likely to result in a

favorable disposition of your case or motion. As explained by Justice Thomas R. Fitzgerald of the Illinois Supreme Court "[t]he lawyers who seem to give the best arguments are [those] who are able to find the most important issues in the case and argue those issues. . . . I think there is a real art in identifying the issues that are the ones that give them the best chance of success." Daniel C. Vock, *Appellate lawyers' version of high wire act: Oral argument*, 150 Chicago Daily Law Bulletin 81.

13. **Practice your argument again.** As your final step in preparing for an oral argument, you will probably want to practice your argument some more. This can be done in a formal setting with one or more colleagues who are familiar with the case. It could also be done at home before your spouse or child. Or, it could be done alone in front of a mirror or a wall. The idea is to become as verbally fluent as possible with the key points you wish to emphasize, the authorities and record cites you wish to rely upon, and the structure of your argument including your introduction and conclusion. You should not attempt to memorize a prepared "speech" because the most important part of your argument will be your responses to the questions you receive. Rather, you want to become as familiar as you can with your affirmative argument and the responses you want to give to the questions you have anticipated.

Now that you have completed the preparation for oral argument, it is time to actually deliver your argument. Good luck!

KEY TIPS FOR DELIVERING AN OUTSTANDING ORAL ARGUMENT

Having completed your careful and extensive preparations for argument, it is now time to actually present your oral argument. There are a number of things that you can focus upon to present the best argument possible:

Answer the judge's or panel's questions directly and honestly. The most important element of compelling oral advocacy is to be as responsive to the judge's or panel's questions as possible. This is effectively the "prime directive" of oral advocacy. If an oral advocate is evasive or incomplete in his or her answers to the judge's questions, that advocate will lose credibility with the court, thus harming the advocate's *ethos*. The advocate will appear to lack answers to the questions the court or panel is concerned with, thereby harming his or her *logos*. And the court or panel may become annoyed with the advocate, leading to an episode of *lame-os*. As Judge Richard A. Posner of the U.S. Court of Appeals for the Seventh Circuit has stated "[s]ome lawyers are terribly afraid of answering questions, because they're afraid it's a trap and that their answer is going to be treated as a fatal concession. So they fence and they evade, and that, of course, annoys the judges." Vock, 150 Chicago Daily Law Bulletin 81. Similarly, Judge Kozinski has noted the dangers of interrupting a judge's question or evading it: "Once the judge starts to ask a question, raise your hand in a peremptory fashion and say, 'Excuse me, your honor, but I have just a few more sentences to complete my summation and I'll be happy to answer your questions.' This will give the judge a chance to dwell on the question, roll it around in his mind and brood about it." Kozinski, 23-OCT Mont. Law. 5, at *24.

Quickly deliver your introduction and attempt to adhere to your argument structure. Because you may get little uninterrupted time to deliver your introduction, do so as quickly as you can and move on to your first point. Once your first point has been covered fairly well and there are no questions pending, move on to your second point. But always be mindful of the prime directive that you must answer the tribunal's questions directly and completely. Even if doing so will destroy the structure of your argument, it is more important to answer the panel's questions than it is to retain the structure of your argument at the cost of addressing the panel's concerns. Therefore, it may make sense to move on to another point when there is a lull in the questioning or when your answer to a question presents a natural opportunity to move to do so. This process is more art than science. It is often very difficult to transition from one point to another when your tribunal is particularly interested in your first point. However, that is not usually a bad thing. If you have structured your argument effectively, your first point should be your strongest. Thus, to the extent that the tribunal is focusing on that argument, it should mean that the tribunal is seriously considering it. I think the best advice here is to be flexible. If the tribunal really wants to take up your entire argument time with your first point, let that happen. If you can skillfully move on to your next points, do so, but not to the exclusion of answering the tribunal's questions.

Weave your key message into your answers to the tribunal's questions. An important tactic for delivering an outstanding oral argument is to weave your key theme, message or points into the answers to the questions you are asked. As Judge Posner has stated, the "critical skill" for effective oral advocates is to build connections between your answers and your message: "If the lawyer, having answered the question briefly, then elaborates his answer in order to bring another point he wants to make, that's not going to bother the judge." Vock, 150 Chicago Daily Law Bulletin 81. One technique for doing this is to respond to a question by saying "I have two responses." The first response can directly answer the question, while the second response can reiterate your theme or make an additional point you believe important. Another technique is to answer the question directly and then conclude by explaining that the question underscores the important point you made earlier—at which time you can then reiterate your theme.

Do not under any circumstance disrespect the court or belittle the questions asked. As a corollary to the prime rule of answering the judge's or panel's questions, you should never disrespect the court or panel. Doing so will significantly reduce the *ethos* and dramatically increase the *lame-os* of your presentation. Judge Kozinski has noted that if you really want a seemingly insignificant question to take on "monstrous significance," "[a] good way to start is by ridiculing the question: 'I was afraid the court would get sidetracked down a blind alley by this red herring.' Mixing metaphors by the way, is always a good idea; it makes it look like you're spinning your wheels after you've missed the boat because you went off on a wild goose chase." Kozinski, 23-OCT Mont. Law. 5, at *24-*25. Furthermore, Judge Kozinski warns of the dangers of "cutting off the judge in the middle of a question":

> First, it's rude . . . . [b]eyond that, cutting off the judge mid-question sends an important message: Look here your honor, you think you're so clever, but I know exactly what is going on inside that pointed little head of yours. Then again, cutting off the judge gives you an opportunity to answer the wrong question. When I pointed this out to a lawyer one time, he told me, 'Well, if that's not the question you were asking, it should be.'

Id. at *25. How's that for a advanced case of *lame-os*?

Accurately portray the relevant authorities and facts of your case. It is critical to be direct, honest and forthright with the tribunal. If the tribunal gets the sense that you are misstating the authority or the facts of your case, you will lose great credibility and your *ethos* will suffer. Moreover your ability to present an argument appealing to either the audience's sense of justice or logic will be dramatically reduced. Thus, the *pathos* and *logos* of your presentation will suffer as well. It is also extremely unlikely that a misstatement will go unnoticed. Most judges prepare for oral argument and are relatively well versed in the key authorities and facts of your case by the time of the argument. It is possible that if an authority or fact is trivial, the court may not be aware of it and may not follow up on your misstatement at oral argument. But if the authority or fact is trivial, why misstate it in the first place? If the authority or fact is significant, it is very likely that the tribunal will realize that you have misstated or inaccurately portrayed that authority or fact.

A corollary to the rule against misstatements is the principle that you should not overclaim the strength of your case. As Judge Kozinski has explained (*Id.* at *24):

> A good way to improve your chances of losing is to overclaim the strength of your case. When it's your turn to speak, start off by explaining how miffed you are that this farce—this travesty of justice—has gone this far when it should have been clear to any dolt that your client's case is ironclad. If you overstate your case enough, pretty soon [the judge] will take the bait and ask you a question about the very weakest part of your case. And, of course, that's precisely what you want the judges to be focusing on—the flaws in your case.

Don't make a jury speech. Oral argument presents a wonderful opportunity to focus the court or panel on the critical points, authorities and record citations you wish to emphasize. Don't waste that opportunity by making an unbridled appeal to *pathos* in the manner that an effective trial lawyer may do before a jury. Adjudicatory tribunals are much less likely to be swayed by one party's bad conduct, ad hominem attacks on the opposing party (even if justifiable), or blunt arguments that a certain outcome would just be "wrong." Such tribunals are usually much more interested in how the key authorities apply to the facts of your case and whether that application prescribes the outcome your client desires. As Judge Kozinski has explained in the analogous context of appellate argument:

> When a lawyer resorts to a jury argument on appeal, you can just see the judges sit back and give a big sigh of relief. We understand that you have to say all these things to keep your client happy, but we also understand that you know, and we know, and you know we know, that your case doesn't amount to a hill of beans, so we can go back there in the conference room and flush it with an unpublished decision. (*Id.* at *25)

Be very careful using analogies or maxims in your argument. Aristotle believed strongly that the use of analogies or maxims could be very helpful in persuading a court or judge to act as an advocate desired. He was right. An analogy, maxim or story that fits well can enhance your argument and help your chances of winning your case or motion. One of my colleagues recently argued a statutory-interpretation case before the U.S. Supreme Court. He argued that his opponent's interpretation, while possibly supportable by the language of the main sentence itself, could not be reconciled with the language of the rest of the statutory provision in which it was located. To conclude his argument, my colleague referred to the parable of the blind man who comes upon two thick trees, unable to understand that the soft tube between them was really the trunk of the elephant that he stood before. My colleague's use of that parable was extremely effective, and he won his case. But an advocate must be very careful using such devices at oral argument. It is very easy to have a seemingly excellent analogy fall apart under questioning, or worse, be turned by one's opponent. In an argument several years ago, an advocate used a baseball analogy to describe his case for the court, only to have his opponent quickly co-opt that analogy to describe how the advocate had swung and missed with each of his three major arguments and had "struck out" with his case. The point here is not that you can never use an analogy, maxim or parable. But you must be very careful. It may make more sense to use such a device to conclude an argument, rather than earlier when it might be more exposed to attack or co-option. If you think there is any risk that your analogy or maxim could be turned against your position, don't use it.

Deliver your argument clearly and at a moderate pace. When we get nervous, many of us speak very quickly, our voices raise, or we may garble certain words. Keep these possibilities in mind. Speak too quickly, and you will lose your audience (unless your audience is a group of college cross-examination debate coaches). Speak too slowly, and you will annoy your audience. Enunciate clearly. Avoid monotones. But avoid excessive drama as well in your manner of speaking. It is also a helpful technique to use pauses to underscore important points as well. The goal is to have a conversation with the court. In doing so, an effective advocate may often use very short or clipped sentences. You may wish to answer a question by saying "No, for two reasons" or "Let's look at the legislative history." The point is to communicate effectively, not produce a beautiful transcript. If you are comfortable doing so, you may wish to use slow, smooth (rather than hard and choppy) hand gestures to emphasize a point. But do so only if you naturally use such hand gestures. It may help to speak as if you are having a conversation with a good friend. Use a conversational tone and approach and you should be able to communicate with your audience.

Be very careful with use of any visual aids. If you have decided to use visual aids during your argument, be very careful with them. If the judge or panel seems irritated or is not following your use of the visual aids, abandon them. If using your visual aids is bogging down the argument, seriously consider only using a few of them. Most importantly, do not allow your use of visual aids to hamper your responsiveness to the court's or panel's questions. There was a recent argument in which the advocate used a significant number of PowerPoint slides during an extended presentation of over one hour in length. While the advocate's use of the slides was mostly effective, at one point, the judge stated that he would like the advocate to "take a break" from his presentation to answer questions that were troubling him. It is very important when using visual aids is to do so without creating the appearance that the presentation is more important than responding to the court's or panel's concerns. Otherwise both your *ethos* and *logos* could suffer substantially.

Act professionally at all times. It is critical to your *ethos* to act as a professional at all times during an argument. Do not raise your voice. Do not show anger, even if legitimately provoked. Do not in any way suggest you believe any questions to be either irrelevant or ill-conceived. When sitting at counsel table, speak in a quiet whisper, if you must speak at all. Do not vigorously shake your head or make facial contortions during the proceedings. Treat your colleagues and opponents with respect at all times. Be aware that when delivering an argument in court, there will almost always be one or more law clerks present in the courtroom well before the judge arrives on the bench. They will watch and scrutinize everything you say or do in the courtroom. If you interact with any of your colleagues in the presence of the judge, panel or any of their staff, treat your colleagues with respect at all times. There was a trial a number of years ago during which one attorney would verbally abuse his legal staff while the judge and jury were absent, but while the judge's law clerk was in the courtroom. It quickly became apparent that the judge as well as his staff viewed that attorney as a "jerk." If you act professionally at all times, your behavior will never come back to haunt you.

Dress professionally. While this is not usually an issue with most oral arguments and advocates, it can be very important. When I was a law clerk to an east-coast appellate judge many years ago, there was one case where an advocate delivered his argument in a loud orange jacket and cowboy boots. Suffice it to say that the most memorable thing about his argument, and the primary element that was discussed by the law clerks, was the advocate's attire. An advocate has to be sensitive to the standards of decorum of the forum in which he or she will argue. In certain parts of the country, wearing cowboy boots to court is commonplace and accepted, while other more formal attire may not be. Indeed, I remember a case in which I was involved a few years ago where local counsel warned me and my colleagues that cuff links and pocket squares were too "east coast" and should be avoided in the courts of his locale. As a general rule, understated and conservative business attire is usually appropriate. But it always helps to speak with local counsel if you have never appeared in court in a particular area to learn the local practice and customs.

Be very careful in using humor. As a character in a *Star Trek* movie once remarked, "humor is a difficult concept." Most experienced oral advocates would likely advise never to use humor at oral argument. That may be too stringent. On rare occasions, a judge or panelist with a good sense of humor may make a joke that could effectively be responded to with a humorous statement. Also on rare occasions, a line of self-deprecating humor might be effective. In such circumstances, the use of humor can improve the *ethos* of your presentation by lightening the mood and showing that you have a sense of humor. But you do have to be very careful. The use of humor in an inappropriate circumstance or before a judge or panelist who does not appreciate the use of humor, or does not appreciate your sense of humor, can do great damage to your credibility.

Watch and listen carefully to the arguments that precede yours. You can often learn a great deal about the approach and demeanor of the judge or panel by listening to arguments which precede yours. You can also learn if there are any special procedures or courtroom etiquette of which you are unaware. If you are fortunate, you may also be able to determine whether there are any special characteristics of your judge or panel that you should bear in mind—the judge hates to be interrupted or prefers to be called "your honor"; the judges seem to have a good sense of humor; or the judge is exhausted and looks ready to fall asleep.

CONCLUSION

Oral argument presents a great opportunity to focus your audience on the key points of your case. By bearing in mind Aristotle's time-honored principles of *ethos*, *pathos* and *logos* and the associated concept of *lame-os*, you can deliver a credible, logical and emotionally compelling oral argument. If you also prepare carefully and thoroughly, you can become an outstanding oral advocate and significantly advance your clients' interests. Speak up. The legal world is listening.

Using the Lessons of Aristotle to Present Outstanding Oral Arguments: Part II

By Lawrence D. Rosenberg

In the previous issue, we examined Aristotle's fundamental concepts of *ethos, pathos* and *logos* (and the associated concept of *"lame-o"s*). Those concepts relate respectively to persuading your audience through your credibility as a speaker, your appeal to the audience's emotions, and the precise logic of the your arguments, and the associated principal of trying to avoid looking like a complete idiot. We now examine how to implement those concepts in preparing for and delivering outstanding and compelling oral arguments.

THE KEY STEPS TO PREPARING FOR AN ORAL ARGUMENT

Preparation is in many respects the key and most important process necessary for delivering a compelling oral argument. In all but the simplest and most limited of circumstances, it is impossible to deliver a compelling and persuasive oral argument without significant preparation. Quite simply, an advocate must know his or her case inside and out to be able to deliver an outstanding oral argument. This means that the advocate must be intimately familiar with the important issues in the case, the primary authorities relevant to the case, the record and facts of the case, and the audience before whom he or she will argue. The advocate must also anticipate what his or her opponent is likely to emphasize and what questions the court or ADR panel will likely have. Moreover, most excellent oral advocates practice their argument and the answers they likely will give to the court's or ADR panel's questions many times before they actually deliver their argument. While excellent oralists may differ in their views of exactly how to prepare for an oral argument, or the order of steps that should be taken to prepare, I would be very surprised to find any excellent oral advocates who would disagree about the importance of preparation. I suggest the following steps to preparing for oral argument; these steps already assume a very good

From the **Appellate Practice Journal**/Spring 2006/ABA/Section of Litigation
(*The author would like to thank his college debate partner, Peter Smiley, his former colleagues at the U.S. Department of Justice, and his present colleagues at Jones Day, most notably, Donald B. Ayer, Glen D. Nager, Robert H. Klonoff, and Gregory A. Castanias, for having discussed their views on oral argument preparation and delivery and for shaping the author's approaches to these subjects.*)

working knowledge of the case, which is a prerequisite to serious oral argument preparation:

Select the key issues for oral argument. Once an oral advocate has a good working familiarity with a case, I think the first step to preparing for oral argument is to isolate the key issues that you want to emphasize at oral argument. While at the end of the preparation process, there should in most circumstances only be one, two or three key issues for oral argument, at the beginning of the preparation process there can, and in some cases should, be more than this. After all, part of the purpose of preparing for an oral argument is to winnow down the issues that you will want to emphasize. With this said, there should be some initial paring down of the issues. There is no magic number, but in most cases there shouldn't be more than five or six issues that you seriously will consider emphasizing at oral argument. Paring down the issues at this initial stage will improve the logos of your argument and will make it much easier to focus the remainder of your preparations.

Become intimately familiar with the record and the facts of your case. Once you have pared down the issues that you may emphasize at oral argument, it is critical that you carefully evaluate the record and the facts of your case, particularly with respect to those issues that you have chosen to focus upon. You should know every detail relevant to those issues and where that detail can be found in the record. Obviously, the extent of this task will depend upon the stage of the case at which your argument has arisen. If your argument relates to a motion to dismiss in a trial court, the "record" may consist of the complaint and the briefing on the motion to dismiss and little else. If your argument relates to a summary judgment motion or mediation, there may be a voluminous record containing briefs, discovery responses, deposition transcripts, and other materials. And if your argument is part of an appeal of a trial court's disposition, the record may be even more voluminous. It is important to realize that at whatever stage of a case your argument has arisen, the court or ADR panel will likely have questions about the facts of your case and how the key authorities should be applied to those facts. Without intimate knowledge of the record and the facts, an advocate simply will be unable to answer many of the questions that are likely to be asked at the oral argument. As Judge Alex Kozinski of the U.S. Court of Appeals for the Ninth Circuit has put it, "[t]here is a quaint notion out there that facts don't matter on appeal—that's where you argue about the law; facts are for sissies and trial courts. The truth is much different. The law doesn't matter a bit, except as it applies to a particular set of facts. So you will find that judges at oral argument often have a lot of questions about the record." Hon. Alex Kozinski, *How You Too Can . . . Lose Your Appeal*, 23-OCT Mont. Law. 5, at *23-*24 (Oct. 1997).

Become intimately familiar with the primary authorities relevant to your case. It goes without saying that an oral advocate is expected to know every primary authority very well and to be able to discuss those authorities at oral argument. Accordingly, an oral advocate should very carefully read those key authorities and note the important points from each case or other authority that he or she may wish to emphasize at oral argument. This is not to say that an advocate must be intimately familiar with every case cited in every pleading filed during the course of litigation. Rather, the advocate should become intimately familiar with all of the important cases pertaining to the issues that the advocate wishes to emphasize at oral argument or that may become the subject of discussion at oral argument. In making such preparations, it is better to be overinclusive rather than underinclusive. Thus, if you are not sure what cases might become important at oral argument, you should become familiar with all of the cases that might be raised.

Carefully analyze how the primary authorities apply to the facts of your case. The real "trick" to the logos of your legal argument is to convey effectively to the court how the primary authorities, when applied to the facts of your case, compel the result your client seeks. Therefore, it is very important to determine how the key authorities apply to your case and how that application shows that you should win. As Judge Kozinski has noted, "[e]ach case is different insofar as the facts are concerned. Where the lawyer can really help the judges—and his client—is by knowing the record and explaining how it dovetails with the various precedents. Familiarity with the record is probably the most important aspect of appellate advocacy." Kozinski, 23-OCT Mont. Law. 5, at *24. This process may be time consuming, and occasionally frustrating, but it is critical to crafting a compelling oral argument.

Anticipate the main arguments that your opponent will make. In most circumstances, oral argument in the United States involves both sides presenting their arguments about a particular issue. It is important to anticipate what arguments your opponent will emphasize, what authorities he or she will attempt to use to support those arguments, and what facts in the case he or she is likely to highlight. By carefully thinking through what your opponent is likely to do at oral argument, you can determine how best to respond to those arguments or how to preempt them with your affirmative arguments. One way to approach this part of the preparation process is to pretend that you are delivering your opponent's argument. By doing so, you can focus on the best authorities and facts for his or her side of the case. Some advocates even go so far as to deliver what they see as their opponent's best arguments to colleagues who have familiarity with the case, so that those colleagues can help determine the best ways to counter your opponent's arguments.

Anticipate the questions your panel is likely to ask. A critical component of the preparation process is to determine what questions the court or ADR panel is likely to ask during the course of your argument. In one sense, this may be the most important part of the preparation process. After all, one of your main goals at oral argument is to satisfy the concerns of the court or your ADR panel. One way to anticipate the panel's questions is to carefully examine the weaknesses on both sides of the case. Quite often a judge or ADR neutral will seize upon such weaknesses to determine whether those weaknesses are fatal to your case or to one of your main points. Another useful tactic is to have colleagues who are familiar with your case or have worked on it draft a set of possible questions that they think the court or panel may ask. It also is helpful to examine any confusing or controversial aspects of your case and of the primary authorities to determine questions that such aspects may suggest. Once you have determined what questions the court or panel may ask, you should then attempt to craft your best answers to each of those questions. By doing so, you will gain even greater familiarity with your case and will help to prepare for the critical function of answering the questions that you actually will receive at oral argument. U.S. Supreme Court Chief Justice John Roberts emphasized this point in an article he wrote while in private practice: "Given the prevalence of 'hot' benches and abbreviated argument times," "your preparation should place a premium on making points concisely: you should have at your fingertips 30-second answers to the most likely questions." John G. Roberts Jr., *Thoughts on Presenting an Effective Oral Argument*, School Law in Review 1997, at 7-2 (available atwww.nsba.org/site/docs/36400/36316.pdf). By undertaking this exercise, you will likely provide better answers at the oral argument, thus enhancing the logos of your advocacy. You will also likely gain confidence in your presentation, thereby bolstering the ethos of your advocacy.

Find out as much information as possible about your judge or panel. While this step can be undertaken earlier in the preparation process (and you should do it earlier if you know the identity of your judge(s) or ADR panel/neutral well before your argument), if you have not yet done so, and once you have become intimately familiar with your case and your opponent's likely arguments and determined what questions will likely arise at the oral argument, you should find out as much as possible about your judge or panel. You will want to know how the argument will be conducted, the applicable time limits, where you will stand to present argument, and the order of presentation at argument. You will also want to know whether your judge has written any decisions relevant to your case and the issues that may arise at argument, whether the judge or panel is likely to ask many questions or just a few, whether the judge or panel members have any particular academic or ideological philosophy. And you should also try to find out if the judge or any panelists are personally familiar with any of the lawyers who will attend the argument. If you are able, it is generally a good idea to observe your judge or panel before the day of your argument to get a feel for how the proceedings are managed. Once you have acquired all the information possible about your judge or panelists, you will want to reexamine the questions that you determined are likely to arise at oral argument to see whether there are additional questions that you think might arise in light of the information you have acquired.

By gaining all the information you can about your audience, you are likely to be able to enhance all facets of your presentation. Your comfort level with the particular judge or panel will likely increase, thus enhancing the ethos of your advocacy. You may determine ways to appeal to your audience's sense of justice or fairness, thus enhancing the pathos of your presentation. And you are likely to determine the most effective ways of delivering your key analytical points, thus strengthening the logos of your advocacy. Finally, you may discover any particular approaches or tactics that your judge(s) or panel particularly dislike, thereby helping you to steer clear of "lame-o"s.

Prepare an oral argument outline or "cheat sheet." Once you have completed the prior steps, it would be useful to prepare a concise oral argument outline or "cheat sheet" that includes the key points you want to address at oral argument along with the key authorities and citations to the record that you believe will likely arise at argument. As part of this process, you likely will pare down your list of key issues even further, possibly to its final form, or possibly to four or fewer issues. I recommend that for each issue you list your primary authorities and record cites with a one sentence description of the key points from each authority and record cite. From this, you can create either an outline of approximately one page for each issue, or a "cheat sheet" that is written on or fastened to a folder for which each surface corresponds to one of your main issues for argument (*e.g.*, the front for issue 1, the inside for issue 2, and the back for issue 3).

While many advocates differ on exactly what kind of outline they may prepare, it is very useful to synthesize the knowledge of your case that you have gained during the preparation process by creating such an outline or "cheat sheet."

Craft your introduction, conclusion and argument structure. Once you have completed your oral argument outline (or as part of that process), it is helpful to craft your introduction and the structure of your argument. Your introduction should include a statement of the main theme of your oral argument as well as a short preview of the points you wish to emphasize at oral argument. Typically, it should be 30–90 seconds in length, depending on your judge or panel and how likely you are to be able to speak uninterrupted for a given period of time. As noted above, your theme can be something very simple such as "under the controlling law, plaintiffs have failed to state a claim for relief, and thus their complaint should be dismissed," or "my client is entitled to summary judgment because the defendant has, as a matter of law, violated the federal antitrust laws in two independent ways." Your introduction should include a very brief statement of the main two or three points you want to emphasize in the order that you intend to present them during your argument. Your best and most persuasive point should go first. Your introduction should also include a very brief statement of the relief you seek. You should also craft a very short conclusion—of perhaps ten to fifteen seconds in length—that summarizes your argument and restates the relief you seek. It could be something such as "accordingly, defendant's expert is unqualified and has not used an appropriate methodology in his analysis; his testimony should be excluded at trial."

Determine whether you wish to use any demonstratives or visual aids. The topic of using demonstratives or visual aids during oral arguments is one that could merit pages of discussion and that engenders severe disagreement among experienced advocates. Certain advocates (in my experience, a minority) believe that visual aids are critical whenever an advocate is communicating orally and attempt to use visual aids in arguments before trial and even appellate courts. They may use boards with documents, charts, graphs or key argument points, more complicated computer presentations, or even play video clips when a court or ADR panel will permit such visual aids. Other advocates believe that oral argument (especially on legal motions before trial courts and on appeals) primarily represents an opportunity to answer the questions troubling the judge or panel. Such advocates usually avoid visual aids except in compelling circumstances such as very technical cases where one or two visual aids can demonstrate a complex machine, computer algorithm, chemical compound, or the like. My advice is to very carefully consider your audience, the complexity of the case, and the focus of your argument when determining whether to use visual aids. I have used them and seen them effectively used in trial court arguments and presentations to ADR panels when the case or issue involved complicated facts that had to be understood by the judge or panel to address the main subjects of the oral argument. On the other hand, I have also talked with and argued before a number of appellate judges who very much dislike such visual aids, particularly in cases where the subject of oral argument is primarily a legal issue. Similarly, I have seen trial court judges refuse to permit advocates to use such visual aids even after they have been prepared and set up in the courtroom. And it is virtually unheard of to use any visual aids in the United States Supreme Court. While visual aids are often essential for presentations to juries and may be very useful in certain oral arguments before judges or ADR panels, an advocate must make a careful decision whether to use them at all and must carefully choose any visual aids that he or she does decide to employ at oral argument.

Perform a moot court or practice argument. After you have put together your oral argument outline and determined whether to use any visual aids, it is usually very helpful to perform a moot court or practice argument. Depending upon the importance of your case and your upcoming oral argument, you could convene a formal moot court with a number of "judges," or simply perform a practice argument before one colleague, legal assistant or secretary who is familiar with your case and who will be able to ask pertinent questions about the case. While excellent oral advocates differ with respect to how they perform such practice arguments (some prefer to treat them much like an actual argument in court, others may prefer simply to have colleagues ask them questions), most generally perform moot courts or practice arguments at least before important or difficult oral arguments. This process can be very important in further paring down your issues for oral argument, examining the weaknesses of your case, and building your confidence as you approach your oral argument. It can also help you to tailor your arguments and your delivery in a manner that will likely achieve the most favorable response from the court or ADR panel. Therefore, this process can strengthen the ethos, pathos and logos of your advocacy. It also can uncover any tendencies you have that are likely to annoy or offend your audience (such as raising your voice when answering a question that you think is stupid), and therefore can help eliminate "lame-o"s.

Revisit your issues for argument and make your final selection of the one, two or three that you wish to emphasize. At this point in your preparation for argument, you should be ready to choose your final list of one, two or three arguments to emphasize at oral argument. You will be intimately familiar with the facts of your case and the primary authorities. You will have carefully considered the arguments your opponent is likely to make and the questions that your judge or panel is likely to have. You will have discovered everything you can about your judge or panel. And you will have subjected yourself to questioning from your colleagues. You therefore should choose the issue or issues to emphasize at argument that are most likely to result in a favorable disposition of your case or the motion you are arguing. As explained by Justice Thomas R. Fitzgerald of the Illinois Supreme Court, "[t]he lawyers who seem to give the best arguments are [those] who are able to find the most important issues in the case and argue those issues. . . . I think there is a real art in identifying the issues that are the ones that give them the best chance of success." Daniel C. Vock, *Appellate lawyers' version of high wire act: Oral argument*, 150 Chicago Daily Law Bulletin 81.

Practice your argument again. As your final step in preparing for an oral argument, you will probably want to practice your argument some more. This can be done in a formal setting with one or more colleagues who are familiar with the case. It could also be done at home before your spouse or child. Or, it could be done alone in front of a mirror or a wall. The idea is to become as verbally fluent as possible with the key points you wish to emphasize, the authorities and record cites you wish to rely upon, and the structure of your argument including your introduction and conclusion. Some experienced oral advocates will practice an argument just one or two times the day before or morning of their oral argument. Other experienced oral advocates will practice their argument many times in the days proceeding their oral argument. The idea is to become comfortable with all of the points and citations you wish to emphasize. You should not attempt to memorize a prepared "speech" because the most important part of your argument will be your responses to the questions you receive. Rather, the idea is simply to become as familiar as you can with your affirmative argument and the responses you are likely to want to give to the questions you have anticipated.

Now that you have completed the preparation for oral argument, it is time to actually deliver your argument. Good luck!

KEY TIPS FOR DELIVERING AN OUTSTANDING ORAL ARGUMENT

Having completed your careful and extensive preparations for argument it is now time to actually present your oral argument. There are a number of things that you can do and focus upon to present the best argument possible:

Answer the judge's or panel's questions directly and honestly. The most important element of compelling oral advocacy is to be as responsive to the judge's or panel's questions as possible. This is effectively the "prime directive" of oral advocacy. If an oral advocate is evasive or incomplete in his or her answers to the judge's questions, that advocate will lose credibility with the court, thus harming his or her ethos. The advocate will appear to lack answers to the questions the court or panel is concerned with, thereby harming his or her logos. And the court or panel may become annoyed with the advocate, leading to an episode of "lame-o"s. As Judge Richard A. Posner of the U.S. Court of Appeals for the Seventh Circuit has stated "[s]ome lawyers are terribly afraid of answering questions, because they're afraid it's a trap and that their answer is going to be treated as a fatal concession. So they fence and they evade, and that, of course, annoys the judges." Vock, 150 Chicago Daily Law Bulletin 81. Similarly, Judge Kozinski has noted the dangers of interrupting a judge's question or evading it: "Once the judge starts to ask a question, raise your hand in a peremptory fashion and say, 'Excuse me, your honor, but I have just a few more sentences to complete my summation and I'll be happy to answer your questions.' This will give the judge a chance to dwell on the question, roll it around in his mind and brood about it." Kozinski, 23-OCT Mont. Law. 5, at *24. Or, as Judge Frank H. Easterbrook of the U.S. Court of Appeals for the Seventh Circuit has warned, don't try to "weasel out of meeting the question" or say "I am coming to that later." Howard Bashman, 20 Questions for Circuit Judge Frank H. Easterbrook of the U.S. Court of Appeals for the Seventh Circuit, available at www.legalaffairs.org./ howappealing/20q/2004_08_20q-appellateblog_archive.html. Answer the questions asked by your judge or panel directly, honestly and immediately. If you do so, you can persuade by the power of your answers. If you do not, you will seriously hurt your argument and your case.

Quickly deliver your introduction and attempt to adhere to your argument structure. Because you may get little uninterrupted time to deliver your introduction, do so as quickly as you can and move on to your first point. Once your first point has been covered fairly well and there are no questions pending, move on to your second point. But in delivering your argument always be mindful of the prime directive that you must answer the judge's questions directly and completely. Even if doing so will destroy the structure of your argument, it is more important to answer the judge's or panel's questions. Therefore, it may make sense to move on to another point when there is a lull in the questioning or when your answer to a question presents a natural opportunity to move to a next point. As you can see, this process is more art than science. It is often very difficult to transition from one point to another when your judge or panel is particularly interested in your first point. However, that is not usually a bad thing. If you have structured your argument effectively, your first point should be your strongest. Thus, to the extent that the judge or panel is focusing on that argument, it should mean that the judge or panel is seriously considering that argument. If you have an extended period of time of 30 minutes or more for your argument, it usually will be somewhat easier to reach your second point and any additional points. However, if you have a shorter argument time of 20 minutes or less, it will be more difficult to follow your argument structure. I think the best advice here is to do your best and be flexible. If the judge or panel really wants to take up your entire argument time with your first point, you should probably let that happen. If you can skillfully move on to your next point or points, do so, but not to the exclusion of answering the judge's or panel's questions.

Weave your key message into your answers to the judge's or panel's questions. Another important tactic for delivering an outstanding oral argument is to weave your key theme, message or points into the answers to the questions you are asked. As Judge Posner has stated, the "critical skill" for appellate lawyers is to build connections between your answers and your message: "If the lawyer, having answered the question briefly, then elaborates his answer in order to bring another point he wants to make, that's not going to bother the judge." Vock, 150 Chicago Daily Law Bulletin 81. One technique for doing this is to respond to a question by saying "I have two responses." The first response can directly answer the question, while the second response can reiterate your theme or make an additional point you believe important. Another technique is to answer the question directly and then conclude by explaining that the question underscores the important point you made earlier—at which time you can then reiterate your theme. While weaving points into your answers is a delicate process, most oral advocates can learn to do this effectively with some experience.

Do not under any circumstance disrespect the court or belittle the questions you are asked. As a corollary to the prime rule of answering the judge's or panel's questions, you should never disrespect the court or panel. Doing so will significantly reduce the ethos and dramatically increase the "lame-o"s of your presentation. Judge Kozinski has noted that if you really want a seemingly insignificant question to take on "monstrous significance," "[a] good way to start is by ridiculing the question: 'I was afraid the court would get sidetracked down a blind alley by this red herring.' Mixing metaphors by the way, is always a good idea; it makes it look like you're spinning your wheels after you've missed the boat because you went off on a wild goose chase." Kozinski, 23-OCT Mont. Law. 5, at *24-*25. Furthermore, Judge Kozinski warns of the dangers of "cutting off the judge in the middle of a question":

> First, it's rude . . . . [b]eyond that, cutting off the judge mid-question sends an important message: Look here your honor, you think you're so clever, but I know exactly what is going on inside that pointed little head of yours. Then again, cutting off the judge gives you an opportunity to answer the wrong question. When I pointed this out to a lawyer one time, he told me, 'Well, if that's not the question you were asking, it should be.'

Id. at *25.

Accurately portray the relevant authorities and facts of your case. It is critical to be direct, honest and forthright with the court or ADR panel. If the court gets the sense that you are misstating the key authority or playing fast and loose with the facts of your case, you will lose great credibility and your ethos will suffer. Moreover your ability to present an argument appealing to either the audience's sense of justice or logic will be dramatically reduced. Thus, the pathos and logos of your presentation will suffer as well. It is also extremely unlikely that a judge or panel will simply miss the misstatement or inaccuracy that you make at oral argument. Most judges prepare for oral argument and are relatively well versed in the key authorities and facts of your case by the time of oral argument. It is possible that if an authority or fact is minor or trivial, the court may not be aware of it and may not follow up on your misstatement at oral argument. But if the authority or fact is trivial, why misstate it in the first place? If the authority or fact is significant, it is very likely that the court or panel will realize that you have misstated or inaccurately portrayed that authority or fact or will follow up on your misstatement after the oral argument.

A corollary to the rule against misstating or inaccurately portraying the authorities relevant to or the facts of your case is the principle that you should not overclaim the strength of your case. As Judge Kozinski has explained:

> A good way to improve your chances of losing is to overclaim the strength of your case. When it's your turn to speak, start of by explaining how miffed you are that this farce—this travesty of justice—has gone this far when it should have been clear to any dolt that your client's case is ironclad. If you overstate your case enough, pretty soon one of the judges will take the bait and ask you a question about the very weakest part of your case. And, of course, that's precisely what you want the judges to be focusing on—the flaws in your case.

Id. at *24.

Don't make a jury speech. Oral argument presents a wonderful opportunity to focus the court or panel on the critical points, authorities and record citations you wish to emphasize. Don't waste that opportunity by making an unbridled appeal to pathos in the manner that an effective trial lawyer may do before a jury. Judges and ADR neutrals are much less likely to be swayed by one party's bad conduct, ad hominem attacks on the opposing party (even if justifiable), or blunt arguments that a certain outcome would just be "wrong." Judges and ADR neutrals are in most circumstances much more interested in how the key authorities apply to the facts of your case and whether that application prescribes the outcome your client desires. As Judge Kozinski has explained:

> When a lawyer resorts to a jury argument on appeal, you can just see the judges sit back and give a big sigh of relief. We understand that you have to say all these things to keep your client happy, but we also understand that you know, and we know, and you know we know, that your case doesn't amount to a hill of beans, so we can go back there in the conference room and flush it with an unpublished decision.

Id. at *25.

While it may be very tempting, resist the urge to make a jury speech. It will hurt the ethos of your presentation, impede the logos of your better arguments, and signal that you are afflicted by "lame-o"s.

Be very careful using analogies or maxims in your argument. Our old friend Aristotle believed strongly that the use of analogies or maxims could be very helpful in persuading a court or judge to act as an advocate desired. He was right. An analogy, maxim or story that fits well can enhance your argument and help your chances of winning your case or motion. For example, one of my colleagues recently argued a statutory-interpretation case before the U.S. Supreme Court. He argued that his opponent's interpretation, while possibly supportable by the language of the main sentence itself, could not be reconciled with the language of the rest of the statutory provision in which it was located. To conclude his argument, my colleague referred to the parable of the blind man who comes upon two thick trees, unable to understand that the soft tube between them was really the trunk of the elephant that he stood before. My colleague's use of that parable was extremely effective, and he won his case. But an advocate must be very careful using such devices at oral argument. It is very easy to have one's excellent analogy fall apart under questioning, or worse, be turned by one's opponent. I recall an argument many years ago where one advocate used a baseball analogy to describe his case for the court, only to have his opponent quickly co-opt that analogy to describe how the advocate had swung and missed with each of his three major arguments and had "struck out" with his case. The point here is not that you can never use an analogy, maxim or parable. But you must be very careful. It may make more sense to use such a device, as my colleague did, to conclude an argument, rather than earlier when it might be more exposed to attack or co-option. If you think there is any risk that your analogy or maxim could be turned against your position, don't use it. Moreover, you may wish to seek the advice of a colleague as to whether using such an analogy or maxim makes sense or could get you into trouble.

Deliver your argument clearly and at a moderate pace. When we get nervous, many of us speak very quickly or tend to garble certain words. And even the most experienced oral advocate often gets nervous when delivering an oral argument.

Nevertheless, it is very important to present your oral argument clearly. An oral advocate must enunciate words clearly. And he or she must speak at a moderate pace. If you speak too quickly, your audience will lose you (unless your audience is a group of college cross-examination debate coaches). If you speak too slowly, you may frustrate your audience or put them to sleep. You should also avoid speaking in a monotone and should use vocal inflection to emphasize important points. Another helpful technique is to use pauses to underscore important points as well. Furthermore, you should not attempt to speak in eloquent complete sentences. The goal is to have a conversation with the court. In doing so, an effective advocate may often use very short or clipped sentences. For example, you may wish to answer a question by saying "No, for two reasons" or "Let's look at the legislative history." The point is to communicate effectively, not produce a beautiful transcript. If you are comfortable doing so, you may wish to use slow, smooth (rather than hard and choppy) hand gestures to emphasize a point. But do so only if you naturally use such hand gestures. If all else fails, try to speak as if you are having a conversation with a good friend. Use a conversational tone and approach and you are likely to be able to communicate with your judge or panel.

Be very careful with use of any visual aids. If you have decided to use visual aids during your argument, be very careful with them. If the judge or panel seems irritated or is not following your use of the visual aids, abandon them. If using your visual aids is bogging down the argument, seriously consider only using a few of them. Most importantly, do not allow your use of visual aids to hamper your responsiveness to the court's or panel's questions. There was a recent argument in which the advocate used a significant number of PowerPoint slides during an extended presentation of over one hour in length. While the advocate's use of the slides was mostly effective, at one point, the judge stated that he would like the advocate to "take a break" from his presentation to answer questions that were troubling him. It is very important when using visual aids is to do so without creating the appearance that the presentation is more important than responding to the court's or panel's concerns. Otherwise both your ethos and logos could suffer substantially.

Act professionally at all times. It is critical to your ethos to act as a professional at all times during an argument. Do not raise your voice or visibly show anger, even if you are provoked or your opponent has said something reprehensible during his or her presentation. Do not give the slightest appearance that you think the judge's or panel's questions are ill-conceived or irrelevant. When sitting at counsel table, speak in a quiet whisper, if you must speak at all. Do not vigorously shake your head or make facial contortions in response to your opponent's presentation or questions from the judge or panel. If you interact with any of your colleagues in the presence of the judge, panel or any of their staff, treat your colleagues with respect at all times. There was a trial a number of years ago during which one attorney would verbally abuse his legal staff while the judge and jury were absent, but while the judge's law clerk was in the courtroom. It quickly became apparent that the judge as well as his staff viewed that attorney as a "jerk." Be aware that when delivering an appellate oral argument, there will almost always be a number of law clerks present in the courtroom well before the judges arrive on the bench. They will watch and scrutinize everything you say or do in the courtroom. If you act professionally at all times, you should never have to worry about offending anyone by what you have said or done in the courtroom.

Dress professionally. While this is not usually an issue with most oral arguments and advocates, it can be very important. When I was a law clerk to an east-coast appellate judge many years ago, there was one case where an advocate delivered his argument in a loud orange jacket and cowboy boots. Suffice it to say that the most memorable thing about his argument, and the primary element that was discussed by the law clerks, was the advocate's attire. An advocate has to be sensitive to the standards of decorum of the forum in which he or she will argue. In certain parts of the country, wearing cowboy boots to court is commonplace and accepted, while other more formal attire may not be. Indeed, I remember a case in which I was involved a few years ago where local counsel warned me and my colleagues that cuff links and pocket squares were too "east coast" and should be avoided in the courts of his locale. As a general rule, understated and conservative business attire is usually appropriate. But it always helps to speak with local counsel if you have never appeared in court in a particular area to learn the local practice and customs.

Be very careful in using humor. As a character in a Star Trek movie once remarked, "humor is a difficult concept." Most experienced oral advocates would likely advise never to use humor at oral argument. I don't necessarily agree. On rare occasions, a judge or panelist with a good sense of humor may make a joke that could effectively be responded to with a humorous statement. Also on rare occasions, a line of self-deprecating humor might be effective. In such circumstances, the use of humor can improve the ethos of your presentation by lightening the mood and showing that you have a sense of humor. But you do have to be very careful. The use of humor in an inappropriate circumstance or before a judge or panelist who does not appreciate the use of humor, or does not appreciate your sense of humor, can do great damage to your credibility. As a rule, I would advise against using humor unless you know that your judge has or panelists have a good sense of humor, a particular opportunity presents itself, and you are very comfortable using humor. Even then, you should never use humor that could be considered disrespectful to anyone or seems "canned." You should not start your argument with a joke or a statement such as "four score and seven depositions ago . . .". If you are not fully comfortable using humor, or are not certain that your judge or panel would appreciate it, don't use it at all.

Watch and listen carefully to the arguments that precede yours. If you have the opportunity to watch an argument or arguments before your case is called, do so carefully. You can often learn a great deal about the approach and demeanor of the judge or panel by doing so. You can also learn if there are any special procedures or courtroom etiquette of which you are unaware. If you are fortunate, you may also be able to determine whether there are any special characteristics of your judge or panel that you should bear in mind—the judge hates to be interrupted or prefers to be called "your honor"; the judges seem to have a good sense of humor; or the judge is exhausted and looks ready to fall asleep.

CONCLUSION

Oral argument presents a great opportunity to focus your audience on the key points of your case. By bearing in mind Aristotle's time-honored principles of *ethos*, *pathos* and *logos* and the associated concept of *lame-os*, you can deliver a credible, logical and emotionally compelling oral argument. If you also prepare carefully and thoroughly, you can become an outstanding oral advocate and significantly advance your clients' interests. Speak up. The legal world is listening.

Lasting Impressions: The Role of Closing Argument
By Linda L. Listrom

THE ROLE OF CLOSING ARGUMENT

Let's begin by talking about what closing argument is not. Closing argument is not the time in the trial to begin to tell the jury your story. Nor is closing argument the first time you articulate your theory or themes. If you have tried the case properly, you began the trial by telling the jury a story in opening statement. And this story was thematic—that is, it connected to key values possessed by most jurors. Then, as the trial progressed, you developed the evidence which supported that story. If you have failed to tell a thematic story, and if you have failed to develop the evidence which proves that story, you cannot win the case in closing argument. If you have tried the case properly, closing argument will be an extension of everything else you have done during the trial. If you have tried the case improperly, closing argument will be irrelevant.

The purpose of closing argument is to give the jurors the tools that they need to reach a verdict. You must tell the jurors what is important to their decision and why. You must also explain what is unimportant, and why. You must remind them of the evidence they have heard during the trial and explain why this evidence entitles you to a verdict. In short, you must give the jurors the ammunition that they need to argue your case effectively to the other jurors.

Closing argument is the *only* time in the trial when you can do this effectively. In contrast to other phases of the trial, in closing argument you are permitted to argue. This means that you can not only remind the jurors about the evidence they have heard, you can also explain to them why it is important to the decision they must make. Argument is a powerful tool. Below we discuss how you can use this tool effectively.

ORGANIZING THE CLOSING ARGUMENT

Your decision as to how to organize the closing argument is crucial, for several reasons. First, and most obviously, a well-organized closing argument is easier for the jury to follow. This is particularly important if your case is complex or your closing argument will be lengthy. Second, and even more importantly, when you organize the closing argument you have an opportunity to emphasize what is most important to your case. Organized properly, the closing argument will emphasize

From the **Trial Practice Journal**/Summer 2005/ABA/Section of Litigation

the strengths of your case and minimize the weaknesses. Organization is just another tool available to you to show the jury which evidence you consider to be most important. Here are some suggestions for how to organize your closing argument effectively.

Organize your argument by topic. The topical method of organization allows you to organize and present the facts in the manner that is most persuasive. Do not organize your closing argument chronologically. Sometimes, we are instinctively drawn to chronological organization because we have heard so often that during a trial we must tell the jurors a story. What better way to tell a story than chronologically? But when you organize your closing argument chronologically, you may be forced to juxtapose two events because they occurred close together in time, even though these two events are completely unrelated to one another. As a result, the point that you are trying to make may become muddled or even lost. By organizing your argument around key topics you have the flexibility to present the facts in a way that is most persuasive.

To select your topics focus on your theory, themes and story. Ask yourself the following question: What is the reason that the jury should return a verdict in favor of my client? You should be able to answer this question in a sentence or two. If there is more than one reason, what are the two or three most persuasive reasons? The answers to these questions will be your topics for closing argument.

In arranging your topics in order, use the principles of primacy and recency. Research teaches us that jurors are most likely to remember what they hear first in your argument and what they hear last. Among other things, the jurors are likely to be most attentive at the beginning of your closing argument and at the end. You should follow these principles of primacy and recency in organizing your closing argument. If you have three topics, you should discuss the two strongest topics first and last.

Build up your theory before rebuffing your opponent's theory. In closing argument you must give the jurors a reason to return a verdict in favor of your client. In a civil case, your reason must be something other than: My opponent is wrong. Whether you represent the plaintiff or a defendant you must help the jury understand why a verdict in favor of your client is a fair result. You must present an affirmative view of the case that they will embrace and use to reach their verdict. In closing argument, you must start by building your affirmative case and then, and only then, rebutting your opponent's view of the case.

In rebuttal, use your agenda, not the defendant's. If you represent the plaintiff, you can prepare a detailed outline for your initial argument in advance, but it is more difficult to plan your rebuttal. You will not know what points you need to rebut until you have heard the defendant's argument. However, you should not make a list of the defendant's arguments in the order in which the defendant makes them, and go through the list of points in order, rebutting each one. By organizing your rebuttal in this way, you are ignoring your agenda—the topics which you believe are important—and, instead, you are using defendant's agenda—the topics which the defendant believes are important. Your rebuttal will, inevitably, sound defensive. Instead, you should organize your rebuttal argument around the same topics that you used in your opening argument.

Tell the jury how you have organized your argument. It will be much easier for the jurors to follow your argument and remember your key points if you use signposts to guide them. There are several ways that you can use signposts in your closing argument. The simplest way is to explain at the beginning how you have organized the argument: "I am going to be talking about three different topics. First, I will talk about. . . . Then, I will talk about . . . and finally, I will talk about . . ." An even better approach is to list your topics on a demonstrative exhibit entitled, "Plaintiff's Closing Argument" or "Defendant's Closing Argument." You can list the topics on a board, which is prepared in advance by a graphics consultant, or, you can simply write the topics on a pad of paper which you place on the easel. At the beginning of your argument, you can refer to the exhibit and its list of topics. Throughout the argument you should leave this exhibit up on the easel. You can then use the exhibit to transition from one topic to the next: That concludes our discussion of the first topic, "What the Plaintiff Did." Now lets move on to the second topic, "What the Defendant Did." With this device the jury always knows where you are in your argument, where you have been, and where you are going next.

CHOOSING THE CONTENT FOR YOUR ARGUMENT

Once you have selected your topics and arranged them in the most persuasive order, you are ready to select the content for your closing argument. Here are some suggestions for how to make those choices.

Frame the issues for the jury. In closing argument it is your job to tell the jury what they must decide. You should explain to the jury what is important to their decision. You should also explain what is *not* important to their decision. Rarely, if ever, are all of the facts in dispute. Often, the plaintiff and defendant disagree, not about what the facts are, but about which facts or issues are most important. If in your view, the jury only needs to decide one issue in your favor, tell them so. If your opposing counsel is confusing the jury by arguing a point that is irrelevant, explain why it is irrelevant. In short, as an advocate, it is your job to frame all of this for the jury, so that when they retire to their deliberations, they know exactly what they need to decide.

Be selective. You do not need to describe every piece of evidence in your closing argument. In any trial, the parties present facts which are not particularly relevant. If you have chosen your topics correctly, you can then use those topics as a guide. For each topic, you will want to discuss the evidence that relates to that topic. Any evidence which does not relate to one of your topics is unimportant to your argument and can probably be ignored. Does this mean that you must use every piece of evidence which relates to one of your topics? Not necessarily. In deciding how much evidence to use to support a topic, you should ask yourself: Is this topic in dispute? If not, you probably should describe your best evidence on the topic, but you probably do not need to remind the jury of every piece of evidence they heard. On the other hand, if the issue is one that is in dispute you will probably want to remind the jury about all of the evidence that supports your position.

Use your best, most persuasive, evidence. The best evidence is, of course, an admission by the opposing party, whether in a document or in testimony. Undisputed evidence is also very persuasive and in almost every trial at least some of the evidence will be undisputed. Equally important, but often overlooked, is evidence that is persuasive based upon common sense and everyday experience.

Show the jury the evidence. Don't just tell the jury about the evidence. Show it to them. Do not assume that just because the jury saw a document earlier in the trial, they remember it now. If a document is important to your theory, show it to the jury again in closing argument. If you are using a courtroom presentation system, document camera or overhead projector, display the document on the screen. Remind the jurors about what the document says, by highlighting a key passage and reading it to them, slowly and with emphasis. Then, explain to the jurors why the document is so important. Similarly, if a witness gave important testimony, read from the trial transcript or, better yet, display the transcript on a screen, highlight the key testimony and read it to them. The precise words of the witness, as recorded in the trial transcript, are much more effective than your paraphrasing of testimony.

When you read from the transcript, you should also remind the jurors who the witness is by connecting the witness to the case. The jurors may not be able to connect names with testimony. They may not remember the witness named "Mr. Jones." But they will probably remember if you explain, "You remember Mr. Jones. He was the store clerk who was standing on the curb when the plaintiff tried to cross the street. He saw everything that happened."

Use Jury Instructions and Verdict Forms. In most jurisdictions, there is a jury instruction conference in advance of closing argument. If you know how the judge is going to instruct the jury, you can use the jury instructions in closing argument. Of course, you do not want to use all of them or even most of them. How do you choose which ones to use? Think of the jury instructions as another piece of supporting information. If a jury instruction provides support on an important topic in your argument, you may want to either read from it or refer to it.

Do not ignore bad facts. The jury will undoubtedly remember them. Rather than ignoring bad facts, you should explain why a bad fact does not matter.

Resolve conflicts in the evidence. Sometimes the evidence is in conflict. In these situations, you should argue to the jury why your evidence should be believed. For example, if the testimony of the witness contradicts a contemporaneous memorandum or letter, counsel should argue to the jury that the document, written at the time of the events in question, is more reliable than the witness's memory of what happened five years ago. Whenever possible, you should try to reconcile the conflicting testimony of witnesses without accusing one of the witnesses of lying. Jurors are reluctant to conclude that a witness has lied. Moreover, the jurors often must base such a conclusion on their impressions of the witness, which are necessarily subjective. While you may be convinced that the opposing party is lying, it is difficult for you to know how the jurors have reacted to the witness. Usually, it is possible to resolve conflicts in the evidence without making this accusation.

As counsel for the defendant, anticipate the plaintiff's rebuttal argument. Defense counsel must, at least to a certain extent, anticipate the plaintiff's rebuttal and respond to the plaintiff's arguments before he or she makes them. But you may be concerned that if you anticipate an argument and then counsel for the plaintiff does not make this argument on rebuttal, you have unnecessarily undermined your own case. Moreover, it is difficult to anticipate the plaintiff's arguments without sounding defensive. On balance, you should anticipate and rebut the plaintiff's key arguments. You should not, however, try to anticipate each

231

and every argument that the plaintiff may make. You should take care to organize your closing argument so that you do not end your argument on a defensive note, rebutting the plaintiff's theory.

Consider motive. In most civil cases, motive is legally irrelevant, that is, it is not a legal element of the plaintiffs case and it is not a legal element of an affirmative defense. When the judge instructs the jury, he or she will not instruct them that they must find motive. But jury research tells us that the jurors always ask the question: "Why? Why did the plaintiff behave in this way? Why did the defendant behave in this way?" To persuade the jury, you must give them an answer to these questions. If there is motive, the story becomes more logical and therefore more persuasive.

Use Demonstrative Exhibits. During closing argument, you can use any demonstrative exhibit that you have used earlier during the trial. However, do not feel that you have to use all of your demonstrative exhibits during closing, or, indeed, any of them. By the time you reach closing argument, you may have used a particular exhibit so many times that it no longer has any impact on the jury. So, be selective. Use a demonstrative exhibit only if you think it will make a difference. In addition to the demonstrative exhibit that you have used throughout the trial, you can create demonstrative exhibits specifically for closing argument. And, unlike the demonstrative exhibits you have used during witness examination, the demonstrative exhibit which you create for closing argument can and should be argumentative. At this stage of the trial the only restriction on demonstrative exhibits is that they must be based on the evidence. One of the best demonstratives for closing argument is one that summarizes or lists the key pieces of evidence on a particular topic. Another effective demonstrative exhibit for closing is one that lists the opposing parties arguments on a particular point, along with your responses to each argument.

Arguing damages. Unless the trial has been bifurcated, the plaintiff's lawyer should always argue damages. But the defense lawyer has a choice. Some defense lawyers are loath to argue damages, while others are not willing to put all of their eggs in the liability basket. They recognize that in most cases there is at least some risk that the jury will return a verdict for the plaintiff on liability and that, for this reason, it would be imprudent to ignore damages. This is a strategic question that you will need to resolve long before closing argument. If you do choose to argue damages, this will present some challenges for you in organizing your argument. Using logic as your guide, you would begin your argument by arguing the liability issues, and then conclude by arguing damages.

However, this approach causes two problems: not only are you ending your argument on a defensive point, you are ending with an argument which assumes that the defendant is liable. The solution for this problem varies, depending upon the facts of your case and the points that you plan to argue. But, in ordering the topics in argument it is crucial that you find some topic to end your argument other than damages.

DELIVERING THE CLOSING ARGUMENT

Be yourself. You have your own style. Use it. Don't copy someone else's. You may admire an accomplished trial lawyer who has an informal conversational style of argument. He weaves into his argument humor and stories about life in his home state of Alabama. Unless you are from Alabama, and unless you can use humor naturally and effectively, you should not emulate him. You will undermine your credibility with the jury by coming across as phony and insincere. You are better off choosing a style that comes naturally to you, even if that means that you give a formal and highly logical argument, without any funny stories.

Do not read your closing argument. Do not prepare a script and read from it. If you read from a script, your delivery will be boring and monotonous; it will lack energy and passion. Moreover, when you are reading from a script you cannot make eye contact with the jurors. Unless you are looking at the jurors you cannot read their reactions. Throughout closing you should be watching the jurors carefully, noting how each one reacts, and making adjustments accordingly. If a juror seems puzzled by a point, you should stop and explain further. If a juror seems bored, you may want to get his attention by, for example, moving out from behind the lectern. If you are glued to a script, you cannot make these necessary adjustments.

Give your closing argument from an outline. Although you should not write out your closing argument word for word and read it, this does not mean that your closing argument should be spontaneous. To the contrary, it should be carefully planned. The best way to take advantage of careful planning, but leave room for some spontaneity, is to prepare an outline for your closing argument. Your outline should list, in shorthand form, all of the points that you plan to make and the order in which you plan to make them. There are two advantages to an outline.

First, an outline gives you a crutch. Some lawyers are able to give an entire closing argument without using any notes. Most of us cannot do that comfortably. If you have a well organized outline, you can use it when you need it. You may be able to argue for 5 or 10 minutes from memory, without looking at your outline. Then, when you need to refresh your memory, you can refer to your outline. It is easier to find your place in an outline than in a script.

Second, an outline gives you flexibility. If, while watching the jurors, you feel that some jurors are not yet fully persuaded about a particular point, you can embellish with additional detail. If, after hearing the plaintiff's argument, you need to add an argument, you can do it. In fact, when I prepare my closing argument outline, I usually insert blank pages at critical points throughout the outline. If, after hearing the plaintiff's argument, I decide to add a point to my argument, I write the new point in the appropriate blank space within my outline. Then, when I stand up to argue, not only do I have a list of the additional points I want to make, I also have an outline which tells me when to make these points.

Memorize your beginning and ending. The first few minutes and the last few minutes of your closing argument are critical. In the first few minutes of the closing you must grab the jurors' attention. In the last few minutes of the closing you must hold their attention while you build towards a powerful conclusion. To grab and hold the jurors' attention, you must maintain eye contact with them. It goes without saying that you cannot make eye contact with the jurors if you are looking at your outline. The beginning and ending of your argument are sufficiently important that you should script them in advance. These moments are too important to trust your ability to be extemporaneous. So, script the beginning and ending and memorize the script.

Move around. Done properly, movement can add interest and emphasis to your closing argument. For example, when you walk over to a chart that is displayed on an easel, you are emphasizing to the jurors that the chart is important. By walking towards the chart you also break up the monotony. By moving away from the chart you can signal a transition to the jury. You can use this type of movement to tell the jurors that you are starting a topic. As with anything else, do not overdo it. Movement is effective, only if used selectively for emphasis.

Vary your voice. You can also add interest and emphasis to your closing argument by varying the speed, volume tone, and inflection of your voice. Once again, the key is variety. A lawyer who speaks in a slow monotone voice is boring. But so is a lawyer who speaks loudly at the same rapid pace throughout his argument. In fact, one of the most effective, and underused, tools in closing argument is silence. By pausing before you make a point you signal to the jury, "Listen carefully; this is important." By pausing after you make a point, you give the jury time to reflect on what has been said.

Use gestures. Most of us have natural gestures. You should use the gestures that come naturally to you. But, you want to avoid using the same gesture over and over again. A single repetitive gesture can become annoying and distracting. The best way to avoid this problem is to watch yourself on videotape. It will probably be a painful experience, but you will see exactly what gestures you use and how frequently you use them.

Insert nonverbal cues into your outline. Most of us do not make good spontaneous use of movement, pauses, and gestures. But like the content of your closing argument, the delivery can also be planned in advance. When you prepare your outline, identify the points that you want to emphasize and decide how you want to emphasize them. Then, write nonverbal cues, such as "pause here" or "step away from the podium" into your outline. When you practice your closing, practice not only the words but also the movement, the changes in your voice, and your gestures too.

CONCLUSION

In closing argument, unlike at any other time during the trial, you have the opportunity to argue to the jury. In other words, you have an opportunity to explain—explain what is important and what is unimportant; explain why the evidence supports your theory and does not support your opponent's theory; and explain why the evidence should lead to a verdict in your favor. During closing argument you also have an opportunity, not just to present the evidence, but to package it. You should choose the topics which emphasize the strengths of your case and deemphasize the weaknesses. You should organize your topics and evidence in a way that is most persuasive. You should plan your argument carefully. This means planning, not just the content, but also the delivery. When you deliver the argument you should connect with the jurors. You should grab their attention at the beginning and hold it throughout the argument. Done properly, the argument should give the jurors all the tools that they need to decide the case in your favor.

Motion Practice

Effective Motion Practice In Trial Courts
By Luther T. Munford and James W. Shelson

You only win the case for your client if you ask the court for relief and get it. You ask by submitting your request in a motion. This article discusses both how to write persuasive motions and supporting briefs, and how to persuade a judge that you are right—that you should win.

PERSUASIVE MOTIONS AND BRIEFS

1. **The Purpose of Motions and Briefs is to Persuade**
   The motion and brief should state your legal theory and the reasons why your client should prevail. Persuasion depends on what you have to say, whether you say it in a professional manner that bolsters your credibility, and whether the judge is willing to listen. Make what you send a judge accurate, complete and "reader friendly." As Judge Richard Posner has said, the receptiveness of the judge depends on the distance he has to move philosophically and his resistance to moving that distance. Narrow arguments narrow the distance. A short, accurate brief lowers the resistance.

2. **The Contents of Persuasive Motions and Briefs**
   a. **Tell the judge immediately what you want and why you should win**
      You should tell the judge immediately what relief you want and why you are entitled to that relief. Do this in the first paragraph if possible, and certainly no later than the first page. The court can understand what comes next if it first gets the big picture. These examples illustrate sloppy introductions and suggested improvements:

      EXAMPLE NO. 1
      Defendant Washington County School District's Motion For Partial Summary Judgment

      In accordance with Rule 56 of the Federal Rules of Civil Procedure, Defendant Washington County School District ("WCSD") moves for Partial Summary Judgment regarding the claims of Plaintiff John Smith as follows:

1. This is a personal injury action in which Sharon Smith, a minor, alleges that WCSD negligently supervised a high school athletic banquet, allowing John Doe, a coach at the school, to "entice" her away from the banquet and engage in sexual intercourse at a local hotel. The Complaint also alleges WCSD knew or should have known of alleged past similar conduct of Doe, and failed to supervise him or to protect the students from him.

2. Both Sharon Smith and her father, John Smith, claim actual, compensatory, and punitive damages for "mental pain, mental anguish, mental suffering, emotional damage, fees paid for counseling and medical treatment, future medical treatment and fees, counseling and fees, a fear of being subjected to such treatment again and again, fear of a party or parties who have held themselves out to be in a position of trust."

3. With limited exception, Mississippi follows the "zone of danger" rule with regards to emotional distress-type injuries, and a father who was not present for the sexual activities of his daughter cannot recover for damages allegedly resulting from these activities. WCSD should not be forced to bear the burden and costs of extensive discovery regarding the claims and alleged damages of John Smith when no facts would make them legally viable. No amount of discovery will raise genuine issues of material fact with regards to Mr. Smith, and WCSD is entitled to summary judgment on the claims of Mr. Smith as a matter of law.

SUGGESTED REVISION NO. 1

Washington County School District's Motion For Judgment Against The Student's Father

Defendant Washington County School District moves under Fed. R. Civ. P. 56 for a summary judgment that dismisses the claims of plaintiff John Smith, the father of plaintiff Sharon Smith. The father did not witness the abduction and seduction that gives rise to his daughter's claims and so was not within the "zone of danger." In more detail:

1. Plaintiff Sharon Smith, a minor, has sued the School District and Coach John Doe in tort. She alleges that, because the School District negligently supervised a high school athletic banquet,

the coach was able to entice her to a motel where he seduced her.

2. Her father has also sued for his own mental suffering caused by the coach's actions.

3. It is undisputed, however, that he did not witness either the enticement nor the seduction that are the basis for the daughter's suit.

EXAMPLE NO. 2
Defendants' Response To Plaintiff's Objections To Magistrate Judge's Rulings And Application For Review

Introduction
Plaintiff Jerry Jones ("Carpenter") has filed Objections to the Magistrate Judge's Rulings and Application for Review ("Application for Review") requesting that this Court vacate or modify the July 18, 2005 Order staying discovery. Plaintiff requests relief from the Magistrate Judge's Order to allow plaintiff to conduct discovery to support his allegations of personal jurisdiction against the various defendants in this matter. Defendants submit that the basis for the Magistrate Judge's Order is sound, although not reflected in the Order, and therefore the Magistrate Judge's Order staying discovery should be left in place. In order for this Court to make an informed decision on the Application for Review, an explanation of the procedural history of this matter may be helpful.

SUGGESTED REVISION NO. 2
Defendants' Response To Plaintiff's Objections And Application For Review

Introduction
Plaintiff Jerry Jones erroneously asks this court to vacate or modify the magistrate judge's July 18, 2005 Order that stayed discovery. In this breach of contract case, he asks for more discovery to support his allegations of personal jurisdiction over individual defendants with whom he never dealt.

But the first issue before the court is not personal jurisdiction. Rather it is subject matter jurisdiction. Plaintiff does not request any discovery on the subject matter jurisdiction question, nor does he need any. This court should hold that it has no subject matter jurisdiction and dismiss the case. It need not reach either the personal jurisdiction question or any right to discovery relevant to that question.

b. **Think about how you present the facts**

Judges know, or think they know, the law. What they readily concede they don't know is the facts. So tell them. Stick to the relevant facts. Add record citations. Doing these things makes the judge's job easier and enhances your credibility. Most of the time, chronological order works best. Some courts may, however, prefer witness by witness summaries. If there are a lot of facts, break them down into groups with headings that will help the judge understand them. Just say the facts, don't argue them. Obvious overreaching raises a question as to whether or not the judge can trust what you say.

c. **Speak plainly and be brief**

Use simple words and plain English. Use short sentences. Use short paragraphs. Be concise. Try to read a paragraph that covers a whole page. Then break it up. You will find it much easier to read. The following example and suggested revision illustrate this point.

EXAMPLE NO. 3

Memorandum Brief In Support Of Taxpayers' Appeal Of Denial Of Request For Refund Of Income Taxes From Review Board Order No._7999

Introduction

This Brief is prepared in support of Petitioner's position with regard to the denial of the refund of income taxes requested for the calendar years 1999 and 2000 (the "Refunds") by the Mississippi State Tax Commission (the "Commission") with regard to Thomas and Margaret Dumas (the "Taxpayers"). The Refunds are as follows:

> As part of the Firm's liquidating distributions to the Taxpayers, the asset representing a potential fee recovery in asbestos litigation (the "Contract") was distributed to the Taxpayers. However, because the Asbestos Arbitration Panel had not yet ruled on the amount of the fee recovery, if any, the Contract did not have an ascertainable value on the date of liquidation, November 5, 1998. At the time of liquidation, the amount of the anticipated fee award was only speculative, and thus, the Contract was not capable of valuation. Because the Contract could not be valued, that portion of the Taxpayers' capital gain resulting from the liquidating distribution and associated with the Contract could not be determined on the date of liquidation. Therefore, the Taxpayers treated the receipt of the 1999 and 2000 fee

recovery payments made to the Taxpayers as part of the liquidation transaction. As such, the fee payments were reported
as capital gains on their 1999 and 2000 Individual Income Tax
Returns (see attached Exhibit I). However, because gains from
the sale of stock in domestic corporations held for more than
one (1) year are not recognized pursuant to Miss. Code Ann.
§ 27-7-9(f)(10)(A), the Taxpayers have requested a refund of the
income tax paid on the reported capital gains resulting from the
liquidation of the firm. The Commission has denied the Taxpayers' request for refund of income taxes from which Tax-
payer hereby appeals.

SUGGESTED REVISION NO. 3
*Memorandum Brief In Support Of Taxpayers' Appeal Of Review Board
Order No. 7999 Which Denied Them A Refund*

Introduction
The taxpayers made a mistake on their 1999 and 2000 returns.
Because they have sought to correct that mistake in a timely fashion, state law gives them the right to a refund. Miss. Code Ann.
§ 27-7-9. The Review Board's ruling that denied them a refund is
wrong as a matter of law. The Commission should reverse that ruling and give them the refunds. The future payments they are to receive are capital gains from the liquidation of a domestic corporation, and should not be treated as interest or rent.

In 1998, the taxpayers liquidated the corporation formed for
their legal practice. They took from the liquidation a contract to receive future payments from the settlement of a case against several asbestos companies. But the amount of the annual payments
is subject to various contingencies, and so the exact amount will
not be known until each payment is made.

In the years in question, the taxpayers properly treated these
payments as capital gains from the sale of stock. But they failed to
assert their rights under Miss. Code Ann. § 27-7-9(f)(10)(A), which
allowed them not to recognize those gains for tax purposes. The
commission staff wrongly claims they are interest or taxes and so
are not eligible for non-recognition.

But the payments are capital gains. Several things support this
conclusion. The treatment given claims for subsequent years, federal law, and common sense. The payments are a return on the liquidation. Nothing more has to be done to earn them. Each payment diminishes the amount the taxpayers are entitled to receive

and, when the last payment is made, the taxpayers will not have anything left.

Legalese does not show the court you are a "real lawyer." Instead, it diminishes your work product. Judges, we hope, think in plain English, or at least they are more likely to do so. Study has shown that they find plain English more credible. So use it. The following is an example of legalese and a suggested revision:

EXAMPLE NO. 4

Plaintiff's Rebuttal To The Defendant's Response To Plaintiff's Motion For Judgment On The Pleadings

Comes now the Plaintiff, New Day Credit Company, LLC ("Plaintiff"), by and through counsel, and pursuant to Rule 12(c) of the Mississippi Rules of Civil Procedure, and files this Rebuttal to the Defendant's Response to the Plaintiff's Motion for Judgment on the Pleadings, and would show unto the Court as follows:

> On or about November 8, 2004, the said Plaintiff filed with the Court its Complaint in Replevin against Crossbow Farms ("Defendant"), alleging default under certain Retail Installment Sales Contracts and Security Agreements ("Contracts"), and seeking a judgment of possession and an award of interest, costs and attorneys fees. On or about February 10, 2005, the said Defendant filed its Answer and Affirmative Defenses ("Answer"). On or about August 8, 2005, the said Plaintiff filed its Motion for Judgment on the Pleadings ("Motion"), alleging that the said Defendant had created no issue of material fact and that the said Plaintiff is entitled to judgment as a matter of law. On or about August 18, 2005, the said Defendant filed its Response to the Motion ("Response"), alleging that due to unforeseen circumstances it is not in default and asserting its right to assert affirmative defenses.

SUGGESTED REVISION NO. 4

Plaintiff's Reply In Support Of Its Motion For Judgment On The Pleadings

Plaintiff New Day Credit Company, LLC asks this court to grant its motion for judgment because the response submitted by Crossbow Farms has no legal merit. The response admits the debt, but offers the novel defense of "unforeseen circumstances." Because on the facts pled here there is no such defense, the motion for judgment in favor of New Day should be granted.

Plain language communicates best. "Would show unto the court" and "said plaintiff" belong to the Dark Ages. Let them stay there.

d. Use argumentative headings

Use argumentative headings to outline the structure and progress of your argument. Say "The skid marks, the affidavit, and the expert report establish the defendant driver's fault." Do not say "Point Three," or "The evidence entitles plaintiff to summary judgment." The use of headings and sub-headings to set off separate points makes it easier for the judge to follow the argument.

e. Case citations

Motions or supporting briefs must cite cases, statutes and other legal authorities before a judge will find the argument credible. But some citations are better than others. For example:

- First, cite a few authorities that directly support the argument. If you go beyond three, the judge's interest begins to decline dramatically. Rather than simply list citations without explanation, make it easy on the judge. Add a parenthetical that explains the citation's importance.
- Second, if you must use string citations, put them in footnotes.
- Third, if you can paraphrase a poorly written legal quotation, do so.
- Fourth, say what the block quotation says before you quote it. Some judges skip over block quotes. But the selective use of block quotations can convey the importance of the cited authority and convince the judge that it really does say what you say it says. Try a lead-in that makes a substantive point, such as:

    The court recognized that there are nine elements of a fraud claim, and held that they must be established by clear and convincing evidence.

    The statute establishes that no claim is permitted against a state hospital unless the injured party first notifies the hospital of the claim ninety days before filing suit.

    Because the plaintiff did not file his claims within three years of the accident, the court held that his claims were time barred.

f. Visual aids

A picture may be worth a thousand words. Do not hesitate to include an important photograph, diagram, chart or other drawing in the text of your motion or brief. The following is an example of the use of a chart to summarize an argument regarding the statute of limitations:

> A three-year statute of limitations applies to plaintiffs' claims. Plaintiffs have each identified the date on which they discovered the alleged product defect. The date on which plaintiffs filed their complaint is a matter of record. Given this information, Chart F.1 [below] demonstrates that plaintiffs' claims are time barred because plaintiffs did not file their complaint within three years of when they discovered the alleged product defect. This lawsuit should be dismissed with prejudice.

Chart F.1

Plaintiff	Date Plaintiff Discovered Defect	Date that Claim Is Barred by the 3-Year Statute of Limitations	Date Complaint Filed
Jim Williams	June 7, 1996	June 7, 1999	May 17, 2004
Steve Smith	September 1, 1997	September 1, 2000	May 17, 2004
Chad Morrison	December 22, 1999	December 22, 2002	May 17, 2004

g. Reserve time for editing

Write your motion and brief and set it aside for a day or so before giving it a final edit. This period of detachment will improve your editing, and will result in a better work product.

PERSUASIVE ORAL ARGUMENT

1. Tell the Judge Immediately What You Want and Why You Should Win

As with motions and briefs, you should tell the judge immediately what relief you want and why you are entitled to that relief.

2. Do not Merely Repeat What is in Your Motion or Brief

You don't have time. Try to figure out what the one point is that the case is most likely to turn on. Then attack it like a bulldog. You might even get time to make three points, but no more. If you discover some important fact in the record while you are preparing for argument, share it with the court. Judges like to hear something extra, so long as it is related to the arguments made in the briefs.

3. Do not read to the Judge

Do not read your argument to the judge. Likewise, few things are less well received than reading a lengthy quote to the judge. If you don't believe us, try having a lawyer in your office read a lengthy legal quote to you.

4. Respond Directly to the Judge's Questions

If the judge asks you a question, answer it directly. Do not attempt to avoid the question, or to give an answer that is not responsive to the question that the judge asked. Do not tell the judge that you will answer his or her question later. And do not interrupt a judge. You are there to please the judge. The judge is not there to please you.

5. Use Simple Visual Aids

Show the judge. The selective use of photographs, charts and diagrams can enhance your argument. If possible, show the judge the actual object at issue. For instance, in a products liability case, if the product is small enough, show it to the judge. Like jurors, judges will better remember what they see over what they hear.

6. Be professional

Be civil and courteous. Do not personally criticize your opponent. Do not berate him or her. Address the judge, not counsel opposite. Be professional at all times. Judges genuinely like that.

Reflections on Motion Practice
By Louis B. York

TIME IS PRECIOUS

I have some thoughts on motion practice that I would like to impart to fellow members of the bar. These thoughts are culled from viewing an uncountable number of motions I have ruled on during my eighteen years on the bench. My suggestions are concerned with motion practice before busy metropolitan trial judges with large case loads. To us time is precious. Supervising jury selection, presiding at trials, deciding motions and keeping abreast of the latest decisions, makes time precious. The lawyer who understands and considers this is the one who will achieve the most success in motion practice.

BE SUCCINCT

It is not the length of the brief or memorandum that has the best chance of success, but the one that addresses the issues head on succinctly and clearly. Emulating the style of Ernest Hemingway rather than that of William James is what I am suggesting.

REFRAIN FROM STILTED LANGUAGE

Lawyers (and judges sometimes) have a tendency to use stilted, archaic phrases. Bad draftsmanship is illustrated in this example: "Heretofore, the plaintiff herein articulated to said driver that the aforementioned accident was the proximate cause of the injuries suffered by the plaintiff . . ." Why not, "Beforehand, the plaintiff told the driver that the accident caused plaintiff 's injuries." If you don't constantly edit and re-edit your language to eliminate verbosities and repetitions, I guarantee that you are going to cause the reader's mind to wander or, worse still, to throw down the brief in disgust, never to pick it up again.

ORGANIZING YOUR BRIEF

It is good practice to start with a short introductory paragraph to orient the reader about the theories or issues you intend to pursue. Example: "The defendants will show that by tolerating their activities over such a long period of time the plaintiffs waived any rights to remove them. Moreover, by accepting payments while these activities continued with-

From the **Committee on Trial Evidence**/Fall 2005/ABA/Section of Litigation
The Honorable Louis B. York is Supreme Court Justice of the State of New York.

out uttering a word of protest, plaintiffs are estopped from enforcing those rights." This usually gives the Court a good idea of what the brief is going to be about, and tends to stir the Court's interest in seeing how the brief writer is going to back.

It is important to separate your different theories into segments and to precede your argument by a brief summary of what you are going to argue. Consider this heading: up what he/she contends and what authorities he/she will rely on.

POINT 1: Plaintiff has waived its right to go forward with the eviction because it accepted the rent while these activities were going on and never raised an objection.

Always start out with your strongest argument. That will insure that the Judge will digest your arguments before his mind tires and starts to wander. There is a division of authority over whether less important or tangential arguments should be raised at all. Some say that you can never be sure what arguments the judge will latch on to. Therefore, raise every argument or theory you can think of. The contrary point of view stresses the annoyance you may engender by increasing the length of the brief with what the Judge may view as innocuous arguments. The overwhelming majority of jurists agree, however, that if you're going to do it, at least save it for last. Personally, I get annoyed by an attorney who raises irrelevant arguments which together with the authorities set forth occupy too much of my time.

DESCRIBING THE FACTS

This bring us to several more important points. Be fair and accurate in describing the relevant facts. Of course you should describe them in a way that is most sympathetic to your case and best illustrates the theory of the case. Nothing irritates a judge more than inaccurately stating the facts and misstating the holdings of the authorities cited. It is surprising how often this occurs. Do not cite a case that you haven't read and haven't shepardized to see if it's been subsequently modified, reversed or overruled. Failure to do so will lessen that attorney's credibility with the judge, not only on the present case but possibly on all appearances thereafter.

Someone should proofread your brief or memorandum as well as yourself to eliminate misspelling (although now a spell check on your computer can do so) and grammatical errors. Where too many of these errors exist, your stature with the judge reading your brief may be diminished.

KNOW THE JUDGE

It is always a good idea to do a little research on the judge who will be deciding your motion. His/her past decisions may shed light on the kinds of arguments that he/she like or dislikes. Don't forget articles he may have written (such as this one) where his/her proclivities may be better revealed than in his/her decisions. Also try to find out what others have written about him. There are a few publications that give information about judges which are derived from attorneys who have appeared before him/her. Finally, speak to the attorneys in your immediate vicinity. Some of them will have the latest and probably the most reliable and useful information. This can be of value not only in writing the brief, but in oral argument as well.

ORAL ARGUMENT

Most of the things I have discussed, apply equally to oral argument of motions. I have just a few additional observations. Never read motions from a script. It's ok to keep a list of talking points or even a brief outline to avoid not missing any important points. But reading the argument is a sure fire way to create disinterest and boredom. Try to be discreet when disagreeing. Saying things like "you're wrong" or "that doesn't make sense" will not endear you. It's better to say something like "I think that if you examine the authorities I have cited that you might see . . ." or "there are authorities who take a contrary point." Once you see that the judge has decided a particular point after hearing both sides move on. There is nothing so irritating as endlessly pressing a point when the judge wants to get to the next point and then to the next argument in a crowded courtroom. Above all, be prepared. Know the facts and know the law. A well reasoned and well thought out argument will always be appreciated.

Some of these observations may be obvious, others not so. But all of them are included because a practitioner, even an experienced one, should keep all of them in mind when submitting a brief or arguing a motion. I hope that you find them useful.

New Standards of Legal Sufficiency
To Survive A Motion To Dismiss?*

*By Judge Samuel A. Thumma***

Fifty years ago, in *Conley v. Gibson*,[1] the United States Supreme Court set the standard for a motion to dismiss for failure to state a claim upon which relief could be granted. *Conley* held that such a motion should be denied unless it appeared "beyond doubt" that plaintiff could "prove no set of facts in support of" the claim that would entitle the plaintiff to relief.[2] In the decades that followed, the Supreme Court approvingly cited this "no set of facts" standard on several occasions and state courts in more than half the states followed the standard.[3]

In 2007, the Supreme Court issued two decisions in a two-week period—*Bell Atlantic Corp. v. Twombly*[4] and *Erickson v. Pardus*[5]—casting doubt on whether *Conley*'s "no set of facts" standard remains applicable. Indeed, these two recent cases have caused much speculation about whether the *Conley* standard has been displaced, was modified, or remains intact.

This article discusses these three cases—*Conley*, *Twombly*, and *Erickson*—in considering whether *Conley*'s "no set of facts" standard remains in play, quoting substantial portions of all three decisions for context. It is too early to tell with precision whether *Conley* has been displaced, whether *Twombly* (a complex antitrust case) will be limited to the context in which it arose, or some middle ground. What is clear, however, is that prudent counsel should carefully consider these recent decisions when briefing motions to dismiss for failure to state a claim.

From the **Appellate Practice Journal**/Winter 2008/ABA/Section of Litigation
Arizona Superior Court, Maricopa County, Phoenix, Arizona.
*This article originally appeared in the Summer 2007 issue of the ABA's Committee on Pretrial Practice and Discovery newsletter. It is reprinted here with the permission of Judge Thumma and the Committee.
**The views expressed are those of the author and do not represent those of the Arizona Superior Court. The author wishes to thank Cid Regal Kallen, ABA JIOP intern from Phoenix School of Law, for his editorial assistance in preparing this article.
[1] 355 U.S. 41 (1957).
[2] 355 U.S. at 45-46.
[3] *Bell Atlantic Corp. v. Twombly*, 127 S. Ct. 1955, 1978 & nn. 4 & 5 (2007) (Stevens, J., dissenting) (citing cases).
[4] 127 S. Ct. 1955 (2007).
[5] 127 S. Ct. 2197 (2007).

A. *CONLEY V. GIBSON*

Conley involved a Railway Labor Act claim by African-American union members asking "that [plaintiffs'] collective bargaining agent be compelled to represent them fairly."[6] The district court dismissed, and the Fifth Circuit Court of Appeals affirmed, on independent grounds and without reaching defendants' argument that "the complaint failed to state a claim upon which relief could be given."[7] After rejecting the grounds relied upon by the district and circuit courts, the Supreme Court addressed whether the complaint failed to state a claim upon which relief could be granted, given that the issue had "been briefed and argued by both parties" as an alternative ground.[8]

In finding that the complaint substantively stated a claim upon which relief could be granted,[9] the unanimous *Conley* Court set forth in a matter-of-fact way the procedural standard to use in addressing a motion to dismiss:

> In appraising the sufficiency of the complaint we follow, of course, the accepted rule that a complaint should not be dismissed for failure to state a claim unless it appears beyond doubt that the plaintiff can prove no set of facts in support of his claim which would entitle him to relief.[10]

Conley found that, if the allegations in the complaint were supported factually, there was "a manifest breach" by defendants.[11] *Conley* then quickly rejected defendants' claim that plaintiffs improperly failed to plead specific facts:

> [T]he Federal Rules of Civil Procedure do not require a claimant to set out in detail the facts upon which he bases his claim. To the contrary, all the Rules require is 'a short and plain statement of the claim' that will give the defendant fair notice of what the plaintiff's claim is and the grounds upon which it rests. The illustrative forms appended to the Rules plainly demonstrate this. Such simplified 'notice pleading' is made possible by the liberal opportunity for discovery and the other pretrial procedures established by

---

[6] 355 U.S. at 42.

[7] *Id*. at 44.

[8] *Id*. at 45.

[9] *Id*. at 45 (citing cases substantively construing the Railway Labor Act).

[10] 355 U.S. at 45-46 (footnote omitted; citing cases).

[11] 355 U.S. at 46.

the Rules to disclose more precisely the basis of both claim and defense and to define more narrowly the disputed facts and issues. Following the simple guide of Rule 8(f) that 'all pleadings shall be so construed as to do substantial justice,' we have no doubt that petitioners' complaint adequately set forth a claim and gave the respondents fair notice of its basis. The Federal Rules reject the approach that pleading is a game of skill in which one misstep by counsel may be decisive to the outcome and accept the principle that the purpose of pleading is to facilitate a proper decision on the merits.[12]

This rationale was widely followed in federal and state courts for decades to follow.[13] *Conley* has been cited nearly 80,000 times—approximately 1,600 times per year—since the decision was issued.[14] *Twombly*, however, took exception to at least some of the *Conley* rationale.

B. *BELL ATLANTIC CORP. V. TWOMBLY*

In *Twombly*, the district court dismissed an antitrust complaint for failure to state a claim, with the Second Circuit Court of Appeals reversing and finding that the district court "tested the complaint by the wrong standard."[15] The Supreme Court, by a 7-2 majority, held that the complaint failed to state a claim and should have been dismissed.[16]

1. *Twombly Majority*

The *Twombly* majority addressed what a plaintiff must plead to properly state a violation of Section 1 of the Sherman Act, which prohibits "a 'contract, combination . . . ., or conspiracy, in restraint of trade or commerce.'"[17] Unlike *Conley*, *Twombly* noted that the substantive requirement to make such a factual showing was not pristine:

---

[12] 355 U.S. at 47-48 (footnote & citation omitted).

[13] *Bell Atlantic Corp. v. Twombly*, 127 S. Ct. 1955, 1978 & nn. 4 & 5 (2007) (Stevens, J., dissenting) (citing cases).

[14] June 23, 2007 Westlaw search, showing that *Conley* had been cited 78,790 times by courts and commentators.

[15] 127 S. Ct. at 1963.

[16] 127 S. Ct. at 1961.

[17] 127 S. Ct. at 1961 (quoting 15 U.S.C. § 1); *see also Leegin Creative Leather Products, Inc. v. PSKS, Inc.*, 2007 WL 1835892, at **5-28 (S. Ct. June 28, 2007) (holding manufacturer's policy of requiring retailers to follow suggested retail prices should be viewed under a rule of reason analysis; overruling *Dr. Miles Medical Co. v. John D. Park & Sons Co.*, 220 U.S. 373 (1911), which established a per se rule analysis).

Because § 1 of the Sherman Act "does not prohibit [all] unreason-able restraints of trade . . . but only restraints effected by a contract, combination, or conspiracy," "[t]he crucial question" is whether the challenged anticompetitive conduct "stem[s] from independent de-cision or from an agreement, tacit or express[.]" While a showing of parallel "business behavior is admissible circumstantial evidence from which the fact finder may infer agreement," it falls short of "conclusively establish[ing] agreement or . . . itself constitut[ing] a Sherman Act offense." Even "conscious parallelism," a common re-action of "firms in a concentrated market [that] recogniz[e] their shared economic interests and their interdependence with respect to price and output decisions" is "not in itself unlawful."

The inadequacy of showing parallel conduct or interdependence, without more, mirrors the ambiguity of the behavior: consistent with conspiracy, but just as much in line with a wide swath of rational and competitive business strategy unilaterally prompted by common per-ceptions of the market. Accordingly, we have previously hedged against false inferences from identical behavior at a number of points in the trial sequence. An antitrust conspiracy plaintiff with evidence showing noth-ing beyond parallel conduct is not entitled to a directed verdict, proof of a § 1 conspiracy must include evidence tending to exclude the possibil-ity of independent action, and at the summary judgment stage a § 1 plaintiff's offer of conspiracy evidence must tend to rule out the possi-bility that the defendants were acting independently[.][18]

The specific issue before the Court was "the antecedent question of what a plaintiff must plead in order to state a claim under § 1 of the Sherman Act."[19] *Twombly* acknowledged that every complaint is re-quired to set forth "'a short and plain statement of the claim showing that the pleader is entitled to relief,'" citing *Conley* for the requirement that a complaint give "fair notice" of the claim and the grounds upon which it rests.[20] Continuing, *Twombly* stated:

While a complaint attacked by a Rule 12(b)(6) motion to dismiss does not need detailed factual allegations, a plaintiff's obligation to provide the "grounds" of his "entitle[ment] to relief" requires more than labels and conclusions, and a formulaic recitation of the elements of a cause of action will not do. Factual allegations must

---

[18] 127 S. Ct. at 1964 (citations omitted)
[19] 127 S. Ct. at 1964.
[20] 127 S. Ct. at 1964 (also citing Fed. R. Civ. P. 8(a)(2)).

be enough to raise a right to relief above the speculative level, on the assumption that all the allegations in the complaint are true (even if doubtful in fact).[21]

As applied, *Twombly* held that a Section 1 claim "requires a complaint with enough factual matter (taken as true) to suggest that an agreement was made. Asking for plausible grounds to infer an agreement does not impose a probability requirement at the pleading stage; it simply calls for enough fact to raise a reasonable expectation that discovery will reveal evidence of an illegal agreement."[22]

Twombly characterized plaintiffs' "main argument against the plausibility standard at the pleading stage is its ostensible conflict with a literal reading of" *Conley's* "no set of facts" standard.[23] Acknowledging that the "no set of facts" standard could be read "in isolation" as requiring "that any statement revealing the theory of the claim will suffice unless its factual impossibility may be shown" on the pleadings, *Twombly* rejected such an approach.[24] Stating that "judges and commentators have balked at taking the literal terms of the *Conley* ['no set of facts'] passage as a pleading standard,"[25] and that the phrase "has been questioned, criticized, and explained away,"[26] *Twombly* found:

> To be fair to the Conley Court, the passage should be understood in light of the opinion's preceding summary of the complaint's concrete allegations, which the Court quite reasonably understood as amply stating a claim for relief. But the passage so often quoted fails to mention this understanding on the part of the Court, and after puzzling the profession for 50 years, this famous observation has earned its retirement. The phrase is best forgotten as an incomplete, negative gloss on an accepted pleading standard: once a claim has been stated adequately, it may be supported by showing any set of facts consistent with the allegations in the complaint

Conley, then, described the breadth of opportunity to prove what an adequate complaint claims, not the minimum standard of adequate pleading to govern a complaint's survival.[27]

---

[21] 127 S. Ct. at 1964-65 (footnote & citations omitted).
[22] 127 S. Ct. at 1965.
[23] 127 S. Ct. at 1968.
[24] 127 S. Ct. at 1968.
[25] 127 S. Ct. at 1969.
[26] 127 S. Ct. at 1969.
[27] 127 S. Ct. at 1969 (footnote & citations omitted).

As applied, the *Twombly* majority found "that nothing contained in the complaint invests either the action or inaction alleged with a plausible suggestion of conspiracy. . . . [W]e do not require heightened fact pleading of specifics, but only enough facts to state a claim to relief that is plausible on its face. Because the plaintiffs here have not nudged their claims across the line from conceivable to plausible, their complaint must be dismissed."[28]

2. *Twombly Dissent*

In a sometimes-pointed dissent, Justice Stevens (joined in large part by Justice Ginsburg) took exception to the majority's approach, stating this is a case in which there is no dispute about the substantive law. If the defendants acted independently, their conduct was perfectly lawful. If, however, that conduct is the product of a horizontal agreement this is a case in which there is no dispute about the substantive law. If the defendants acted independently, their conduct was perfectly lawful. If, however, that conduct is the product of a horizontal agreement among potential competitors, it was unlawful. Plaintiffs have alleged such an agreement and, because the complaint was dismissed in advance of answer, the allegation has not even been denied. Why, then, does the case not proceed? Does a judicial opinion that the charge is not "plausible" provide a legally acceptable reason for dismissing the complaint? I think not.[29]

Although the parallel conduct alleged in the complaint "is consistent with the absence of any contract, combination, or conspiracy," the dissent found that such "conduct is also entirely consistent with the presence of the illegal agreement alleged in the complaint. . . . As such, the Federal Rules of Civil Procedure, our longstanding precedent, and sound practice mandate that the District Court at least require some sort of response from [defendants] before dismissing the case."[30] Although noting the discovery costs and the risk of jury confusion in the case, such concerns "do not, however, justify the dismissal of an adequately pleaded complaint without even requiring the defendants to file answers denying a charge that they in fact engaged in collective decisionmaking. More importantly, they do not justify an interpretation of Federal

---

[28] 127 S. Ct. at 1970, 1974.
[29] 127 S. Ct. at 1974 (Stevens, J., dissenting).
[30] 127 S. Ct. at 1975 (Stevens, J., dissenting).

Rule of Civil Procedure 12(b)(6) that seems to be driven by the majority's appraisal of the plausibility of the ultimate factual allegation rather than its legal sufficiency."[31]

The dissent turned to Federal Rule of Civil Procedure 8(a)(2), which requires that a complaint contain "a short and plain statement of the claim showing that the pleader is entitled to relief," setting forth historical context for this notice pleading requirement and citing to Form 9, a terse negligence complaint that complies with pleading requirements.[32]

> Consistent with the design of the Federal Rules, Conley's 'no set of facts' formulation permits outright dismissal only when proceeding to discovery or beyond would be futile. Once it is clear that a plaintiff has stated a claim that, if true, would entitle him to relief, matters of proof are appropriately relegated to other stages of the trial process. Today, however, in its explanation of a decision to dismiss a complaint that it regards as a fishing expedition, the Court scraps Conley's 'no set of facts' language. Concluding that the phrase has been 'questioned, criticized, and explained away long enough,' the Court dismisses it as careless composition.[33]

Noting the "no set of facts" standard had been cited with approval by the Supreme Court and adopted in a majority of state courts,[34] the dissent added that none of the parties or amici asked the Court to reject Conley.[35] Taking exception to the majority's "negative gloss" comment, the dissent noted that "the pleading standard the Federal Rules meant to codify does not require, or even invite, the pleading of facts" and that Conley addressed "what a complaint must contain, not what it may contain."[36] After discussing decisions relied upon in Conley,[37] the dissent noted that "Conley's statement that a complaint is not to be dismissed unless 'no set of facts' in support thereof would entitle the plaintiff to relief is hardly 'puzzling' [as stated by the majority]. It reflects a philoso-

---

[31] 127 S. Ct. at 1975 (Stevens, J., dissenting).
[32] 127 S. Ct. at 1975-77 (Stevens, J., dissenting).
[33] 127 S. Ct. at 1977 (Stevens, J., dissenting) (citation omitted).
[34] 127 S. Ct. at 1978 & nn. 4 & 5 (Stevens, J., dissenting) (citing cases); see also id. at 1981-83 (citing Supreme Court cases).
[35] 127 S. Ct. at 1979 (Stevens, J., dissenting).
[36] 127 S. Ct. at 1979-80 (Stevens, J., dissenting).
[37] 127 S. Ct. at 1980-81 (Stevens, J., dissenting) (citing Leimer v. State Mut. Life Assur. Co., 108 F.2d 302 (8th Cir. 1940); Continental Collieries, Inc. v. Shober, 130 F.2d 631 (3rd Cir. 1942) and Dioguardi v. Durning, 139 F.2d 774 (2d Cir. 1944)).

phy that, unlike in the days of code pleading, separating the wheat from the chaff is a task assigned to the pretrial and trial process. Conley's language, in short, captures the policy choice embodied in the Federal Rules and binding on the federal courts."[38]

> Everything today's majority says would therefore make perfect sense if it were ruling on a Rule 56 motion for summary judgment and the evidence included nothing more than the Court has described. But it should go without saying . . . that a heightened production burden at the summary judgment stage does not translate into a heightened pleading burden at the complaint stage. The majority rejects the complaint in this case because—in light of the fact that the parallel conduct alleged is consistent with ordinary market behavior—the claimed conspiracy is "conceivable" but not "plausible." I have my doubts about the majority's assessment of the plausibility of this alleged conspiracy. But even if the majority's speculation is correct, its "plausibility" standard is irreconcilable with Rule 8 and with our governing precedents. As we made clear in [prior cases], fear of the burdens of litigation does not justify factual conclusions supported only by lawyers' arguments rather than sworn denials or admissible evidence.[39]

The dissent added that antitrust claims are "a poor vehicle for the Court's new pleading rule, for we have observed that 'in antitrust cases, where "the proof is largely in the hands of the alleged conspirators,' " . . . dismissals prior to giving the plaintiff ample opportunity for discovery should be granted very sparingly."[40]

Rejecting the majority's conclusion that it was not applying a heightened pleading standard, the dissent had "a difficult time understanding its opinion any other way. . . . [T]he theory on which the Court permits dismissal is that, so far as the Federal Rules are concerned, no agreement has been alleged at all," which is "a mind-boggling conclusion" for a variety of reasons, including that the complaint at least three times alleged such an agreement.[41] "The majority circumvents this obvious obstacle to dismissal by pretending that it does not exist."[42]

---

[38] 127 S. Ct. at 1981 (Stevens, J., dissenting).
[39] 127 S. Ct. at 1983 (Stevens, J., dissenting) (citations omitted).
[40] 127 S. Ct. at 1983 (Stevens, J., dissenting) (quoting *Hospital Building Co. v. Trustees of Rex Hosp.* 425 U.S. 738, 746 (1976)).
[41] 127 S. Ct. at 1984-85 (Stevens, J., dissenting).
[42] 127 S. Ct. at 1985 (Stevens, J., dissenting).

The Court admits that "in form a few stray statements in the complaint speak directly of agreement," but disregards those allegations by saying that "on fair reading these are merely legal conclusions resting on the prior allegations" of parallel conduct. The Court's dichotomy between factual allegations and "legal conclusions" is the stuff of a bygone [code pleading] era.[43]

Going further, the dissent rejected the majority's conclusion of implausibility. "Even if I were inclined to accept the Court's anachronistic dichotomy and ignore the complaint's actual allegations, I would dispute the Court's suggestion that any inference of agreement from petitioners' parallel conduct is 'implausible.'"[44] Based on the allegations in the complaint, the possibility of an improper agreement "sits comfortably within the realm of possibility. That is all the Rules require."[45] Accordingly, even a sworn denial of the allegations "would not justify a summary dismissal without giving the plaintiffs the opportunity to take depositions."[46]

> I fear that the unfortunate result of the majority's new pleading rule will be to invite lawyers' debates over economic theory to conclusively resolve antitrust suits in the absence of any evidence. It is no surprise that the antitrust defense bar—among whom "lament" as to inadequate judicial supervision of discovery is most "common"—should lobby for this state of affairs. But "we must recall that their primary responsibility is to win cases for their clients, not to improve law administration for the public." As we did in our prior decisions, we should have instructed them that their remedy was to seek to amend the Federal Rules—not our interpretation of them.[47]

In conclusion, and in a portion of the dissent in which Justice Ginsburg did not join, Justice Stevens observed:

> Whether the Court's actions will benefit only defendants in antitrust treble-damages cases, or whether its test for the sufficiency of a complaint will inure to the benefit of all civil defendants, is a question that the future will answer. But that the Court has an-

---

[43] 127 S. Ct. at 1985 (Stevens, J., dissenting) (citations omitted).
[44] 127 S. Ct. at 1985 (Stevens, J., dissenting).
[45] 127 S. Ct. at 1986 (Stevens, J., dissenting).
[46] 127 S. Ct. at 1987 (Stevens, J., dissenting).
[47] 127 S. Ct. at 1988 (Stevens, J., dissenting) (citations omitted).

nounced a significant new rule that does not even purport to respond to any congressional command is glaringly obvious.

. . . .

[I]n the final analysis it is only a lack of confidence in the ability of trial judges to control discovery, buttressed by appellate judges' independent appraisal of the plausibility of profoundly serious factual allegations, that could account for this stark break from precedent.

. . . .

If the allegation of conspiracy happens to be true, today's decision obstructs the congressional policy favoring competition that undergirds [the Sherman Act]. More importantly, even if there is abundant evidence that the allegation is untrue, directing that the case be dismissed without even looking at any of that evidence marks a fundamental—and unjustified—change in the character of pretrial practice.[48]

C. *ERICKSON V. PARDUS*

Just two weeks after *Twombly*, in *Erickson*—a per curiam decision—the Supreme Court again addressed the standard for a motion to dismiss for failure to state a claim. This time it considered whether the district court properly granted a motion to dismiss a pro se prisoner 42 U.S.C. § 1983 complaint alleging cruel and unusual punishment when prison officials terminated plaintiff's hepatitis C treatment.[49] Finding that plaintiff's claims were "conclusory," the Tenth Circuit Court of Appeals affirmed the district court's dismissal.[50] The Supreme Court, however, reversed, finding that the dismissal "departs in so stark a manner from the pleading standard mandated by the Federal Rules of Civil Procedure."[51]

Plaintiff's complaint alleged that defendants removed him from hepatitis C treatment in violation of protocol and endangering his life; that plaintiff was suffering continued damage to his liver as a result of the nontreatment and requested relief including damages and an affirmative injunction to provide hepatitis treatment.[52] The Tenth Circuit held

---

[48] 127 S. Ct. at 1988-89 (Stevens, J., dissenting).
[49] 127 S. Ct. 2197, 2197-98 (2007). Justice Scalia voted to deny the petition for a writ of certiorari and Justice Thomas dissented on substantive grounds. *Id.* at 2200-201.
[50] 127 S. Ct. at 2198.
[51] 127 S. Ct. at 2198.
[52] 127 S. Ct. at 2198-99.

that plaintiff improperly had made "only conclusory allegations to the effect that he has suffered a cognizable independent harm as a result of his removal from the [hepatitis C] treatment program."[53] In reversing, the *Erickson* Court noted:

> It may in the final analysis be shown that the District Court was correct to grant respondents' motion to dismiss. That is not the issue here, however. It was error for the Court of Appeals to conclude that the allegations in question, concerning harm caused petitioner by the termination of his medication, were too conclusory to establish for pleading purposes that petitioner had suffered "a cognizable independent harm" as a result of his removal from the hepatitis C treatment program.[54]

Citing cases—including *Twombly* and *Conley*—*Erickson* stated that "Federal Rule of Civil Procedure 8(a)(2) requires only a short and plain statement of the claim showing that the pleader is entitled to relief. Specific facts are not necessary; the statement need only give the defendant fair notice of what the . . . claim is and the grounds upon which it rests. In addition, when ruling on a defendant's motion to dismiss, a judge must accept as true all of the factual allegations contained in the complaint."[55] As applied, *Erickson* quickly found that the complaint met this standard:

> The complaint stated that [the] decision to remove petitioner from his prescribed hepatitis C medication was "endangering [his] life." It alleged this medication was withheld "shortly after" petitioner had commenced a treatment program that would take one year, that he was "still in need of treatment for this disease," and that the prison officials were in the meantime refusing to provide treatment. This alone was enough to satisfy Rule 8(a)(2). Petitioner, in addition, bolstered his claim by making more specific allegations in documents attached to the complaint and in later filings.[56]

Noting that the "departure from the liberal pleading standards set forth by Rule 8(a)(2) is even more pronounced" because the plaintiff was proceeding pro se, *Erickson* concluded:

---

[53] 127 S. Ct. at 2199 (citation omitted).
[54] 127 S. Ct. at 2199-2200.
[55] 127 S. Ct. at 2200 (citation and quotation marks omitted).
[56] 127 S. Ct. at 2200 (citation omitted).

Whether petitioner's complaint is sufficient in all respects is a matter yet to be determined, for respondents raised multiple arguments in their motion to dismiss. In particular, the proper application of the controlling legal principles to the facts is yet to be determined. The case cannot, however, be dismissed on the ground that petitioner's allegations of harm were too conclusory to put these matters in issue.[57]

DISCUSSION

What, then, do *Twombly* and *Erickson* accomplish? To date, commentary has ranged widely, including that (a) *Twombly* overruled *Conley*; (b) *Erickson* was intended to negate any suggestion that *Twombly* adopted a particularly high pleading standard; (c) *Twombly* turned away from notice pleading and *Erickson* did not retreat from *Twombly*; and (d) *Twombly* and *Erickson* are fundamentally very different cases, which may best describe their language.[58] Given such divergence of opinion, *Twombly* and *Erickson* provide confused guidance for parties briefing motions to dismiss for failure to state a claim. Some things, however, are clear.

- At least in the context of a Section 1 Sherman Act claim, the *Twombly* majority was critical of *Conley*'s "no set of facts" standard for a motion to dismiss.

---

[57] 127 S. Ct. at 2200 (citation omitted).
[58] *See, e.g.,* http://williampatry.blogspot.com/2007/06/conley-v-gibson-overruled.html (visited July 1, 2007) ("On May 21th [sic], the Supreme Court overruled *Conley*" in *Twombly*); www.scotusblog.com/movabletype/archives/2007/06/more_on_yesterd_1.html (visited June 28, 2007) ("It seems likely that the Court initially identified *Erickson* as a case that should be held and potentially remanded in light of *Twombly*. Then, in early May (after the *Twombly* opinion was in circulation), it decided to summarily reverse in *Erickson*, likely in order to counteract any impression that could arise that *Twombly* was intended to set a particularly high pleading standard."); http://lawprofessors.typepad.com/civpro (visited June 28, 2007) ("I do not see how some can read [*Twombly*] as 'not turn[ing] away from notice pleading' or 'merely elaborate[ing] on the question what it means for a complaint to give "notice,"' or as 'quite insignificant.' Nor do I see how *Erickson* changes anything."); http://www.josephnyc.com/blog (visited June 28, 2007) ("There appear to be three primary differences between [*Twombly*] and *Erickson*. First, the Supreme Court stressed the pro se status of the plaintiff in *Erickson*—a far cry from the highly sophisticated antitrust counsel in [*Twombly*]. . . . Second, the pleading issue in *Erickson* was harm, not liability. Under Rule 8(a)(2), only "a short and plain statement of the claim showing that the pleader is entitled to relief" is required. . . . Third, *Erickson* was a simple case, [*Twombly*] a complicated one. What more did the defendants in *Erickson* really need to know? Not much.").

- The *Twombly* majority expressly disavowed requiring "heightened fact pleading of specifics," finding that a claim "conceivable" on its face was inadequate as a pleading matter, but that a claim "plausible on its face" would withstand a motion to dismiss for failure to state a claim.[59]
- The *Twombly* dissent concluded that the majority had "announced a significant new [pleading] rule," and expressed uncertainty about whether the majority's approach was limited to antitrust cases, "or whether its test for the sufficiency of a complaint will inure to the benefit of all civil defendants."[60]
- *Twombly* addressed whether a pleading alleging facts with two possible meanings—impermissible agreement *or* permissible conduct—was sufficient, while *Erickson* addressed the somewhat different issue of whether a pleading alleged with sufficient specificity facts that, if proven, would be actionable.
- *Erickson* did not expressly construe, in a meaningful way, *Twombly*.

Beyond these basic conclusions, it is difficult to make broad-brush proclamations about the impact of these two decisions. In the short term, savvy counsel will account for these decisions in drafting pleadings and briefing motions to dismiss for failure to state a claim. Unfortunately, as suggested by the dissent, the ultimate impact of these decisions—including the breadth of their application—"is a question that [only] the future will answer."[61]

---

[59] 127 S. Ct. at 1970, 1974.
[60] 127 S. Ct. at 1988 (Stevens, J., dissenting).
[61] 127 S. Ct. at 1988 (Stevens, J., dissenting).